O9-BUC-706

Notes from a
Young Black Chef

Notes from a Young Black Chef

A Memoir

KWAME ONWUACHI
With Joshua David Stein

ALFRED A. KNOPF   NEW YORK   2019

THIS IS A BORZOI BOOK
PUBLISHED BY ALFRED A. KNOPF

Copyright © 2019 by Kwame Onwuachi

All rights reserved. Published in the United States by
Alfred A. Knopf, a division of Penguin Random House LLC,
New York and distributed in Canada by Random House of Canada,
a division of Penguin Random House Canada Limited, Toronto.

www.aaknopf.com

Knopf, Borzoi Books, and the colophon are registered trademarks
of Penguin Random House LLC.

Library of Congress Cataloging-in-Publication Data
Names: Onwuachi, Kwame, author. | Stein, Joshua David, author.
Title: Notes from a young Black chef : a memoir / Kwame Onwuachi
with Joshua David Stein.
Description: New York : Alfred A. Knopf, 2019.
Identifiers: LCCN 2018036747 (print) | LCCN 2018038324 (ebook) |
ISBN 9781524732639 (eBook) |
ISBN 9781524732622 (hardcover : alk. paper)
Subjects: LCSH: African American cooking. | Cooking, American. |
LCGFT: Cookbooks.
Classification: LCC TX715.2.A47 (ebook) |
LCC TX715.2.A47 O59 2019 (print) | DDC 641.59/296073--dc23
LC record available at https://lccn.loc.gov/2018036747

Jacket photograph by Matt McClain / The Washington Post /
Getty Images
Jacket design by Stephanie Ross

Manufactured in the United States of America
First Edition

I dedicate this book to all the women in my life
who have shaped me into the man I am today.
Mya, Jewel, Tatiana, Annette, Trinity, Madisyn,
Cassie, Momo, Tracy, Joyce, and Peekoo.

Contents

Standing on Stories 3

Egusi Stew.. 24

Dominoes 43

Ancestors 58

The Block 78

Gulf State 111

Finding My Craft 129

CIA Man 150

Blood on the Eggshells 175

From Old Guard to Start-Up 201

Angles 218

The Jewel.. 230

The Lesson 264

Acknowledgments 273

Notes from a
Young Black Chef

Standing on Stories

T he air is so warm in D.C. tonight, it still feels like summer. It's October, it should be night already, but the sun
is taking her sweet-ass time leaving the stage. It's just
too beautiful a day to say goodbye. From where I stand, on the
fifth-floor balcony of the brand-new National Museum of African American History and Culture, the city spread below seems
full of promise. Across the North Lawn, American flags flutter
in the wind around the base of the Washington Monument.
To the east, the Capitol building, with its impressive dome, is
bathed in bright light, and to the south, the White House sits
like a perfectly proportioned dollhouse. In the distance, the red
and blue lights of the carousel at National Harbor glitter in a
tiny festive constellation against the pink-fading-to-blue sky,
guileless and beautiful.

Standing above the scene in my chef's whites, I feel like an
orchestra conductor peering in on my pit as the musicians tune
up. Under the ruby sun, everything glimmers and shimmies
with excitement. Next month is a historic election. Next month
I'll open my dream restaurant. Next month I'll step into the life
I've always wanted. So though it's late in the day, it feels like
the dawn of something new.

"Chef!" A voice behind me cuts short my daydream. "Where should we put the allium shoots?" The voice belongs to Jong Son, one of the team of nine young chefs I brought to cook at the museum with me tonight. "Next to the Ossetra caviar in the reach-in fridge," I tell him. Behind me is a hive of activity as cooks rush to finish their premeal preparation, called *mise en place,* before the guests begin to arrive. My mind turns to the spreadsheets and to the lengthy lists of tasks and quantities through which even the most sublime food—in fact, especially the most sublime food—must pass before it can be made whole again. I turn my back on the view and head in to the kitchen.

With the opening of my first restaurant, the Shaw Bijou, less than three weeks away, my mind churns on overdrive. For the past two years, the project has come to consume my life. It is, by far, the most ambitious thing I've ever been a part of, the most logistically complicated and the most precarious for me personally. It is the expression of years of busting my ass, of constant forward movement, of seizing opportunities manufactured to be beyond my grasp. Though my culinary journey started like so many other chefs', as a child in my mother's kitchen, opening a fine-dining restaurant of my own is the goal toward which all my efforts have been oriented. I'll need every bit of luck, every scrap of knowledge, every shred of strength. I'll need to call on every single connection I have, and tug on the thread of every story I can tell, to open the doors to my very own place.

The experience and knowledge I've gained since graduating from the Culinary Institute of America I hope will help me. My time at some of the best restaurants in the country I hope will prepare me. That I won a national dining competition called

Dinner Lab and that I appeared on *Top Chef* has hopefully given me a national audience that will translate into customers. But you never know. Everyone is famous to themselves. Whether the audience on the other side of the television screen will show up at the Shaw Bijou, I'm not sure.

When I arrived in Washington, D.C., from New York two years ago, I thought by now I'd be the prince of the D.C. restaurant world. Things haven't gone exactly as planned. All ambitious restaurants suffer setbacks, but it seems we were dealt a particularly crummy hand. Already, my partners and I have blown through a handful of opening dates and hundreds of thousands of dollars. Everything that could go wrong has, from broken water mains to boneheaded zoning laws. I've found out that, just as L.A. is a city that's run on movies, D.C. is a city that runs on red tape. But, somehow, we've toiled on and finally we have a date—November 1.

D.C. is a city whose culinary landscape has long suffered from the preferences of deep-pocketed politicians for the unchallenging, dick-swinging food of steakhouses. There is, of course, a small vanguard of fine-dining chefs, but as a young black chef from New York, who has worked in some of the most acclaimed restaurants in the country, my arrival was greeted with a lot of excitement and anticipation.

As the weeks turned into months that turned into years, the food media's fascination with the Shaw Bijou has only grown. Bijou, as we call it, has become like a destination resting somewhere between myth and reality. As each detail leaked out—Washington, after all, is a city with no shortage of leaks—interest grew. There would be only eight tables. True. There would be a members-only club on the second floor. True. We would sell tickets, not take reservations, and those tickets would be nonrefundable. True. That I had parlayed my fifteen minutes of fame on *Top Chef* into a million-dollar restaurant. Not true. My partners and I were already deep into opening Bijou long before *Top Chef* ever came along. But there's a lot out there about me that's untrue.

I took a ton of heat a few months ago, when I announced that dinner at the Shaw Bijou would cost $185 per person, not including tax, tip, or wine pairing. The price tag made us one of the most expensive restaurants in D.C., and it immediately made me a target for populist rage. Who was I, the city's critic class howled, to charge so much? How dare I, new here and so brazen, compete with José Andrés, whose flagship, minibar, was our closest equal, pricewise? To whom had I paid my dues?

I could have responded that our food costs were high and our margins were low. I could have pointed out that $185 is pricey, but when you look at cities with more established fine-dining scenes, cities like New York, a city with five Michelin three-star restaurants, to D.C., where the guide hadn't even arrived yet, $185 is not ridiculous. I could have shown the haters the $150,000 worth of reservations we had presold and said, "Well, the public begs to differ." The truth is, I could have said whatever I wanted to but nothing would have helped. It was an audacious move; part of being audacious is dealing with the blowback.

But the real truth, the truth I keep under lock and key, is that I also sometimes wonder if all the haters are right. This fear I haven't shared with Mya, my fiancée, or my mother, Jewel, or even fully with myself. I haven't dared to give shape to these thoughts with words. But damn, $185 *is* kinda pricey for a first-time chef in a new city. Who *do* I think I am?

It's a question I can't afford to pose so close to opening night. Lately, my life has taken on the rhythms of a boxer in the lead-up to a title fight. I'm in the restaurant, in motion, head down for twelve hours a day. This morning began with me on my knees, for instance, grouting the tiles in the kitchen. Later I crawled into the phone-booth-sized office in the basement to finish assembling recipe books for my cooks. My eyes ache from peering at microcress and obsessing over the angle of a rice chip on a piece of lamb sweetbread. But in the high-wire act that is fine dining, these things matter. Well-grouted tiles matter. Millimeters matter. This frenetic pace is only broken up when I sit down with curious journalists for interviews in which I attempt to appear relaxed, confident, and charming as I make the case about why people should root for us. Then there are the meetings with my partners, in which I try to calm their nerves even as mine fray. Lately these have turned heated but I chalk it up to preopening jitters. And sometimes, maybe once a week, I see Mya, who lives with me a block from the restaurant but whose face I'm more likely to see when scrolling through Instagram or Facebook than in real life.

There are so many moving parts—from staffing and training to menu development to purchasing ingredients—that I shouldn't even be at the museum tonight, but it's too meaningful an opportunity to pass up. One of the lines of attack that pisses me off most in the backlash against the Shaw Bijou is the objection that I haven't paid my dues. To all the morally outraged critics who say I haven't, I want to clap back, "What were the brutal days working for little or no pay at blue-chip kitchens like Per Se and Eleven Madison Park, if not paying my dues? What was hunching my shoulders down toward the cutting board to weather the abuse of a fire-breathing chef but an act of supplication to the fine-dining gods?" Maybe it's that I'm too young, that I haven't been "a member in good standing" for long enough to deserve this chance. True, at twenty-six I haven't put in decades in kitchens around the world, spending the years when I have the most energy, drive, and horsepower in someone else's kitchen. I haven't waited to be summoned for my big moment by a tap on the shoulder from a mysterious, benevolent stranger. It doesn't work that way where I'm from. You make your own opportunities where I'm from.

But more infuriating is the question about to whom I should have been paying dues. It seems like the only ones keeping track are the white guys with tall hats. And how did those guys get into the club? By paying dues to older white guys with even taller hats. As for the thousands of black and brown chefs—dubbed cooks, domestics, servants, boys, and mammies who were kept out of restaurant kitchens or overlooked within them—they were beyond consideration. Their work, like them, was invisible. Invisible men and invisible women cooking invisible food for invisible children. So I get that it must be confusing for those who criticize me as an ingrate upstart—how can I pay dues to people who don't exist?

They exist to me, though, and tonight I'm standing on their stories. In an immediate, physical way, the National Museum of African American History and Culture, on the last undeveloped plot on Constitution Avenue, is both oppressively and upliftingly powerful. Inspired by the angular shape of a Yoruban column from Nigeria, the museum is a three-tiered structure that looks like a futuristic wedding cake. The frame is wrapped in an intricately cut metal shroud that mimics the ironworks found on the gates and balustrades of cities like Charleston and New Orleans. At one time, these ornamental ironworks were fashioned by slaves and installed on the buildings of their masters. But those chains are broken now, and the museum celebrates those who lived bound by them, those who broke them, and all we've done as a people since.

Why am I here tonight? A few months ago, the champagne

maker Dom Pérignon asked me to create an "African American"–themed menu for a dinner to celebrate David Adjaye, the Ghanaian British architect who designed the building. At first I balked at the request. I don't do "African American–themed" menus. I am an African American chef, so if I cook *my* food, isn't every menu I create African American by default?

On the other hand, why quibble? This is a media dinner, not a thesis on race. And anyway, I was gearing up to open a restaurant. Any press is good press, and good press is especially good press.

There's a lot riding on my performance tonight. It's not that a critic might walk through the door (I've checked the guest list for both real names and known pseudonyms). It's not that I'm cooking for forty-seven of the most influential tastemakers in D.C., the people I need to evangelize for me in the name of the Shaw Bijou. It's that I'm cooking for all the people, and to tell all the stories, told and untold, remembered and forgotten, housed in the floors below me.

Before we started prepping, I had a chance to wander the empty halls. Though the building is massive, rising hundreds of feet above the ground, the most harrowing exhibits are housed in three subterranean galleries bluntly called the History Galleries. Dug deep into the soil, the first level—the lowest, the earliest, the most base—is given over to the horrors and heartbreak of the American slave trade. Like any black man in America, I've felt the effects of enslavement through time. Though for me the shackles have been figurative, they're nonetheless very real. In ways spoken and unspoken I bear the offspring of the wounds, welts, and scars whose victims are memorialized beneath me.

Like them, I live with the contradiction between what this country says it is and what it really is, as my mother and father have, as my brothers and sisters have, and as my ancestors have too.

But to come face-to-iron with actual shackles, rusty and real, that once bound the wrists of a kidnapped African child; to see a whip, its leather worn supple with cruelty; to see the splinters on the rough-hewn whitewashed walls of a slave cabin, reassembled here from its home on a Charleston plantation; to see a stack of bricks as high as a man, each representing a slave owned by Thomas Jefferson, is to mainline history straight into my bloodstream. Exhilarating. Edifying. Important. Infuriating.

The misery of the Middle Passage, the transformation of people into property, the anger I still feel when confronted by so much freedom stolen, all are intensified by the contrast between the sadistic insanity visited upon my ancestors and the richness of the lives in Africa from which they were ripped. I have seen both sides. I have been T'Challa and I have been Killmonger. I have grown up in the knockabout projects. In the Bronx, I've been the kid on the corner, but I have also spent time in Nigeria with my grandfather, an Igbo *obi,* where there were no projects, no blocks, no corners.

A long table with a black tablecloth sits on the balcony, with chairs around it and on top an array of slender-stemmed glasses ready to be filled with thousands of dollars' worth of vintage champagne. The empty plates wait for me. Cards with the names of the city's powerful art and culture glitterati are written in elegant gold type. They were placed there by a stressed-out PR woman in a similarly elegant gold dress. A man furiously studies the printout of the names and faces of guests soon to be arriving. Many of the faces are black or brown, a rarity as far as my own experience with black-tie events goes but one of the things that first attracted me to D.C. People here talk about Washington and D.C. as two separate cities. Washington is a city of monuments, marble, and men making deals. D.C., on the other hand, is a city of vibrant culture, with a long-established and flourishing black elite. Harlem had its renaissance, but D.C. never needed a comeback.

Since the National Museum of African American History and Culture cannot and does not attempt to resurrect the stories of all the millions of African Americans, enslaved and free, it is up to us—not just me, not just my guests tonight, but all of us living—to keep the names and stories on our lips. We must realize that those few stories told on the floors below stand for the many that aren't. In my own way, I am trying to do the same through cooking. Keeping their stories alive.

Tonight I'm using the allium shoots (*Allium* being the genus name for onions) Jong asked me about, as a garnish for a reimagined gumbo we are serving as a second course. They are one third of the "holy trinity," the mirepoix of celery, bell peppers, and onions that form the base for much of Creole cuisine. These are the flavors I grew up with. These are the flavors and scents my mother, Jewel Robinson, grew up with. Her father, Bertran, was Creole, an old penny-skinned deep-voiced man by the time I met him in the galley of a ship on the Mississippi, but his daughter filled our Bronx kitchen with his recipes. Gumbo kept me company growing up. As I sat on my fire escape outside our apartment in the summers, the smell of it wafted out the kitchen window. Its taste kept me cozy when it turned cold and the windows were closed and we kept the heat low to save a few dollars.

This is what the bone-tired cleanup crews I cooked for in the aftermath of Deepwater Horizon had grown up with too, the same scent I conjured on a ship's galley floating in the middle of the Gulf of Mexico that transported them back to their own kitchens hundreds of miles away.

Now I am upgrading it with luxury furnishings and a few amenities, but trying to keep the spirit alive. Gumbo's got good bones. These allium shoots, whose flavor is more subtle than that of the more common bulb, sit atop a version made with a rich crustacean broth that will be poured tableside over a knuckle of new-shell lobster, two morsels of king crab, and a quenelle of Ossetra caviar. Though run through the ringer of fine dining and elevated technique, the flavors—rich seafood essence cloaked in a silken roux—would be instantly recognizable to any south Louisianian, and they hold special resonance for a black one.

Gumbo, in its essential form, arrived shortly after 1720, carried in the taste and muscle memories of enslaved West African people. The word gumbo comes from the Gold Coast Twi term *ki ngombo* which means "okra" (itself an Igbo word, the language of my grandfather and my father). It was a staple up and down West Africa, from Benin to Ghana and Nigeria. Ripped from their own country and planted in a new one, these enslaved people sought out what was familiar to them in the fields of Louisiana. In cabins just like the one reassembled below me, these slaves ate their *ki ngombo* mixed with rice, another staple from their homeland. As the okra gave their stew its supple texture, kernels of rice gave it body. This was the start of what we now know as gumbo.

Like stolen labor, this stew became part of a Southern culture whose origins rest on the corrupt scaffolding of slavery. Nothing about what it has become undoes this fact, though the dish never stopped growing and evolving. When Germans arrived in Louisiana, they introduced spicy andouille sausage. When the Spanish took over in the late eighteenth century, they threw in their famous *jamón* and added a salty meatiness to the stew. And after the Spanish government brought fishermen over from the Canary Islands in the late 1700s, shrimp and crab pulled from the Gulf of Mexico were added, and seafood gumbo, my favorite, became common too.

The gumbo I'm making tonight, a preview of what I'll serve at Bijou, is almost ridiculously extravagant. The crustacean broth is made of caramelized lobster, king crab, and shrimp bodies. I've added a dark roux made with the holy trinity, garlic, and thyme, plus my mom's spice blend. The king crab arrived last night from Norway. The new-shell lobster, which tends to be more tender and flavorful than late-season ones, came from Maine and is much more expensive than its hard-shelled kin, and the Ossetra caviar is $395 per seven-ounce tin. If I were a white chef, this luxurious riff on a gumbo might come with a whiff of cultural appropriation. If I were a black chef serving it only to white folks, I would feel uneasy too, as if somewhere in my fancifying lay a secret shame that black folks' food needed fixing. But tonight I'm a black chef serving black-tie food to a largely black crowd, with a black president sitting in the White House a few blocks away. I am proud of this menu, proud of this moment, proud of this museum, proud of my people, dammit, proud of myself.

Every dish on this five-course menu is a part of me, a taste of my past remade for the future. The yams, for instance, I had first known candied in holiday spreads in the Bronx and—later on, in their larger, whiter, and less sweet form—as a deep-fried street food in Nigeria, where as a ten-year-old I was sent to live. Tonight I've transformed the yams into a velouté, a velvety soup thickened with a blond roux. I've cut the sweetness with the muscular earthiness of black truffle puree and added a few toasted pepitas for texture. Instead of marshmallows, which I used to think were the worst part of candied yams, I've made a savory Parmesan foam. The orange, white, and brown Bakelite casserole dishes from my childhood table and these custom-made, matte-finished porcelain soup tureens could not look any more different. But these dishes are anagrams of each other. These flavors—all of them—are my first language, even if the syntax and grammar have evolved with time.

The fifth floor of the museum holds the administrative offices—and some challenges for a chef. There's a lot of carpet we can't mess up and fluorescent light good for board meetings but not really for cooking. Also, a little detail: there's no kitchen. So my team has set up in the cramped freight elevator well; the rest are working in a few conference rooms in a tiny alcove where we've put together a makeshift line. Two tall refrigerators and a hot box we wheeled in this morning hold most of the *mise en place,* and I haven't slept more than a few hours in the past three days working to fill them. There were thirty pounds of lobster to be broken down, poached, cleaned, and chilled for the gumbo. Last night, I was up at 2 o'clock grilling and braising Wagyu short ribs in the kitchen of my apartment to accompany a red-bean sofrito. Everything I own now smells like delicious meat. Not a bad thing at all.

This is the first night the whole Shaw Bijou team—the team on which I've staked my reputation and nearly everything I own—is in it together. We're a mixed bunch, mostly young, all hungry, halfway between strangers and friends, who will be growing more intimate every night in the cauldron of the kitchen. I've known my business partner and general manager Greg Vakiner since my days back at the Culinary Institute of America. We worked together at Eleven Madison Park, lived together in New York, and trust each other completely. Other than that, welcome to the world of social media: most of my team came to me through Instagram or Facebook. A few weeks ago, we posted a listing for cooks. Immediately we were flooded with young chefs, many of whom were people of color looking for a kitchen environment where they might, finally, fit in. There's Jarren, a quiet sous chef with midnight skin from D.C., and Russell, tall and timid. There's Janny and Jong, who reached out via Facebook; Gisell Paula, the head of pastry, was working at Mast Brothers in Brooklyn. Gisell and I had met, officially, only a week before but she'd already become a leader in the kitchen. Tonight she's typically ambitious, preparing not one but four desserts, including a beet butter cake served with cream cheese sabayon, chocolate malt snow, and sorrel; a *mignardise* consisting of a banana pudding tartlette; a yam doughnut fried to order; and a chocolate-covered praline. She's had to produce all of it in the cramped space near the elevator, tucked beside a deep fryer, an immersion circulator, and a dishwashing station. But she's still found time to assert herself to the rest of the team. As I walk by, I hear her telling the other cooks, "Guys, if we fuck up this carpet, we're fucked." She's not wrong.

The kitchen staff around me resembles nothing I've seen before. Not in fancy restaurants, not in the classrooms of the Culinary Institute of America, not on the set of *Top Chef*, nowhere. Fine-dining lines are as white as the tablecloths that cover the tables and the patrons that sit around them. And, from my experience, being the only black guy on the line makes you stick out like a minor note on a major scale. No one lets you forget you don't belong. Though it's gaining more exposure now, the kitchen is about as immune from racism as it is from sexism. I've felt this firsthand in every single kitchen

I've worked in, from the closet-sized belly of a cleanup ship to the gleaming stainless-steel show kitchens of three-Michelin-star restaurants. Sometimes racism takes the form of ugly words and actions. Other times it remains unspoken, communicated by hostile looks and secret snickers. But the most corrosive form, and often the hardest to address, is not being seen at all.

Now that I'm building my own kitchen, I'm not interested in the lip-service inclusivity you read in bullet-pointed lists in employee orientation manuals. Stock images over stockpots and tokenism aren't going to cut it. And I don't want them to. As one of the very few African American chefs in the world of fine dining, it's my responsibility to be inclusive. When I look around tonight, I swell with pride. As a team, we're young, we're gifted, and we're black and brown and caramel and yellow and white.

But just because we're a rainbow coalition doesn't mean it's all going to work out. An inclusive kitchen isn't worth anything if you can't put up good food.

The way these dinner things always work is that you begin with one number of guests and then that number steadily creeps upward. Tonight we were meant to be cooking for thirty-six. Then someone important absolutely needed a plus-one. Plus one turns into plus three. Thirty-six becomes forty, forty-five, and then there are the local society journalists, invited for cocktails but not dinner, who throw a fit, so add two there and all of a sudden there are forty-seven demanding, very judgmental people who must be served four courses with multiple elements each on a limited amount of flatware by a finite number of hands. Brotherhood and solidarity get you goodwill, but nothing stokes discord like an appetizer served late.

The stakes are high but I wouldn't have it any other way. In the kitchen, jittery and pumped up just before the curtains rise,

I'm in my element. I am the son of a caterer, and ever-expanding parties are my birthright. I remember my mother's outward calm when a client would call to say the party just doubled in size, moments before she loaded chafing trays of mesquite chicken wings and jollof rice into her van. Catering is like low-grade war games: hope for the best, prepare for the worst. So I prepare for nearly every eventuality. I'm so organized my systems have systems. A successful kitchen runs on plastic quart containers and paper towels, strips of tape and Sharpies. On the doors of my fridges are taped elaborate spreadsheets breaking down each dish into its component parts and assigning each element to a team member. Now I just have to trust the system.

Dinner was supposed to start at 7:00 p.m. but it's 7:15 now and the guests are still happily mingling on the floor below, so we hurry up and wait. As they eventually begin to file in, the two tables that serve as our pass are spotless. Six of us chefs stand behind it wearing our custom-made dark-purple Shaw Bijou aprons. We project calm—excited, let's-crush-this calm, but calm nonetheless. But past the conference room in the narrow vestibule to the elevators and out of view, it's all rattle-and-hum. Every square inch of space is occupied. Empty crates for the glasses and plates form cardboard towers. The space is crowded with people. Sylvia, our dishwasher, has set up her station at the only industrial sink in the kitchen. John Gray, Lester Walker, and Pierre Serrao, from the Bronx-based cooking collective Ghetto Gastro, have stopped by to lend support, and also because those guys love a party with free champagne. Lester, with his phone out, is narrating the entire evening for his followers on Instagram. Pierre is working on the line and Facebook Live simultaneously, and John Gray is looking for a spot to crash tonight, if they go to sleep at all.

I step off the line to review guest aversions with Greg, who is heading up the team of servers. It's up to him to connect what comes out of the kitchen with those for whom it is intended. This is simple if no one dies when they come into contact with peanuts. It's much harder when dropping a plate can result in death. "Kwame Onwuachi Murders Society Doyenne" is not a headline I need right now. Anyway, this is good practice. We live in the era of the bespoke. One reason I feel comfortable charging so much at the Shaw Bijou is that we've made a promise to our guests that we will work around them. Dinner will be truly customized, so it's best to get in practice now.

Tonight is typical. There's a red-meat aversion, a dairy aversion, and a few gluten aversions. Maybe a few years ago, it would have been enough to just lose the Parmesan foam in the first course, sub more red-bean sofrito for the Wagyu short rib, and serve the butter cake without the cream cheese sabayon. But we've moved beyond that. It's not a matter of taking out a piece of the puzzle; we're making a whole new puzzle.

For the red-meat aversion, I've brought two squab that have been dry-aging in my fridge for a week. I grab a sauté pan and switch on the induction burner. I reach for the butter but the butter is gone. Sheepishly, a cook tells me the butter sauce broke and he used all our backup to remake it. I'm pissed but I don't yell. I've been yelled at enough to know that anger breeds anger, not excellence—and anyway, it won't bring the butter back. This is an opportunity, I think, to show my team what they can expect from working for me. I'll talk to the cook later; for now I just have to get this squab ready.

"Arrosé that shit, bro!" says Lester. "Add some herbs, man!" I take his suggestion. I add a few tablespoons of grapeseed oil to the pan, throw a sprig of rosemary in, then the squab, quickly basting the bird with the fat it releases. I cover the pan with a quart saucepan, allowing the smoke to infuse the bird. I pray the smoke alarm isn't sensitive.

By seven forty-five the mingling is over, the sun is setting, the candles are lit, and the beautiful people are finally seated. It's go time. My squad lines up on both sides of the table, ready to work. Every member of the team performs a small but necessary task that if they don't do perfectly every single time, the system breaks down. There are forty-seven bowls, custom-made for us by a ceramicist in Virginia. Each must be warmed with a blowtorch. A cold bowl is death for a warm soup. The warm bowl will be spotted with two dots of black truffle puree, allotted five toasted pepita seeds, filled with two ounces of velouté, and finished with five grams of Parmesan foam.

Plating one dish at your own pass, with your own heat lamps and your own pickup system, is a high-stakes solo act. Nine people simultaneously plating forty-seven dishes with four elements apiece takes a virtuosic ensemble. So we reach over each other—dotting here, dropping there—a tangle of hands and fingers, each relying on muscle memory to tell us what is exactly two tablespoons, or five seeds, or five grams. With so many servings even small errors accumulate, until the poor bastards served last are a few pepita seeds short and search in vain for the black truffle puree they were promised. As each velouté is plated, the dish as it is meant to be served begins to decompose. "Let's go!" I tell the team. "Pick up!" I tell the waiters, who are also new to me and shuffle by without a sufficient sense of urgency for my taste. "Let's go!" I say. "Let's fucking move!"

The servers head out the door, carrying a small bowl in each hand. Two—with bowls for seats 14 and 36—are for the dairy aversions: "Fourteen and thirty-six!" I call out to them as they leave, "don't forget!" Once the waiters pick up, we immediately start plating the gumbo. I twist open the tin of caviar and begin parceling out the beads with a tiny spoon when the PR lady in gold asks if I can come out to speak to the guests. I almost forgot. It's time for *that* Kwame.

There are two of me—well, more than two, but two have starring roles for tonight: Chef Kwame and Kwame All Smiles. Both are me, but not all of me. As any artist with patrons knows, there's a song-and-dance to be done for the guest. Luckily for me, I've spent my life modulating which Kwame to show the world. There was the Kwame of his father's house and the Kwame of his mother's kitchen; Kwame at school and Kwame in Nigeria; Kwame the drug kingpin and Kwame on television. The only Kwame I haven't yet settled on is Kwame Alone, with no one else watching. I'm still figuring out who that one is.

For now, I remind Jong about the caviar—"Only five grams or we won't have enough"— then push out the door onto the balcony. By now, the sky has turned dark. The candles flicker on the tables, casting light onto glasses and the faces that turn toward me. They're filled with pleasant expectation. A tall man from Dom Pérignon, wearing a well-fitting suit, stands up and taps on his glass. He speaks with a French accent. His skin is smooth and tanned. "Ladies and gentlemen," he says, "it is my pleasure to introduce to you chef . . ." He pauses, turns to look at me and then back to the crowd for comic effect. Apologetically, he says "I'm not going to say this right but . . . Kwame?" He says it correctly. He knows how to say it. I briefly tell the story of what candied yams meant for me growing up. Because of where we are, I mention something I won't say to guests at the Shaw Bijou when it opens, that what brought yams to the country in the first place was slavery. But even though this is the story of the people that's told at the museum we're gathered here to toast, I know I need to lighten up. Kwame All Smiles reads his crowd. "For this course," I say, "I made a yam . . ." I pause and turn to the tall Frenchman who introduced me, and say, "I'm not going to say this right but . . . velouté?" He nods. Of course I know how to pronounce velouté too, but the crowd laughs, in on the joke, and he feels benevolent. I take the opportunity to rush back toward the kitchen to prepare the next course.

But just before I head inside, I pause for a second to take it in the enormity of the moment and my small role in it. Five stories up and I'm still standing on hallowed ground. Caskets and chains and splintered beams of slave ships, knives and forks and salt shakers, Woolworth stools and mammy figurines, freedom and blood, progress and pain, voices raised and voices silenced, courage. The purpose of this museum is to resurrect the dead, to honor their lives, to celebrate their progress, to remember their suffering, to never forget their stories. This building is an argument that these stories, traditions, this suffering, this history, matters. In three weeks, I will open my restaurant and with it, I'll have a chance to add my voice to that chorus. To prove that my story, like the millions of voices behind and beneath me, matters. As I push open the kitchen door, the last of my smile fades and I get back to work. I'm standing on stories, and this is my own.

Gumbo

YIELD: 6–8 servings

---

1 pound butter, melted

2 cups flour

1½ cups onions, small dice

1 cup celery, small dice

¾ cup green pepper, small dice

2 tablespoons garlic, minced

2 tablespoons canola oil

Kosher salt

1 tablespoon Cajun spice

2 quarts shrimp stock

1 quart chicken stock

2 andouille sausages, 1 whole, 1 sliced

1 whole chicken, quartered and skinned

2 cups lump crabmeat

---

1. Preheat oven to 350° F.

2. **Make the roux** In an ovenproof loaf pan, whisk the butter and flour together until smooth. Bake, uncovered, stirring every 30 minutes for approximately 2 hours. Reserve half of the roux for your gumbo; the remainder can be kept in the freezer for up to 3 months.

3. In a large saucepan, sweat the onions, celery, green pepper, and garlic until tender in the canola oil with a pinch of salt.

4. Add the Cajun spice and stocks, and bring to a simmer. Slowly whisk in the roux to create a thick, smooth liquid.

5. Add the whole sausage and chicken and simmer for 20 minutes. Season to taste with salt. Skim excess oil as needed.

6. Remove the whole sausage and add the crabmeat and sliced sausage.

7. Serve with Thyme-Scented Rice (page 23).

Thyme-Scented Rice

---

2 cups long-grain white rice	Kosher salt
1 fresh thyme sprig	4 tablespoons butter

---

1. In a medium saucepan with a lid, combine rice, 3 cups of water, thyme, and a pinch of salt, and bring to a boil. Cover and reduce heat to low. Simmer for 15 minutes.

2. Remove from heat and let sit, covered, for 5 minutes. Add butter; fluff with a fork.

Egusi Stew

I always loved the nights when Mom made *egusi* stew. It meant that my parents were at least trying to get along. The smells of cooking on my mother's side of the family were soft: peppers frying in butter, onions turning translucent and garlic turning golden, the buttery perfume of a roux and the sea-shack scent of shrimp.

My father, Patrick, was Nigerian, a skinny man with a hot temper. And just like him, the food of his people was sharper and more unyielding. My nostrils flared with the bitter smells of *egusi* stew, the scent of stockfish softening in a broth. That my mom was cooking his family's food was at least a gesture of harmony. Or maybe she just liked the flavors. They were, admittedly, delicious.

My mother and father met in January 1989 at a political rally at City College in New York. They came together by chance and almost certainly wouldn't have stayed together had I not been born. But I was born, that November, and so, with my mother facing the prospect of raising both me and my half sister, Tatiana, alone, having already lost one husband to a car crash, she decided to try to build something—a life, a family, a future—with the near-stranger who was my dad. They were thrown together, rather than drawn; two ships that should have passed each other in the night but somehow collided and sailed, briefly, under the same flag.

As those smells crept under the bathroom door one summer night, they found me sitting on the floor, a three-year-old boy blissfully watching his mother prepare to go out. As she worked the comb through her hair, she curled her lips into a smile. Or perhaps it was a grimace. I was too young to read between the lines, to know the difference between a smile and a grimace, or when the former hid the latter. When my mother leaned over the counter in that cramped bathroom, almost knocking over the bottles of straighteners, outlandish curlers that looked like toys, and paddle brushes that looked like instruments of torture, I *thought* her expression was a smile.

This was on a quiet block on a warm night in the Bronx, in 1992 or thereabouts. Yes, the Bronx, the Boogie Down Bronx, the Burning Bronx, the terrifying Bronx that gave birth to Big Pun and KRS-ONE. Not everyone from the Bronx comes from the streets, a correction I find myself having to make even now. Actually, we might be from the streets but many of the streets are like mine, Waring Avenue, tree-lined and quiet, bordering the dense parkland of the New York Botanical Garden. And in the houses that lined those streets, there were many moments like these, magical, mundane.

Sitting on the floor of the bathroom as my mother got ready, each one of her gestures was a deposit into a secret joint savings account between us. Four of us lived in that apartment: me, my mother, my father, and Tatiana, who was three years older than me. It was an 800-square-foot two-bedroom, not a small apartment, at least not by New York standards. But the four of us were rarely alone in arrangements of our own choosing. That's why the moments when just my mother and I were together meant so much to me.

Her doll-sized lip liner pencils, the miniature tubes of mascara, and the secret mirrors of her open makeup case beat my action heroes by a mile. Just being there, as my private mother became a public one and I was the only audience, that was the best thing of all.

Mom headed into her bedroom and I, as I often did when left alone, tottered into the kitchen. For as long as I can remember, I was drawn to that room like a marble rolling down a hill. It was where I came to rest. The place was modest—none of those new Bronx gentrified condos—and our kitchen was the original. It didn't gleam with state-of-the-art stainless-steel appliances, but it was well used. A groove had formed in the linoleum in front of the stove where Mom spent hours cooking. Next to that were four indentations from the little wooden step stool on which I often stood to watch her. I followed my mom around like a puppy, and just like a puppy, when she was in the kitchen you couldn't slip a piece of paper between us. So as she cooked I watched her work, my head just peeking above the counter. Despite her job as an accountant for a television production company and a social life that would put most millennials to shame, my mother somehow managed to always be in the kitchen. There was always something bubbling on the stove or cooking in the oven. She, like me, gravitated there to find a moment for herself.

I come from a long line of restaurateurs, from a family whose roots were made of gravy and whose blood ran hot with pimentón. My mother, Jewel Robinson, was born in Beaumont, Texas, in 1963. Her father, Bertran Ronald Robinson, was from Crowley, Louisiana, a town in the south of the state that called itself "the rice capital of the world." He named my mother Jewel after his own mother. Jewel and her husband, Floyd, owned two bars in the small town: the Mellow Inn, which was not nearly as mellow as it sounds, and Jewel's Place, a larger establishment where a guy could get a plate of Floyd's slow-smoked brisket with his beer. My mother's mother, meanwhile, was born in Ville Platte, Louisiana, a speck of a town in the center of Cajun Country that proclaimed itself "the smoked meat capital of the world."

Bertran loved to cook. After he met my grandmother, Cassie, the family moved to Beaumont, where he began to work as a chef, though he'd laugh if he heard me say that. "I'm a cook," is what he used to say to my mother, "plain and simple." He helped support his family—which grew to include my mother and her two brothers—by working in whatever kitchen would have him. Whether or not he could be a chef was, at least for most of his life, moot. Because of the color of his skin, he wasn't allowed off the fry line even if he'd wanted to move up.

After they settled in Beaumont, my grandparents set up a private bar of their own called the Little House, located behind their modest clapboard home. It had fifteen seats, a long wooden bar my grandfather built by hand, and a bathroom so small you could barely sit down. There was no décor to speak of. No inside kitchen, no draught lines, no nothing. What there was, however, was safety. Part of the reason they built the Little House was to have a place to hold fish fries and barbecues on hot summer days and to nurse Lone Stars long into the night unmolested. Southern Texas wasn't an easy place to be black in the 1960s—or now—and outside the house, outside the Little House too, the threat of harassment dogged every step a black man or woman took. Since it was impossible to relax when you had to keep your guard up, private bars like the Little House and the others that discreetly dotted the neighborhood's back lots and alleys offered refuge.

The Little House proved popular, especially given my grandfather's knack for frying shrimp into golden curls and slowly smoking ribs on the outdoor pit so the meat fell from the bone in ways still talked about fifty years later by my mother. My grandmother was the beautiful matron, though matron is too uptight a word. She was the mistress of the house, the heart, the jewel, always in the center of the crowd. Her stories, everything from reminiscences of life in Ville Platte to neighborhood gossip, were tied in bundles with frequent peals of laughter. Or so my mother tells me.

My grandmother, like her daughter, was fun-loving but steel willed. Opportunities were few and far between in Beaumont, and she wanted something better for her children. Plus, Bertran, though a talented chef, was a less talented husband, one prone to violent rages. After her brothers moved to Lansing, Michigan, to work in the auto industry, in 1968, my grandmother piled her three kids into a green Buick Skylark and followed him north. Of the long trip, my mom tells me, she remembers peeing by the side of the road and sleeping in the car. A single black woman with three children was welcome precisely nowhere.

Left alone, my grandfather sold the house and headed to the galleys of riverboats on the Neches River, where he worked as a cook in kitchens the size of cubicles for the rest of his life, gradually losing touch with my mom.

My mother and her family weren't alone in heading north. They were part of the exodus of black families from the South called the Second Great Migration, which stretched from 1940 to the 1970s and included up to five million people. And like the other refugees, my grandmother carried her family's recipes with her. Having for years worked as a cashier at the Astrodome, she got a job in the sales and marketing division at the beauty company Revlon in Chicago and moved the family there. But her personnel file, which was then complete with a photograph, caught the eye of a Trinidadian man named Winston in the company's New York HR division. He called and offered her a job on Long Island, which just happened to be closer to him. They got married soon thereafter.

As the family made its way east, the recipes from Jewel's Place and the Mellow Inn and the Little House, from the kitchen table and from Jewel's own life, came with them. Now, with the addition of Winston's curries and pepper sauces, the aromas of those recipes filled that house on Long Island and, when my mother had a family of her own, they filled our kitchen too. We still had distant family in Texas and Louisiana, and when one of these Southerners headed north, they brought packages of Gulf shrimp, boudin, spicy andouille, crawfish, and red beans. These my mother stored in our pantry and refrigerator, and carefully rationed. She never knew when the stocks would be replenished next. But they formed a little embassy of the Deep South in the north Bronx, a haven where gumbos and jambalayas were stirred, jerk chicken wings sizzled, and peel-and-eat shrimp were peeled and eaten.

M y mom has roots that wrap around America. My father, on the other hand, is from a no-man's-land, caught between being Nigerian and Nigerian-American. His father, an academic named Patrick Chike Onwuachi, had emigrated to the United States from Nigeria in the 1950s. The son of a prominent Igbo family, my grandfather was born in Zaria, in northern Nigeria, and had attended university in Lagos before leaving to continue his studies in Paris, then in London, then—improbably—in Fargo, North Dakota, and finally in St. Louis, Missouri, where he earned a PhD in sociology and anthropology. Granddad was a major player in the Pan-Africanism and African Liberation movements for many years. As a professor at Howard University, he taught that the influence of Europeans on African culture was deeply destructive, a sort of colonialization not just of land but of minds too, and he advocated for reembracing the richness of African culture. It was during these years that my father, the only son among six children, was born in 1961.

In 1973, my grandfather decided to move back to Nigeria, first settling in Lagos and then moving six hours east to his ancestral village, Ibusa, where he planned to build a Pan African Center on a huge parcel of land he'd bought. My father, also named Patrick Onwuachi, then twelve years old, went back with him. He grew up partly in the diaspora and partly in the motherland. As a boy, he had been raised in the United States during the tumultuous throes of the civil rights movement, in which his dad played a small but important part. And he came of age in Africa, during the heat of the African Liberation movement. Eventually, my father left Africa behind for good, moving to the States just like his father had, in order to study architecture, where he met my mom.

Our Bronx pantry when I was a boy was filled with neat packages of *fufu* powder, ground crayfish, and *egusi* seeds we bought from the Nigerian market on Arthur Avenue. Though my father seldom cooked, he had enough family in the area— and later my mother—to turn these ingredients into fragrant stews that could appear any time during the day. There were the Crayola-red onion-studded stews he preferred for breakfast but which for me were no match for Frosted Flakes. There were stews with tinned *banga* (palm fruit), beef, and castor seed seasoning from the Delta State, and spicy ones thick with peppers and tripe from the Yoruban people in northern Nigeria. But my father's favorite was *egusi* stew. Making the stew was a labor of love, a multihour process that included rendering the hard dried stockfish soft, then thickening the stock with ground-up *egusi* seeds, adding onion, chili, bitter leaf, crayfish powder, and palm oil. That my mother made it at all shows me that she was at least trying to make my dad happy. She hadn't learned the recipe from him but from his cousin, a doctor named Ozubike living in Harlem.

The kitchen was perhaps the only place where my mom could make my dad love her. My mother, for whom experimenting in the kitchen was as natural as walking, learned to refine her own jambalaya recipe until it resembled more closely its ancestral jollof rice. She added peanut and ginger powder to her spice rubs, marrying the ribs of her grandfather with the *suya* spices of her in-laws.

It had gotten into my toddler head that the stew needed to be stirred. I had, after all, watched my mother tend it for the better part of the afternoon. I pulled over my step stool, grabbed a wooden spoon from the counter, and tried vainly to reach the pot. Had I succeeded, disaster and third-degree burns surely would have followed. But the pot was on the back burner and just out of reach. Even as I struggled for it, I braced for my mother's stern voice behind me: "Kwame, get down from there!" But the voice never came, and eventually I gave up.

Growing bored, I began tottering aimlessly around the apartment. The stew continued to bubble, and I wondered where everyone had gotten to. It had been only moments before when all was warm and safe as I sat with my mother. Now the apartment seemed cold and empty, and I was scared. I began to cry, thin high cries. I plopped down in the living room, wailing in the existential anguish of a three-year-old. Normally, this was the cue for my mother to swoop me up in her muscular arms and soothe me gently. But she didn't appear, so I stumped over to the hallway outside my parents' bedroom to cry there. Through the door I heard the voices of my mother and father rising with the muffled ferocity adults use so as not to alarm their children. Occasionally, I heard Tatiana let out a small cry. That I had found everyone was the good news, but that they were inside and I was on the other side of the door was bad. *What could they be doing in there?* I wondered. And if they were all in there and I was outside, surely it must have been something I had done. I sat there listening, wondering why my mother got dressed up just to go into the bedroom, wondering if my parents had forgotten about me, if they had forgotten about the stew, and what would happen if it burned. The voices rumbled like distant thunder, quiet but foreboding. Eventually they erupted into unrestrained anger. The shouts came hot, like flames, from the closed door.

My father was not an easy man. It's not that he wasn't fun or couldn't be charming, because he could be both and frequently was. But his moods could turn dangerous without warning. One moment his face would be open and smiling, his long and lanky body a jungle gym for a toddler to climb as he relaxed on the couch after work. The next his brow would furrow and his eyes behind his glasses flashed with menace and his back would turn. He could be mean, cuttingly mean, real mean. There's nothing more unsettling than unpredictability, and I'm sure that my mother, like me, felt rudderless in the unnavigable waters of his moods. This, I soon learned, was the storm that raged behind the closed door.

When the door finally opened, I was shocked to see that my mother—her hair still as perfect as it was when she'd left the bathroom—was crying. Mascara ran in watercolor rivulets down her cheeks. She had my sister's cheerful My Little Pony backpack slung over one shoulder and in the other hand she held Tatiana's small arm by the bicep. Tatiana's eyes were wide with terror. Tears ran down her cheeks too. But my mother paid no heed to them, or to me either. Her jaw was grimly set on action. She glanced down at me, crying at her feet, but did not smile. She let go of Tatiana's arm, bent down, and looked me in the eyes for a long time. She gave me a tight hug, so tight it scared me, and whispered "I love you, Kwame." Then she stood back up, turned to my father, and said, "Bye, Patrick."

She closed the bedroom door, now with only my father behind it. My mother and my sister walked straight to the front door, opened it, walked through it, and shut it again. I stood in the hallway wondering what had just happened.

When you're a child, everything is about you. That night as my mother walked out the door, as my life changed in a way I couldn't yet understand, I was positive that I had somehow started the fight, that it was my fault. Had it been the stew? I wondered. I really shouldn't have tried to stir it.

In the immediate aftermath of my mother's leaving, in the hours and days that followed, an unsteadiness crept into my life that hasn't left me yet. That moment introduced a new cast of characters into my world, a new vocabulary of trauma. Worry—that I had done some vague thing wrong but didn't know what it was; confusion—as my mother rushed past me, as she held my sister's arm and left; an asphyxiating sense of anxiety—as my father paced in his room and I, cried-out and tired, sat on the floor silently waiting for . . . something.

A week later my new life began. My mother moved out and my father got his own place on Amundson Avenue, even farther north in the Bronx. From then on, I mostly lived with my mother but I never asked why she left me that night with the bitter *egusi* stew and my raging father. The question still simmers in my mind.

I saw my father on weekends, and when I did, I no longer had my mother to protect me from his wild moods. He had a girlfriend, a woman named Jennifer, but she did little to calm the emotional earthquakes. A day could sour if, for instance, I accidentally dropped a glass. "Why the fuck would you do that?" my father would scream. "What the fuck were you thinking?" And as I scooped down to pick up the shards, I would cry. And as I cried he would tell me, "Stop crying. Only faggots cry."

He was demanding, not like a dad who wants his son to succeed but in a way that seems engineered to ensure failure. And each time I failed, a gleam would enter his eye. When I was a little older, seven or eight, he made me create a chart on poster board that he kept taped to the wall in the kitchen. He made me note with an *X* every time I had committed an infraction. If I didn't line up the equal signs perfectly in my math homework, I would have to walk over to the chart and mark an *X*. If the two legs of the *K* didn't meet perfectly in the center of the line in my name, an *X*. Ditto the *W, A, M,* and *E.* Though I had been named after my dad's friend—the late son of the singer Kwame Olatunji—and for my grandfather's friend—the activist Stokely Carmichael, who had changed his name to Kwame Ture—I hated my name because the letters were so complicated to form. See, after a certain number of *X*s had accumulated—five, ten, does it matter?—I had "earned" an ass-whooping, and this my father did with a wooden-handled leather whip he said was from Africa.

I remember that whip and its origin in particular because a few years earlier, I had taken a weeklong trip with my father to Nigeria. It was the first and only time I had been there. We had stayed at resorts in Lagos and ventured to Ibusa to see Granddad's Pan African Center, then just a field. Though now hazy, my memories are of the farm animals and lush oases, blurs of color, hot sun, dusty roads, and a feeling of joy. *And this,* I thought as he beat me a few years later, *this whip is what you brought back from Africa?* Rage and pain and sadness and fear took root inside me, planting their toxic seeds in my heart.

My father beat me on my arms until the braided leather lacerated the skin. He beat me on my ass and my legs, through my pants and sometimes not, so I could hardly sit down. Sometimes he delivered these beatings as soon as the chart was updated. Other times, out of the blue while we were watching television or hanging out, when everything seemed cool, he'd casually say, as if just noticing, "Kwame, get the whip." Once he beat me so hard the whip broke and he made me repair it with duct tape. All Jennifer could do—or all that she did—was hold me as I cried and put ice on my skin to soothe the pain.

He was a sadistic man who could barely contain his rage at the world. He was an architect by profession, a career built on predictability and straight lines on the assumption that every angle aligns just right. He was a man who valued plans and sticking to them. That the world was messy, that I was messy, he took as a personal insult. And so he punished me every time I diverged from the plumb line of what he said, his plan for what he thought I should do or be. And in some ways he was successful, because even now I share his mania for precision.

Since my father had beaten me for as long as I could remember, I never mentioned anything about it to my mother. Mom had her rules, and I guessed Dad had his. Surely, I thought, she must have known. When you're a kid, it doesn't occur to you that adults have secrets from each other as well. More to the point, I never mentioned to my mother that my father abused me because I didn't know he had. I thought that it was normal to have to wear sweaters in summer to hide the bruises. Now, when I look back on it, I wonder how my mom could not have seen the welts covering my body when I got back from my father's house, and why Jennifer never spoke up, and why I didn't say anything.

Understandably, I tried to spend as much time as I could at my mother's house. Our new apartment was much smaller, in a six-story elevator building between Pelham Bay Park and Eastchester Bay, where I shared a bed with my mom. Tatiana slept next to us in her own tiny bed. There was no living room to speak of, and the bedroom was so small the two mattresses took up the entire floor space, so the only place we could gather as a family was the kitchen. There Tatiana, my mother, and I would assemble around the wooden table.

Some people deal with a failed relationship by taking to drugs or drink. My mother began to cook with a fury. Tatiana and I loved her macaroni and cheese, made from scratch and bubbling on the stovetop. She'd make her own versions of Hamburger Helper and Chef Boyardee. At the time, I just wanted the boxed versions I saw on television, but had I tried them, I would have realized I had it so much better. When she had the time, she'd make Cajun shrimp and etouffée, red beans, oxtail stew, chicken wings she jerked on the fire escape. Occasionally, when we could afford the crab and shrimp, she'd make seafood gumbo too.

Shortly after my parents' divorce, my mother was laid off. The production company she worked for moved their accounting department to San Francisco. And with the dissolution of both her employment and her marriage, our financial situation went from modest but comfortable to precarious.

My mother often says I was the only good thing that came out of her marriage with my dad, but she forgets a woman named Piku Ashley. Piku was a friend of my father's, a radiant woman with long dreadlocks, born in Liberia but raised in Sierra Leone, who always wore a brightly colored dashiki. As soon as they were introduced, my mother and Piku became fast friends. They are both incredibly social women for whom storytelling and hospitality come easy. Even after my parents got divorced, we spent a lot of time at Piku's rent-controlled loft in Hell's Kitchen. What I remember most were the parties. They were an exciting blend of African and African American culture. Everybody who passed through New York at that time or was a part of the black cultural elite stopped by Piku's. Fela Kuti, Spike Lee, and Baba Olatunji were frequent guests. There were fashion shows, healing circles, and impromptu concerts and lots of dancing. Of course, as a kid, I didn't know any of the boldface names. Who is Spike Lee to a five-year-old? But I can still recall the giddy excitement of staying up *way* past my bedtime. While Tatiana and I would run around with Piku's kids, pushing through guests' legs just as my mother had done at Jewel's Place, our mothers made West African dishes of jollof rice, bitter leaf rice, and *egusi* stew.

When my mother was laid off in 1992, these informal catering gigs became the backbone for a career. She tried cobbling together enough income to raise a family by working as a catering waiter, as a cook at a bar in the Bronx called Café Lou's, and trying to find a foothold as a caterer. She'd always loved cooking, but she had no professional experience other than being around caterers on photo shoots and in Piku's kitchen preparing for her parties. Nonetheless, she thought she could do better than the lackluster spreads she encountered on craft services tables.

My mom had a magical ability to turn everything into a glamorous adventure. She used to tell Tatiana and me about how she'd bring a change of clothes to a gala she was catering and, after her shift was done, slip in as a guest. This trick went both ways. Sometimes she'd sneak into parties she wasn't working, using the white shirt and black bow-tie uniform of a waiter as cover. My mother is a charming, chatty woman, always the center of attention. She, like her mother in the Little House, can wrap a room around her pinky. This is a useful skill when you're starting a business. Soon enough, our small kitchen was commandeered into service as a professional *mise en place*. Our plates and glasses were pushed to one side. Sheet pans and stockpots replaced them. Our meager closet space was filled with chafing dishes and Tupperware. The fire escape turned into the not-quite-legal stage for a smoker.

Piku became something of our family's guardian angel. Through word of mouth, much of which started as chatter at her parties, Catering by Jewel quickly became the go-to caterer for many of the black musical acts and magazine shoots in New York. Between Piku's hype and my mom's connections at the production company, soon her clients included Queen Latifah and Naughty by Nature, as well as shoots for magazines like *Essence* and *Ebony*. For the most part, her clients just wanted the no-frills classics: fried chicken, barbecued shrimp, rice and beans, simple salads. It wasn't groundbreaking cuisine, but my mother made all her own spice mixes and seasonings from scratch. And just as important as the menu was the fact that Catering by Jewel was a black woman–owned business devoted to satisfying the tastes of successful African Americans.

It was a lot for one woman. By now I was five or six, old

enough to be put to work on the days my mom had to cook. Perched on a step stool, I spent my afternoons peeling shrimp and dividing their legs and bodies into two separate bowls, or stirring roux for gumbo to make sure the flour didn't burn before it turned a dark chocolaty brown. I stuck to the cooking while Tatiana gravitated toward baking, and we both helped my mother stir and scrape and knead. The chopping was left to Tatiana and Mom—I was too young to handle a knife—but we formed our own well-oiled miniature kitchen brigade. I had never seen my mother as radiantly happy, a happiness that came, I know now, from being completely in her element. As she summoned complex flavors from the holy trinity of celery, onion, and bell peppers for her gumbo, as she allowed the marrow of chicken bones to turn a pot of water into a rich stock, she cocooned herself and us in love. I was too young to be of real use but she showered me with praise. It didn't matter if I peeled one shrimp per minute, she'd laugh and give me a kiss and say, "You're doing great, Kwame."

Then as now, the neighborhood between Morris Park and Parkside was extremely diverse. Our neighbors were Indians and Puerto Ricans, Albanians, Italians, and Jamaicans. To roam through our apartment building's hallways was to waft through the aromas of the world. I remember one day when my mother and I were working in the kitchen, the thick fragrant smell of curry came on so strong both of us stopped what we were doing and looked up. Our nostrils twitched. "Let's go find it!" my mother said. I, of course, was only too happy to oblige. We rushed out of the kitchen and into the elevator. I pressed all the buttons. At each floor I'd race out and take a quick lap, letting my nose lead me. No curry on the fifth floor. None on the fourth. But on the third, the smell got even stronger when the doors opened. I bolted down the hallway until I came to a door that might as well have had curry fumes billowing from it like smoke. Catching up, my mother looked down at me and giggled. "Should we go inside?" I thought she was crazy but she was my mom, so of course I said yes. We knocked. After a few moments a tiny Indian woman maybe in her fifties, her head wrapped in a white linen scarf, opened the door. "Excuse me," said my mom. "My name is Jewel. This is my son, Kwame. We live on the sixth floor. We couldn't help but smell your curry." The woman's face flickered with fear. Were we going to yell at her? Were we going to threaten her? I got the feeling it wasn't the first time she had heard a knock at the door, and I'm sure she thought we were going to complain about the smell. But my mother continued, "It smells wonderful. I don't know how to say this, but we'd like to try it!" At that the woman's entire demeanor changed. Her face crinkled into a smile and she stepped back, opening the door and gesturing for us to enter. On the walls I noticed framed photographs of her with what I guessed were her grandkids, two boys with mops of dark hair and an older girl with a long face. Walking to her kitchen, I saw the children grow up, captured first in baby pictures, then school portraits and cap-and-gown graduation photos. Our host grew up too, the smoothness of her cheeks crinkling up like aluminum foil and her hair, once dark like her daughters', turning rougher and snow white. Judging from the tidiness of the house, she was alone now. But out of force of habit, I suppose, she still cooked for a crowd.

As she led us into her kitchen—same flooring, same lighting, same setup as our apartment, I saw an uncovered pot of golden-colored curry steaming on the stove, releasing an aroma I'd never experienced.

"What is that?" asked my mom, peering at it with a professional eye.

"It's called kokum curry," said the woman. "It comes from the south of India."

The liquid in the pot was near a boil.

"What is that smell?" I asked.

The woman didn't regard me as a child asking a rude question and neither did my mother, who must have been wondering too.

"That?" the woman said with a chuckle. "That must be the *hing*. It has quite the odor, doesn't it?"

It did. The *hing*, also called asafetida, gave a pungent funky note to the curry.

Later, as the demands of the catering business intensified, this woman would become my babysitter, bringing with her up a few flights not just *hing* but recipes for curry chicken and potatoes too.

Unfortunately for us, catering is a feast-or-famine business, while a family needs to eat year round. Like farming, catering is largely seasonal, and when business was slow we had no cushion. For weeks on end dinner was tuna fish sandwiches on white bread. And sometimes my mother would play a game called Lights Out, in which we gathered in the living room and ate by candlelight. Only years later did the reason why we did this occur to me.

My father lived a few subway stops away, and since he was an architect, had plenty of money. But given a choice between being hungry but loved or fed but terrified, I chose the former. After a few weeks of scraping by, another gig would come and my mother would spring into action with me by her side. Then our kitchen would fill with the aromas of her cooking that were—and still are—the scents of family.

Egusi Stew

YIELD: 8 servings

---

4 cups small onions, diced

2 tablespoons garlic, minced

2 whole tomatoes, chopped

2 tablespoons ginger, minced

1 teaspoon Scotch bonnet pepper, minced

1 cup palm oil

2 cups ground *egusi* seeds

1 teaspoon crayfish powder

3 Maggi cube

¼ teaspoon iru

2 quarts chicken stock

1 pound goat shoulder, cubed

Kosher salt

2 tablespoons canola oil

2 cups pumpkin leaf or spinach, strained dry

---

1. In a large saucepan, over medium heat, sweat the onion, garlic, tomatoes, ginger, and Scotch bonnet pepper in the palm oil until vegetables are translucent, about 10 minutes. Add the *egusi* seeds and toast in oil for 10 minutes. Add crayfish powder, Maggi, iru, and chicken stock and simmer for 30 minutes.

2. Meanwhile, in a separate pan, over high heat, season the goat meat with salt and sear in canola oil until browned on all sides, about 7 minutes. Add the goat meat to the egusi mixture and simmer together for about an hour, or until the meat is tender. Add the pumpkin leaves during the last 20 minutes of cooking. The sauce should be thick and most of the liquid should have simmered off.

3. Season to taste with salt. Serve with *fufu* or pounded yam.

Dominoes

A few years ago in New Orleans I was walking backward down Bourbon Street in the blazing sun during peak Mardi Gras. It was so packed you couldn't see the cobblestones under your feet. You could barely see the sky. Standing on the wrought-iron balconies with beer cozies in hand, revelers rained brightly colored plastic beads down like joyful plastic hail. There wasn't a sober soul in the parish.

It was no accident that I found myself in New Orleans, and it wasn't just for the party. In one way or another, with varying degrees of directness, all roads lead back to that low-lying port city. New Orleans holds a unique place in American culture, a spiritual home baptized by suffering and joy, the birthplace of jazz, the graveyard of Katrina, as proof of my people's indomitable spirit. Despite centuries of discrimination, the saints just keep marching. It's almost impossible to write about New Orleans without lapsing into hyperbole, but that poetic magic is exactly why the city of 391,000—about the size of Wichita, Kansas—has always loomed tall in the American mind. And in my mind, especially.

My connection to the city runs through my grandmother, who grew up in Ville Platte in western Louisiana before joining the migration north in the 1960s. My mom always carried Louisiana with her, in her cooking, in her accent, in her outlook. She never left. And after raising me and my sister in New York, by 2007 my mother had had enough and moved back home. First she settled in Baton Rouge, where she worked as an executive chef at a hotel. By the time I was down there for Mardi Gras, she had settled in a small but tidy shotgun apartment in the Garden District in New Orleans, working as a private chef for some of the city's wealthy families.

As I was walking, looking up and back but not forward, I stumbled hard into the body in front of me.

"Watch where you're going!" I said angrily, spinning around with more than a tinge of Frozen Hurricane–fueled aggression.

"*You* fucking watch out!" said the other guy. That was all I needed to hear. I cocked my arm, ready to knock this guy out. But just as I was about to deck the asshole, I paused. The guy's face—broad, pale, somewhat flushed now, with greenish-blue eyes—and mop of tawny hair was familiar. He didn't look that different from any of the thousands of frat boys who arrive in New Orleans en masse, like popped-collar locusts, to rage, but somehow I knew this kid. He wasn't just any frat boy.

"Holy shit," I said, searching my memory to match a name and a face. "Michael?"

The kid's scowl broke into a wide familiar grin "Kwame!" he shouted.

We hugged as drunk old friends do when meeting in an unlikely place after a very long time: tightly and with extreme affection.

Michael and I used to be like family. Not "like family," but like literal family. The Gallaghers—Michael, his twin

brother, Patrick, their mother Fran and their father Dennis—
lived on Astor Street, not too far from where I grew up in the
Bronx. I first met the twins when we were five years old, at
the start of first grade. The summer before, I had scored high
enough on the Gifted and Talented test that a parallel world of
education opened up to me. I don't remember much about the
exam except that my mother was nervous, that I wasn't, that
I had to match patterns of circles and squares, and that I was
excited I got a fresh pencil on testing day.

That I was there taking the test at all represented a small victory. My mom drove me, like a gas pedal caught in the down
position. She, and by extension I, occupied the upper stratum
of have-nots. We were poor but had just enough resources to be
aware of and eager to take advantage of programs that gave me
at least a fighting chance of moving on up. But I have to give
him credit: it was my father who registered me for the Gifted
and Talented test. The test cost nothing but it required the
time and the skill to navigate the Department of Education's
bureaucracy. For some of the kids I met growing up, and for
many I later met in the projects, it didn't matter how talented
and gifted they were, since their parents didn't know the test
existed.

That test determined my future in ways too vast and varied
to chase down. Instead of attending the Dickensian, chroni-
cally underfunded and overcrowded school in my neighborhood, I took the bus every morning to P.S. 153 in faraway
Baychester, a school nestled amid the brick buildings of Co-Op
City.

Since kids tested into the program from around the city, our
little classroom looked like an image from a fancy postracial
preschool brochure. In my classroom there were Dominican
kids, African kids, Indian kids, Japanese kids, Eastern Euro-

pean kids, Irish kids. It was a real rainbow, with Michael and Patrick as the white stripes.

At that age, friendship is mostly fermentation. You just need the right conditions—physical proximity, natural warmth, and a little time—and affection takes root. The Gallagher twins were goofy, friendly, and open kids, just like me, and that was enough for a friendship to form. They had identical sandy brown hair, fair skin, freckles, and cockeyed smiles. Michael was outgoing, adventurous, and a little obnoxious. Patrick was quieter and introverted but funny as hell when you got to know him, and doggedly loyal.

We quickly established our dynamic. Michael and I would stir the pot. Patrick, whose angelic demeanor endeared him with authority figures, covered for us. He had such an air of responsibility, and innocent saucer-like eyes, the teachers took his word over clearly observable facts. Michael and I would have stolen ketchup packets—destined for the edge of a toilet seat—spilling out of our pockets, but wide-eyed Patrick would swear up and down that "No, ma'am, Kwame and Michael certainly never sneaked out to the cafeteria." He's a math teacher now, back in the Bronx, but he'd have done great testifying before Congress.

Because we couldn't drive or otherwise make plans on our own, we were dependent on our parents to keep the friendship alive outside of school. Luckily their mother, Fran O'Leary—which is a cliché of an Irish moniker but really her name—and my mother became fast friends. My mother was a boisterous peeled-almond-skinned Creole woman who had left behind the corporate world to scrape by as a caterer and chef. Mrs. Fran was a lily-white hard-nosed prosecutor for the New York City criminal court. But when she wasn't at work, she was just as fun-loving and outgoing as my mom. Even if I hadn't gotten along well with the boys—which, thankfully, I did—the two liked each other so much I still would have been at the Gallaghers' house every day or they'd have been at mine.

I preferred to go there. Unlike our cramped quarters, the Gallaghers' home was a spacious three-story brick house around the corner from the Bronx Zoo. It was much more suburban and quiet than my neighborhood. Kids scampered around the blocks like extras in the *The Sandlot,* all Chuck Taylors and wholesomeness. They left bikes outside. Unlocked. And when they came back, the bikes were still there. It was crazy.

The Gallagher house was a jumble of stuff, a mess of life. No space on the wall was bare, no inch of carpet uncovered. There were stacks of newspapers and magazines, shelves full of mugs and framed photographs and knickknacks. Books, ranging from thick novels with leather binding to Danielle Steel thrillers, were everywhere, next to cups full of pens. So many pens. The place was lived-in, and the clutter—clean but not tidy—gave it a friendly vibe, as if everyone and everything in it was so comfortable they could let their guard down.

After surviving the boredom of the school day, the twins and I usually just took it easy. We watched television, played Pokémon, or Legos, or K'NEX. And dominoes. The Gallagher boys were proud owners of the most epic set of dominoes I had ever seen: 2,000 black-and-white tiles they kept in a huge tin box in their bedroom. As soon as we arrived at their house, we'd dump them all out and start building. With Patrick acting as supervisor and master planner, Michael and I would arrange the tiles to form great lines that snaked down the hallway, through doorways, down stairs, over boxes and piles of magazines. We weren't simple single-snakers, either. Our dominoes had more bypasses and detours, jug handles and forks than a New Jersey road. The tumbling of one tile set off the clack-clack of two branches, and these, like a river rushing around a rock, would surround table legs and G.I. Joe figurines before joining up again. Even though we couldn't sit still during the school day, Michael and I were focused, precise, and disciplined in our pursuit of domino domination.

For children, especially like me, who have so little power in the world, the predictability of dominoes is more than a game. It's proof that you can plan; proof that you can choose your path; proof that sometimes things work out. But that wasn't the only thing that was comforting about life at the Gallaghers': I came for the dominoes but stayed for the dinners.

Usually we'd play until six, when Mrs. Fran came home from work. The garage door would grumble open and, like a dog spotting a squirrel, we'd stop what we were doing and scamper to the kitchen to meet her. The kitchen was the undeniable heart of the Gallagher house, seemingly untouched since it was built in the 1970s. The cabinets and counters were an eye-piercing bright yellow that never existed before that decade and ceased to exist after. Upon putting down her briefcase, Mrs. Fran would give us all a hug and start cooking dinner immediately. She didn't even change out of her work clothes, skirts over tights with sneakers. Unlike my mother, Mrs. Fran was not an adventurous cook nor, with a full-time office job, was she able to spend time experimenting and perfecting recipes the way my mom could. She fed her family a simple rotation of dinners: London broil, meatloaf, boiled chicken, and, when she was feeling adventurous, pierogies. Fish never made an appearance, nor did any of the staples of my childhood kitchen: no goat, no rice, no curries, no stews, nothing spicy or even flavorful.

I remember the first time I had London broil at the Gallaghers'. It was about a year into our friendship, on the night of my first sleepover. When done right, London broil can be tender and juicy. The meat is marinated for hours and then simply and quickly broiled. But if you overcook it—or undermarinate it— it becomes extremely tough, which was the best way to describe Mrs. Fran's: tough as leather.

When she handed me a plate with a few slices of grayish meat, a couple of marble potatoes, and a mound of Stovetop Stuffing I peered at it with apprehension and muttered, "Thank you, Mrs. Fran." As soon as I put the steak into my mouth and chewed it, I thought, *Man, this is tough.* But stranger than the texture was the flavor, or lack of it. It was completely flavorless, not good, not bad, just . . . nothing. I asked incredulously, "What's wrong with this? It doesn't taste like . . . anything." Mrs. Fran was not pleased. Patrick and Michael stared at their plates, embarrassed. But I honestly didn't know what was going on with the food in front of me.

Until that point I had really only eaten my mother's cooking, a combination of her family's Creole and Caribbean recipes as well as the Nigerian dishes my father's cousin had taught her. At school I never went near the lunch lines. The smell of industrial cleaning supplies, prefrozen burgers, and cardboard milk containers kept me away. Often I'd wait to eat until I got home, welcomed by the familiar scents of garlic and thyme. My palate was used to the supersaturated flavors of *mojos* and curries and jerk. But this meat, this meat was like nothing I had tasted before.

"If you don't like it, Kwame," said Mrs. Fran sharply, "you don't have to eat it. But that's what is for dinner."

I blushed, ashamed. I didn't say anything but began dutifully sawing through a slice of the meat.

Like every child I was learning about the world by trespassing on it. Etiquette, like not criticizing someone's cooking, was a tripwire I had just stumbled over. I'm sure Mrs. Fran doesn't remember that night, but to me both the realization that sparked the question and the shame of asking it return with undiminished intensity every time I look back.

The kitchen, as I said, was the heart of this home but clearly not because of the food. It was the family spirit that gave the room its magnetic power. Much of this warmth came from Mrs. Fran. But the person who struck me as most responsible for the hominess of the Gallagher house was Patrick and Michael's dad. Mr. Gallagher couldn't have been more different from my own father. First of all, he was a cop. In fact, if you close your eyes and picture "Irish cop," you probably wouldn't be too far off. He was a big guy with a beer belly and a mustache that sat heavily on his upper lip like hay on an overloaded wagon. It was a total cop 'stache. By the time he turned in his badge in the early aughts, he was captain of New York City's organized crime task force. When I was hanging around, though, Mr. Gallagher was a detective. This was in the nineties, at the tail end of the Gambino family rule, so it's safe to say he had seen a lot of dark and ugly things. But when he opened the kitchen door, he seemed to leave all that stress and darkness outside. You could tell that he could be scary as hell if he got mad, but I never saw that happen. Not once.

Every night I was there, Mr. Gallagher came home just as we were sitting down for dinner. It seemed like a magical coincidence. Sweeping in, he'd take off and drape his NYPD coat over the back of a chair in one fluid motion. Then he'd work his way around the table, with a hair tousle for me and a kiss or hug for Michael and Patrick before ending up in front of Mrs. Fran, who turned to greet him, her face upturned and ready for a kiss. To Michael and Patrick this was normal everyday stuff. To me it was remarkable. Mr. Gallagher and Mrs. Fran seemed to fit each other like jigsaw puzzle pieces.

The easy way in which the twins received his affection and unselfconsciously reciprocated filled me with the sadness of a window-shopper. I could see it, feel it, come close to it, but their family life would never be mine.

The time I spent with my father was marked by pain and fear. Even when he was in one of his playful moods, I was never sure when the switch would flip and he'd go off on me. At my mother's house the situation was becoming more complicated. It was no surprise that a woman as talented and beautiful as my mom would find someone else, and in retrospect, I'm glad she did. But at the time she met Westley, I wasn't as magnanimous. All of a sudden there was a new man in the house, not quite my father but also not *not* a father figure.

Westley was a big guy, muscular, with a trim goatee and watchful eyes. Looking back on it now, all things being equal, he was probably the best thing I had going for me father-wise. He had been a well-known streetball player in Harlem when he was younger. By the time he met my mother, he was working for the City Parks Department as a venue manager for Summer-Stage, a series of concerts held in Central Park. He and my mom met there at a Roy Ayers concert. Piku, the social butterfly who had first introduced my mom and my dad, introduced them too.

As my mom tells it, she was hanging out with her friends at the concert. They were all passing around a Poland Spring bottle filled with vodka, too savvy to pay $15 for a watery beer or a tiny plastic cup of wine. My mom, being maybe a little naïve, had no idea and, to cool herself off, dumped the bottle's contents over her face. She yelped in pain and surprise. "My eyes are burning!" she cried. Piku, who knows everyone, acted fast. She led my mom to Westley, who was on duty that night, and he shepherded my mother to a bathroom backstage where she could rinse herself off. When she could finally see again, she noticed his gentle eyes and the confident way he loped along and the care with which he took her back to her friends. They immediately dug each other.

West already had a son and a stepdaughter from an earlier marriage, and he knew how to be a father when he moved in with us a few months later. He even had a damn good idea of how to be a stepfather. A stepdad is like a substitute teacher. The position holds power but the person who holds it lacks credibility. West knew he wasn't my father and didn't try to act like he was. Certainly he didn't try to act like my real father.

One night, after I'd returned from the Gallaghers', he found me crying hysterically in my room. He came in and sat down on the bed next to me.

"What's going on, Kwame?" he asked gently.

Through gulps of breath I said, "Why doesn't my dad treat me the way Michael and Patrick's dad does?"

I don't remember whether West had an answer for that. I'm not even sure there is one. But what I remember is feeling that finally I had a father figure not too far from Mr. Gallagher, someone who would listen and put his arm around me and give me a hug.

As Michael, Patrick, and I grew up, the distance between their world and my own became more pronounced. Michael and I were always goofing off at school, but in second grade my trouble took on a different character and the consequences became more severe. Though the Gifted and Talented program was racially a rainbow, bias was not absent. As has been shown over and over again, black kids are more likely to get into trouble for the same behaviors white kids engage in, and I certainly could feel the story that I was a problem taking shape around me.

If Michael was caught throwing a spitball at another kid, he'd get a stern warning from the teacher. But if I was, I was immediately sent to the principal's office. If we were both caught roughhousing at recess, the aide might say to him, "Michael, we don't want to see you getting in trouble anymore" but he would turn to me and say, "Kwame, you're becoming a troublemaker."

But I also can't lay it all on the school. Life at home was like a noose getting tighter, and so I did act out during school hours. Despite the positive influence of Westley in my mother's house, my relationship with my father continued to be a source of suffering. Some of the trouble I got in, like the time I banged chalkboard erasers together and produced a cloud of dust that almost killed the asthmatic student in our class, seem like bad luck. Other instances, like the time I threw a boy off a jungle gym so hard he fractured his wrist, weren't that innocent. Like a lot of other kids, I talked back to teachers. What headstrong second grader doesn't try to prove he's right? But none of the other kids shouted, "You're a worthless piece of shit!" the way I did. None erupted in torrents of abuse, screaming, "You're a stupid idiot!" or "What's wrong with you?" Naturally my teachers were alarmed, so they sent me to the principal and eventually to the school therapist, a nice lady in a beige room. "Kwame," she asked, "who taught you those words?" I told her I didn't know, but of course I did. It was my father. It was his voice coming out in my higher register. The same things he shouted at me, I was shouting back at the world.

Soon I had cemented my reputation as a troublemaker, and I thought *If the suit fits, wear it*. On field trips to the American Museum of Natural History or to community theaters, I was the one preemptively told not to ruin it for the class. In the classroom my teachers stopped trying to engage me at all, and from my desk in the back of the room, I became louder and even more disruptive in response. Trips to the principal's office became even more frequent, though over time their purpose became less rehabilitative. Eventually I just sat there, seen by the entire school as a nuisance.

I guess that's one reason I grew to love the terrible London broil. The Gallaghers' home became like a spit of solid ground where I could just be myself, a boy, a child, guard down and heart open, even as the world seemed to settle into its own conclusion about who I was. No matter what others thought, at the Gallagher house Mrs. Fran still served her flavorless food with a side of unconditional love, and Mr. Gallagher still swept in at dinnertime with a hug and a kiss and a pat on the back.

In fifth grade, Michael, Patrick, and I all transferred to a private Catholic school called Mount Saint Michael. That began our slow drift away from closeness. Since the school was much farther away than P.S. 153, you either had to take a school bus or the subway. The Gallaghers could afford the extra $300 a semester for a bus but my mom, who could barely cover the tuition, couldn't. So every morning I took the 2 train to the 6 train, getting off at Nereid Avenue then catching the Bx16 fourteen blocks to the school. The commute was the real dividing line between the middle-class kids who went to Mount Saint Michael and the poor ones like me. It was also the first time I had been around other kids with my skin tone. I watched them on the train, fascinated as they brushed their hair into waves. I hadn't known how to train my hair but I began to learn, first by watching and then, after buying my own brush, by doing. Eventually these guys became my friends. We'd meet up on the platform on Pelham Parkway and head to school together.

Something, more than just that their skin was the same color as mine, resonated with me.

I began to wear do-rags, keeping them in my pocket until I left my house so as not to alarm West and my mom and earn the mockery of Tatiana. Then I'd meet up with the Mount crew, smoke a joint, and head to school. It felt good to belong, and even though my new friends didn't seem like educators, they taught me about black culture in New York City.

I still remained friendly with Michael and Patrick but our friendship cooled. We went from hanging out outside of school, to eating lunch together in the cafeteria, to chatting in the hallways, to nodding to each other. Nothing unfriendly, just that I had found a coterie, a new identity. Our paths had diverged.

And then, twenty years later, I'm walking backward on Bourbon Street and bump into the past and he's almost unrecognizable to me. Michael's a lighting designer out in Las Vegas. Patrick is a teacher. And I'm a chef.

"We have to go see Jewel!" Michael shouted at me.

"Yeah!" I agreed. "She'll freak out."

The two of us happily made our way through the French Quarter, threading our way through the hordes to the Garden District apartment where my mother lived. She wasn't back from work yet so we continued the party, raiding the freezer for ice cold bottles of Tito's vodka that steamed in the heat. When my mother walked in a few hours later, she thought I'd just picked up some random drunk white dude. She gave me the quizzical "What are you up to, Kwame?" look I knew well. I liked that look. Unlike my dad's, it was pretty open. My mom could come down hard, but she was also ready to throw down and party too.

Then Michael said, "You know me, Jewel."

"I don't know you," said my mother, taken aback.

"Yes, you do," said Michael, "Think."

He got down on his knees and pulled his best little-kid face, gazing up at my mother with a faux wide-eyed innocence like Martin Lawrence used to do on his show. He looked ridiculous, of course—a grown man, drunk off his ass, on his knees—but then, after an instant her face began to crinkle and melt into a smile.

"Michael!" she cried and hugged him as hard as I'd seen her hug anybody in a long time. "You're all grown up! It's been so long; I didn't recognize you!"

It was a moment full of emotion, for me and my mom and Michael too. I had no idea how he got to where he was, nor did he know of my own troubles and successes. You meet each other as friendly strangers, melt away the years with memory and the heat of nostalgia, and you're a kid again, and friends again, and for a moment you're back at the beginning. The three of us spent the rest of the night and well into the morning together, reminiscing about the Bronx, touching briefly on the vast blank space between then and now, but mostly letting it be. Maybe it was Mardi Gras, maybe it was the Tito's, maybe it was just a trick of memory. But in that moment we were all younger again and lighter too, still untoppled.

Not Mrs. Fran's London Broil

YIELD: 4 servings

---

3 tablespoons extra-virgin olive oil

3 tablespoons balsamic vinegar

3 garlic cloves, smashed

1 jalapeño, quartered

Juice of 1 lime

¼ cup cilantro stems

1 teaspoon salt, plus more for searing

½ teaspoon freshly ground black pepper

2 pounds top round steak

CHERRY SALSA

1 pound cherries, pitted and roughly chopped

¼ onion, minced

2 garlic cloves, minced

2 tablespoons cilantro, chopped

¼ jalapeño, ribs intact, minced

Juice of 1 lime

Kosher salt

---

1. **Make the London broil** Combine the olive oil, vinegar, garlic, jalapeño, lime juice, cilantro stems, salt, and pepper. Place the mixture in a large resealable plastic bag, add the steak, and seal. Refrigerate for 24 hours.

2. Remove the meat from the marinade. Discard marinade. Dry the meat and bring to room temperature.

3. Meanwhile, make the cherry salsa by combining all ingredients. Season to taste. Set aside.

4. Heat a large heavy-bottomed skillet over high heat. Season the steak with salt and sear for about 7 minutes on each side, until the internal temperature reads 130° F. Transfer to a cutting board, tent with foil, and let rest about 10 minutes.

5. Thinly slice against the grain, and serve with cherry salsa.

Ancestors

When I was ten years old, I broke my mother's wooden cutting board. I can't remember how it happened; I'm sure it wasn't on purpose. I'm not a psychopath. But regardless, in that moment both the cutting board and my life split in two. This went down at the end of fifth grade, and it couldn't have come at a worse time. Summer was a nightmare scenario: three long, hot months with a punk-ass kid (that was me), a drama queen (that was Tatiana), a boyfriend (that was Westley), and an overworked matriarch (Mom) packed into a one-bedroom apartment on Pelham Parkway in the Bronx. Everything in our house was cramped. You could literally see and hear everyone else from every corner. The four of us fought for turf like we were in a prison yard. My mother and Westley slept in the living room; Tatiana had claimed the bedroom as her own. Now a sign on that door read Keep Out, and if I wandered in, she'd smack me so hard my ears rang for days. Tatiana hated Westley and me; I wasn't a fan of hers, and gave Westley a harder time than I should have. We all loved my mom, but between her job at Café Lou's and catering, she didn't have that much time for any of us.

Without a bedroom of my own, I slept in a closet. Not a

closet-sized bedroom, an actual closet. There was just enough room to wedge a twin mattress on the floor with a few extra inches on one side. To my mother's credit, she tried to make it room-like. She cleared out the clothes racks and shelves, decorated the walls with posters I got to choose, and installed a moon-shaped nightlight since I was terrified of the dark.

For a while I loved it. It was like being in a hobbit hole. But by the time I was ten, what had been comforting and snug felt like a cell. I was speeding into adolescence, with the usual haywire emotions. I needed a space of my own. More space. It couldn't be at my father's apartment, just twenty minutes away, at 233rd Street and Amundson Avenue. The weekends I spent with him left me feeling even more claustrophobic than my time in the closet. At least the closet was my own. At my dad's house, every single thing I picked up or put down or sat on or lay on, every task I tried to complete, could set him off on an epic rage. An eye roll would "earn" me a beating with the African whip. When I returned to my mom's on Sunday nights after a weekend with him, with bruises up and down my arms and legs and a body full of hurt and rage, I'd throw myself in my closet and lock the door.

No wonder I fought with everybody over everything. Tatiana and I constantly skirmished, over what to watch on TV, who showered first in the morning, on and on. These were nasty, hair-pulling fights, and since my mother was often at work, they lasted for ages. When she was home, I fought with my mother over my tone of voice, her tone of voice, why I was stuck in a damn closet, why she was never around anymore, and why I kept getting into trouble

As I morphed from a fat-cheeked kid to a young man, the world began to see me differently. At Mount Saint Michael, the Catholic private school to which I had transferred, I was surrounded and befriended by much tougher kids, mostly black like me, many of whom had grown up fending for themselves. Many of the teachers, however, were middle-aged or older white women, and they approached us—ten-year-olds—like we were dangerous. They wielded their power like prison wardens. And in their fear I saw reflected back an image of myself I hadn't seen before. At the same time I saw the power my friends possessed, how they could manipulate using fear. As our teachers reprimanded us and, when that didn't work, suspended us, I saw how the kids around me dealt with this anger and frustration. They turned their faces to stone and deadened their eyes like those of statues. They became hard and menacing, and as I saw it then, that hardness meant strength.

At home if I broke a video game cartridge, when West tried to talk to me about responsibility I'd retort that he had nothing to teach me, that he wasn't my dad. At ten years old I'd come home after the streetlights had switched on, smelling of the Newport Lights I had tried to smoke and sometimes high, and challenge West and my mom to say something. I started to hang a red bandana out of my back pocket like I was a junior member of the Bloods (of course I took it out and carefully stashed it in my bag before I went out into the streets). I welcomed any pretext for a brawl. West, who had gotten in trouble himself as a kid and could see some of himself in me, would back off and off until he couldn't back off any more. And then we'd fight, as my mother looked helplessly on. A few times he'd slap me around the small kitchen, more out of frustration than rage, but it hurt just the same. Every time we had an argument like that, it was like a slipknot that cinched a bit tighter in the apartment. The cutting board was the last straw. Soon the fight just became the same one we'd been having for months. My mom said I had to learn respect; I said she couldn't control me. Both were true. That night I stormed into the closet and slammed the door again.

I awoke the next morning to the smell of bacon frying. No matter how rough the week had been or how much we had scrounged for money or how hard we fought on Saturday night, Sunday morning was a chance for our family to hit reset. My mom cooked pancakes until they were perfectly golden brown and fried strips of bacon until the aroma of hot fat filled the kitchen. She turned cans of salmon into little patties we pan-fried together. I loved helping her make scalloped potatoes most of all. She minced the garlic and onions and sliced the potatoes while I layered them in a casserole dish and tended the garlic and herbs as they softened in a hot pan. We never fought in the kitchen. It's hard to, when you're standing side by side at the counter.

West was the egg master and could make eggs like a short-order line cook, any way you liked them. Tatiana, who by this time was attending a Food and Finance High School, bustled around the small space in a cloud of cake flour. When she asked, I fetched her baking powder and salt without complaint, a rare period of cooperation.

In the first few seconds of getting up, I forgot about the cutting board. But as soon as I walked into the kitchen, I remembered. Something was off that morning; I could feel a heaviness in the air.

"What's wrong, Ma?" I asked.

With no preamble she said, "You're going to live with your grandfather."

At first I was confused. Which grandfather did she mean? My real grandfather, her dad, Bertran Robinson? That couldn't be right; she hardly knew him herself. I had met him a few years ago when we had visited him in the galley of a ship where he worked as a cook down in Beaumont, Texas. He had towered over me like an old statue, smelling of fry oil and diesel fuel. Later he had made me fried crawfish and fried shrimp that I ate with my feet dangling in the air off the wooden planks of the dock, looking at the water below. But that was the last I had seen of him.

Maybe she meant her stepfather, a laid-back Trinidadian guy named Winston who lived in Virginia with her mother. We were very close, but that was unlikely too, since we all called him Papa.

"No," said my mother, "with Granddad."

"Granddad!" I yelped. "But he lives in Africa!"

"Yes, I know that," said my mom. "You're going to live there with him."

"When am I leaving?" I asked.

"We're leaving for D.C. this afternoon," she said. "You'll fly to Lagos from there."

"How long will I be gone?" I asked.

She paused for a moment. "Just for the summer."

I loved my grandfather of course. I saw him nearly every summer when he returned from Nigeria to spend time with Auntie Chu-chu at her home in Washington. Not only were my grandfather and my father not close, but Auntie Chu-chu was the eldest, so by tradition she had the right and obligation to host him. Every August all of us New York cousins would pile into a car and head south to D.C. That part of the trip wasn't out of the ordinary. But I hadn't been to Nigeria since a week-long trip with my father five years ago. I couldn't tell whether this was retribution in some way for the cutting board or whether it was just a long-planned childcare solution for the summer that no one had thought to tell me about.

At any rate, the sweetness of breakfast was gone. Soon after, I packed up my few belongings—I had, after all, only a closet. That afternoon I gave Westley a hug before my mom and I began the drive south. I was scared and a little apprehensive, but Africa was cool, if far away, and I was excited to spend time with Granddad.

My grandfather was born in Zaria, in northern Nigeria, but his family hailed from Ibusa, a village in the Delta State that was the cultural center for the Igbo people. Though he studied in Lagos as a kid, most of his adult life had been spent in the States. From the fifties through the seventies, he was a leading academic voice in the Pan-African movement, holding teaching positions at Howard and Fisk Universities, and publishing books on black ideology, on the diaspora and African identity and Black Liberation. But he saw firsthand the assassination of his friends like Stokely Carmichael, and concluded that the government wouldn't let black activists live in peace until they were either in the ground or in a cell. In 1973 my grandfather realized he could never be free, truly free, in the United States. So he moved back to Nigeria, leaving behind his wife, my grandmother Gloria, and his seven grown children, including my father and Chu-chu.

My grandfather first settled in Lagos, where he served as the director general of the Nigerian Institute of International Affairs. But by the time I was sent to live with him, he had returned to Ibusa and assumed the title *obinzor*, or elder. He had built himself a large compound, with a couple of wives and a flock of chickens and a ceremonial hall in which he held court. That we came from noble blood was part of the family lore, I knew it well. In fact, every time we saw him in D.C. he made all the male cousins recite, "As men we must be honorable, respectful, and gentlemen. We must take care of those around us."

When he opened the door of my Aunt Chu-chu's house that evening, my grandfather certainly looked like something out of a history book. He wore a long white embroidered shirt called an *isiagu* and matching silken pants. On his head was a traditional red fez. His face bore the creases of age, his eyes crinkled behind a pair of wire-rimmed glasses and his thin and sinewy arms poked out of his sleeves. He was so foreign-seeming, so . . . African. But his smile was warm as he hugged my mother, and when he hugged me, I hugged him back.

M y grandfather and I were flying alone. But my cousins, Chu-chu's kids Ayana and Shakir, had flown over a few months earlier. They had been sent to Africa on a cultural mission to appreciate their heritage; I was sent to Africa on a cultural mission to get out of my mother's hair. After what felt like a day in the air, we descended into Nigeria's largest city. My grandfather had a car pick us up at the airport, where the chaos of Dulles was repeated but in reverse and with many more smiles, and we began our six-hour journey to Ibusa. As we drove through the traffic-jammed streets, I peered through the windows. The density of the dizzying city gave way abruptly to a low sprawl of buildings and makeshift structures with roofs of corrugated tin, laundry hanging from clotheslines at crazy angles, satellite dishes perched precariously, and streets full of people and carts and motorcycles and cows. Everywhere there was action and people and life. After about an hour or so, the buildings thinned out and the sky opened up.

The landscape of the Delta State was lush and green, with cattle grazing by the side of the road and rolling hills in the distance. Jet-lagged and hazy, I nodded in and out of sleep. I remember only snatches of my grandfather talking to me, explaining, for example, how we had to avoid debris like oranges on the road, since local bandits were known to fill them with nails to puncture the tires of cars so they could ambush disabled vehicles and their occupants. I was too exhausted to be freaked out.

It must have been after dark when we arrived in my grandfather's compound, and he must have carried me to my bed. The next morning I woke up to the loud crowing of a rooster. At first I thought it was a cartoon; I had never heard a real rooster before. I sat up in bed and looked around the room. It was small and spartan, big enough only for a full-size bed. I saw that Shakir was sleeping beside me. *Well,* I thought, *at least it wasn't a closet.* The walls were cinderblock with a thin layer of cracking plaster. A small window opened into the kitchen. And though it was only seven o'clock, the familiar smell of onions frying filled the room.

I explored my new home. Seven people lived in the compound, spread over three buildings. Most of us lived in the big house. Shakir, Ayana, and I lived on the bottom floor. My grandfather and his second wife, a dark-skinned woman from North Carolina I knew only as Mother, occupied the upstairs floor. She'd been in Nigeria since just after my grandfather arrived in 1973 but still spoke with a perfect southern drawl. Granddad's study was on the second floor too. We children were forbidden to enter his book-lined space, with its old desk covered with papers, and traditional sculptures and masks on the walls.

The bedrooms of Nkechi and Chukwuma—technically my aunt and uncle, but only a few years older than me—were on the second floor too. Aunt Mimi, my granddad's second wife, a thirty-something-year-old Igbo woman with light skin who wore lots of makeup, lived in a smaller house connected to the main one by a concrete walkway stretching from bedroom to bedroom across which my granddad would sneak late at night. You could always tell at breakfast when he'd gone to visit Aunt Mimi, because Mother would be even more taciturn than usual but Aunt Mi would be all smiles. The two of them—Mother and Mi—bickered constantly, though occasionally I'd walk in on them laughing at some secret joke.

The third building we called the servants' quarters, though Granddad had no servants (and never had, to my knowledge). It was a simple structure with a long hallway and a series of small bedrooms on either side that were used for storage.

The compound was complemented by a graveyard/parking lot containing functional to semifunctional vehicles. Under a big blue tarp, the RV that Granddad had once driven with Mother on a cross-country trip of America back in the 1960s sat like a great whale. In the dry climate it was remarkably well preserved, and the cabin, blue-tinged and dark through the tarp, was like a *Twilight Zone* time machine. I have no idea how or why he had brought it to Nigeria, but there it was. Then there were the Mercedes, at least four of them, in various conditions. The cars were an exact measure of social standing in the compound. Granddad had the newest—and by newest I mean from the 1980s—followed by Mother's older model and then Aunt Mimi's, which was beat-up and dusty and hardly worked.

Between the wheels darted a flock of twelve chickens who slept in a coop near the water pump. They weren't the only animals. There was a goat I named Goaty and a Ram I named Rammy. (My nicknames were admittedly not exactly creative, but at least they were clear.) The chickens had names too. The red one I called Red. The rooster with the floppy comb who flounced around in the dirt I dubbed Goofy.

For the first few weeks I was there, I tried to re-create my

Bronx apartment. Like any ten-year-old I gravitated to the television, but to my dismay only four channels came in. And when the electricity didn't work—not at all an unusual occurrence—there were none. It was just as well. Every time she saw me on the couch or peered through the kitchen window and saw me on my bed, Mother would holler, "Boy, get outside. There's work to do." And there was. We pumped water from the well near the cars into plastic jugs, poured the water from the jugs through a filter into more jugs, then into bottles, and then carefully washed out used bottles and jugs, stacking them to form a plastic wall waiting to be picked up. I fed the chickens, scattering feed around the yard and laughing as they rushed at me. I kept Goaty and Rammy fed, groomed, and watered. I went with Mother to the market, where I was tempted by the fragrant skewers of beef *suya* grilling on the street. But she pulled me away by the hand, hissing, "We don't eat street food!"

I passed the first few weeks of the summer bored but happy, cataloguing the heat, the dust, the work, and the dusty conditions as future stories to tell my friends back in the Bronx. I chased Red and Goofy around the yard and kept mostly on the compound grounds except for a few forays into town. These were long hot days playing knock-off Nintendo games with Shakir, watching Aunt Mi and Mother go back and forth, and playing hide-and-seek among the Mercedes and the RV.

E very morning I awoke to the strong smell of onions wafting into my room as Auntie Mi stood at the stove making red onion stew and rice. She caramelized the onions, added tomatoes, and then let the stew simmer. It was not, to my ten-year-old American mind, breakfast food. I survived the first few months on cheese puffs (the Cheez Doodles of Nigeria); peanuts, which we called groundnuts; and *fufu,* a doughy ball we made in the Bronx with yam powder but that here Auntie Mi made with actual yams. At first I had no idea that the groundnuts, which we kept in glass jars, were the same snacks I ate out of small packages on the streets back in the States. These were so much nuttier, so distinctive, so full of flavor. They didn't just taste like salt or roasting.

Auntie Mi and Mother competed in many different ways, but perhaps the most hotly contested battle occurred in the kitchen. And I have to say, Auntie Mi won. Early in the morning I would follow her out into the dusty yard. She carried a machete that she dragged in the dirt behind her and I followed the trail to a stand of thick, sawtooth-leaved, bumpy-trunked oil palm trees. She hefted the machete up and used the side of the blade to knock down a few of the bright red palm kernels that clustered like grapes at the top of the trunk. We kids would pick up the kernels, about the size of a macadamia nut, and as the chickens clustered around us, rinse them and pick off their shells. While my cousins and aunts and uncles ran around in the yard, I sat in the kitchen with Mi as she simmered the palm kernels. When they were soft, we'd drain them and place them in a giant stone mortar and pestle. Auntie Mi sat down, wrapped her legs around the mortar, and gripping the pestle in both hands, began to rhythmically grind the kernels into a red mush.

When the consistency was right, she added dried crayfish, hunks of tan and sandy-colored stockfish, and other funky things to the pot, and let it simmer for three hours. This was the *banga* stew we'd have for dinner that night, eight hours from cultivation to plate. It didn't matter what continent I was on, in my mind food and love were being mixed together.

———

As we got to the end of summer, Mother drove me an hour and a half over bumpy roads to the nearest internet café so I could call my mom. It was hot as balls, and we were in Mother's Mercedes with no air-conditioning. My bare skinny legs stuck to the leather of the back seat as we bumped along the road, with me trapped between my cousins in the middle seat. Everything in the café was covered in dust. Hell, everything everywhere was covered in dust. As Mother waited outside I took my place at a long dirty counter, thin dividers offering the merest gesture of privacy between me and the young men with drawn-out faces calling parts unknown. I dialed my mom's number.

"Yo, Mom," I said. "It's almost September. When am I coming home?"

At first I thought the call had been dropped, which happened more often than not in those parts. There was only silence, but then, amid the static, her voice came on sounding a million miles away and very small.

"You're not coming home. Your home is there now."

Silence. Static. Flies buzzed. Men around me chattered in Igbo I couldn't understand.

What. The. Hell. We made this drive every week so I could talk to my mom, and she had never, not once, let on that I wasn't going to start sixth grade with the rest of my friends. I had been dreaming of coming home. It wasn't that I didn't like it in Nigeria, but I wanted to turn on the water and there would be water to drink, to turn on the lights and there'd be electricity, to return to New York and, for the love of God, to her, my mom.

"You're not coming home," she said again, "until you learn respect."

Respect. The word that hung between us like a wall. What

did she know about respect? How could she know what I'd learned about respect? She was four thousand miles away, leading her own goddamn life, and here I was, holed up in a filthy internet café in the middle of the Delta State. Maybe I was full up to my ears with respect—respect for myself, respect for Granddad, respect for what I had back in the Bronx. She wouldn't know. You had to be there to know.

Of course, I didn't say any of this. I just began to cry, tears tracing a path through the dirt on my cheeks. I dropped the receiver, letting it dangle inches from the floor. As I got up I could hear my mother saying, "Kwame? Kwame? Are you there?" No, I wanted to shout, I'm not there. I'm here. I'm stuck right here.

I returned to the compound. The gate opened and shut. I had nothing to do but settle in for the long haul. That I didn't want to be there, that I missed my mother, that I missed my home, none of that mattered. The walls of the compound kept the world outside and kept me locked in. The difference between a home and a prison is in the mind of the occupant. Yet at the same time, staying in Nigeria for the indeterminate future allowed me to fully put my weight on the ground. My life wasn't a future story to tell my friends. It was just my life. The Kwame who dropped the phone, the heartbroken Kwame who wanted to go home, I locked him up too; gate open and gate shut. I rearranged my mind to make space for the fact that my mother didn't want me back. I'd wanted space. Now I'd gotten it.

A few weeks later my cousin Shakir, Chukwuma, and I began going to the city's only private boarding school, Santa Maria College II. It was a three-story building, red and white, that looked like an abandoned motel. There were windows but no windowpanes, doorways but no doors. The kids who lived there—drawn from around the Delta State, dropped off by their parents not to be seen again for months on end—slept in barrack-type bunk beds. Even in my school-issued yellow polo shirt and tiny bright blue shorts, knee socks and sandals, I stood out. That I was American immediately conferred prestige.

"How do you say 'little boy' in American?" asked the boys, crowding around me the first day.

I said "little boy," in my best American accent, which sounded like a newscaster's from the 1960s.

They exploded into peals of laughter, misunderstanding what I'd said. "Noodle boy! Noodle boy!"

From then on, I was Noodle Boy. I didn't love it, but there was no malice intended.

Gradually I learned to decipher the Nigerian accent, a sort of ornately overenunciated version of my own English, and my classmates learned to decipher my "American." Our lessons consisted of copious amounts of note-taking on subjects like Nigerian history and science. Even our phys ed classes involved taking notes, in this case on the dimensions of a basketball court and the rules of the game.

When the Nigerian method of discipline became clear, I quickly shed my troublemaker persona. Back in the States, detention was cool. Here, punishments included digging a hole equal to your height and carrying a cinder block across the dusty soccer field. Talking back to my teachers suddenly lost its appeal.

But it wasn't just that. What I remember most of all was how differently our Nigerian teacher treated us. We were just boys, students, some of us better than others. What we weren't were problems. At the time I couldn't put into words or thoughts exactly why I felt the way I did—lighter than usual, more joyful than I was in the Bronx—but now I know that this was it. I was fundamentally not seen as a problem first and a person second.

As the days turned to months, I felt more and more at home. After a long breakfast hunger strike, I finally surrendered to Mimi's menu of red onion stew and rice. To my great surprise, I loved it. I even grew to love those Nigerian lunch staples, corned beef sandwiches, canned sardines, Scotch eggs, and minced-meat pies, vestiges of British rule. And then there was Auntie Mi's jollof rice and red stew waiting for us when we returned to the compound in the afternoons, filling the open kitchen with pungent aromas that drew me in like tractor beams.

What I looked forward to most was when my granddad would preside over meetings of the village council. As an *obi*, or village elder, my grandfather frequently hosted meetings in a large open-walled building he had constructed across the dirt road from the compound. One of the few times I was allowed out the gate alone was to take him bowls of bright pink bitter kola nuts during these meetings, which the men would chew and spit out. It was always me, and not the others, who were chosen, so these days were special. The hall was a big open structure with a dirt floor and a raised platform on one end. My grandfather sat on a large wooden throne that was covered with hides and intricate wood carvings. As *obi*, he acted as a mediator for local disputes, settling small claims among the villagers. In his baggy *isiagu* and red fez, and with heavy beads around his neck, my grandfather looked both small and grand. In front of him scores of men gathered, sitting in folding chairs, waving their hands through the thick hot air to shoo flies and make their points. I couldn't follow their disputes since they spoke in rapid Igbo, but all the men knew me. I was the *obi's*

American grandson, and I'd walk through the crowd's brightly colored *isiagus,* giving high fives and handing out the kola nuts.

Frequently, after these meetings we would host a gathering at the compound for the other elders on the council. Aunt Mi would spend all day in the kitchen, preparing jollof rice, *egusi* stew, *banga* stew, and red stew, and kneading the yam dough to make *fufu,* which she brought out on trays into the courtyard.

Council days had the spirit of Sunday morning mixed with the festive air of a block party. But there was something else too, something that even then I could sense was different from anything I had experienced in America. The air, hot and windless, was also heavy with the past. The Igbo had been holding councils like these for thousands of years, gathering for meals like this for thousands of years, living in households like this for thousands of years. The past connected to the present without a rupture, without a seam, with no distinct lines between then and now.

Much as it was in the other compounds that dotted Ibusa, in my grandfather's he made sure we knew who our ancestors were. And that our ancestors walked among us.

Early one morning my grandfather walked into the kitchen clutching Goofy by his neck. Goofy was the best of the cocks, a floppy-combed rooster with a handsome green neck who reminded me of Gaston from *Beauty and the Beast.* Me and Goofs, we were amigos. He might have been my only true friend in the compound. When I was done with Shakir and the others, Goofy was there to keep me company. This was the same Goofy that grandfather was now spinning by his handsome neck. Granddad did a little dance, shouting gleefully, "We're killing Goofy tonight!" This was a perennial joke he pulled, sometimes with Goofy, sometimes with Red, sometimes with the others. He thought it was hilarious. Me, not so much. I cried every time, never knowing if he meant it. This time, I quickly found out, he did.

"No!" I cried, "please don't kill Goofy!"

"Fine," said my grandfather, relenting. He put the chicken down and Goofy scrammed for the door. "But we have to kill one."

"Kill Red," I said, "if you have to."

"Follow me," said my grandfather, suddenly serious, and we headed to the yard.

Red was only slightly less lovable than Goofy. He didn't have the same sense of humor or a comb as floppy. Still, I was sad as I watched my granddad stalk the bird, grabbing him in a quick motion with both hands and pinning his wings to his body.

Red swung his head around and I could have sworn he looked to me for help. But you never know with chicken eyes. We walked over to a large wooden stump by the water pump. A cleaver hung on a hook on the fence.

My granddad laid Red down on the stump. "Hold its neck," he said, "and do not look in the animal's eyes when it is about to die." That was considered the worst luck. It was too late. I knew what was coming, and Red seemed to know as well. Our unblinking eyes had already connected.

My grandfather took the cleaver from the fence.

Red was dead in seconds, his shocked head lying on the stump next to his chicken body. My grandfather picked up his limp, warm carcass and poured the blood into a metal bowl mounted in a block of whitewashed concrete I hadn't noticed before. As the hot blood splashed into the bowl, my grandfather uttered a few words in Igbo. "This is a prayer to our ancestors, Kwame," he told me when he was done. "We offer them this life as gratitude for everything they've given us."

My grandfather slowly began to reveal more about our ancestors, parceling out bits of information at just the right rate for me to absorb them. Over the next year and a half that I spent in Nigeria, the concept of ancestors seeped into me, so much so that after a while, I stopped even thinking about them and they became a part of me. The bowl devoted to them; the statues in Granddad's office; the recipes Auntie Mi and Mother cooked—these all traced a line directly to where I came from, to who I was. My grandfather, who had devoted his professional life to encouraging the African diaspora to feel pride in their heritage, loved that I had, in fact, come home and felt that pride. I learned what it meant to have space, space at home, space to be who I really was without being penned in by what people *thought* I was.

When my mother finally told me, just after my twelfth birthday, that I was coming home, it wasn't joy I felt but sadness. Though I was excited to see my mother again, to see my friends, I was heartbroken to leave Ibusa, to leave Granddad and the dusty compound behind. And I was heartbroken to leave my ancestors on this continent and return to America. The day before I left, I knocked on the door of Granddad's study.

I didn't often hug Granddad. He wasn't the hugging kind of man. But this time I walked behind the desk and gave him a huge hug. I felt his bony shoulders and torso. I told him that I loved him and that I would miss him, miss it here in Nigeria, miss the presence of my ancestors.

"You can't take this land with you," he said, patting my arms, "but your ancestors will never leave you. They are part of who you are."

Market *Suya*

YIELD: 4 to 6 servings

FOR THE *SUYA* SPICE BLEND

3 tablespoons cayenne pepper

1½ tablespoons roasted peanuts, ground into a fine powder

1 tablespoon paprika

1 tablespoon garlic powder

1 tablespoon onion powder

½ tablespoon ground ginger

2 teaspoons kosher salt

2 Maggi bouillon cubes, crushed

FOR THE *SUYA*

1 pound jumbo shrimp, peeled and deveined

1 pound Wagyu rib eye beef, thinly sliced into strips

1 pound boneless chicken thighs, cut into 2-inch pieces

FOR THE ROASTED TOMATO SOUBISE

2 medium vine-ripened tomatoes, stemmed

1 tablespoon olive oil

Kosher salt

2 tablespoons canola oil

1 medium white onion, thinly sliced

1 cup heavy cream

---

1. **Make the spice blend** In a small bowl, combine all the spice blend ingredients until incorporated.

2. **Prepare the *suya*** In three separate bowls, place the shrimp, beef, and chicken. Divide the spice blend equally among the bowls and mix well to coat the meats. Cover each bowl in plastic wrap and transfer to the refrigerator to marinate for 1 hour.

3. **Make the soubise** Preheat oven to 400° F. On a rimmed baking sheet, toss the tomatoes with the olive oil and salt. Transfer to the oven and roast for 15 minutes, then remove and let cool.

4. In a large skillet, heat the canola oil over medium-high heat. Add the onion and cook until soft and translucent, 6 to 8 minutes. Add the tomatoes and cook until they have fully broken down, 10 minutes. Stir in the cream and bring to a light simmer. Cook, stirring occasionally, until the cream has reduced and become thick. Transfer to a blender and purée until smooth. Season with salt and set aside.

5. Light a grill or place a grill pan over medium-high heat. Skewer the shrimp, rib eye, and chicken on soaked 12-inch bamboo skewers. Grill, turning occasionally, until cooked through, 2 to 3 minutes for the shrimp, 2 to 3 minutes for the rib eye, and 6 to 8 minutes for the chicken. Serve alongside the roasted tomato soubise.

The Block

I left the United States for Nigeria on a jet plane, a small skinny kid with an attitude. I came back two years later a few inches taller but just as skinny and quickly developed the same attitude that got me sent away in the first place. If my mom thought Nigeria would scare me straight, she was wrong. At best it just got me out of her hair for a while. The lessons I learned there, the experiences I'd had, went deep underground somewhere and wouldn't reemerge until nearly a decade later.

Returning to the Bronx felt like stepping back onto a stage and into a character I knew well. Ibusa was a stage too, of course, but with a different cast, a different audience, and very different scenery. I had been a bit player there, traveling through. I was the kid from America, the *obi*'s grandson from the Bronx, Noodle Boy. I didn't get into trouble much those two years; in Nigeria I was too insecure in my own position to rock the boat much. But as soon as I got back home, virtually from the moment I landed, that old rebellion flooded back.

When I got off the plane and walked past security, my mother greeted me with a wide smile and a big hug. "You're so much taller, Kwame!" she said, holding me close as I wriggled

away. "C'mon, Mom," I said. "Let me go." Yet despite the pre-
teen awkwardness, I was so happy to see her. For the first few
moments our conversation was stilted—a lot of "How are you
doing?" over and over again—but she was my mom and soon
we were chatting away as effortlessly as we always had.

Despite the show of joy, I had returned in what was a difficult period for her. Catering by Jewel was going well but my
mother just wasn't making enough money to survive. Especially now that the house included not just Westley and Tatiana
but me too, what she took home every month simply didn't
cover what we needed. She worked herself to the bone, getting
up early to prep for events during the day and hustling for dinners at night. Still it wasn't enough to make the rent. So when
I returned that fall, home was a moving target. In the space
of five years we moved eight times, bouncing from the South
Bronx to 135th Street in Harlem—our apartment overlooked
the Abyssinian Baptist Church and we could see, every Sunday, busloads of white tourists standing patiently outside for
their opportunity to sway to "Wade in the Water"—and back
up to the Bronx. We lived in a purgatory between packed and
unpacked, here and gone.

I didn't realize it at the time, but a lot of our financial inse-
curity had to do with me. Just as she had before I left for Nigeria, my mom scrounged together monthly tuition to send me
to a private school. Now she did it again, this time to Cardi-
nal Spellman, a Catholic high school up in Baychester, Bronx,
where tuition was $8,000. Spellman had a reputation for turn-
ing tough kids around. It was strict—it was Catholic, so that
goes without saying—but with a staff that really cared about
the students. The first time I visited, a few weeks before classes
started, I was so excited about the well-kept building with its
interior courtyard, and a full-size football field, that I really

thought I'd found my place. Compared to Santa Maria College in Ibusa, this was like a resort.

Every morning I'd transfer from the 2 train at Third Avenue to the 5 train to Baychester. That's where I met Jaquan. It wasn't hard to spot fellow students. Who else would be wearing a maroon polo shirt and khaki pants at 7:20 in the morning? I was used to people scowling at me on the train or just ignoring everything, listening to their music. So when Jaquan immediately nodded when he saw me and said, "What's up, man? My name's Jaquan. What's yours?," I noticed. At age thirteen he still had fat baby cheeks, and he wore thick glasses. He was not, to say the least, intimidating. In fact, his nickname on the block, he told me shortly after I met him, was Urkel, after Steve Urkel. That first morning, after he introduced himself I slid over to sit by him. Next to Jaquan was his friend, soon mine, named Marquise. He was slight, very studious and quiet. Marquise's mother was a corrections officer at Sing Sing, and you could just tell looking at the kid that he was kept on a tight leash.

Like Jaquan, Marquise was disarmingly friendly. He didn't bother with macho posturing or intimidation. We immediately got along. I was new to the school and in need of friends. We'd eat lunch together in the cafeteria, play basketball at recess, and goof off. It was like me and the Gallagher twins all over again. Sort of.

Because we all got on the train at different stops, I didn't know exactly where Jaquan or Marquise lived. And because we all wore the same school uniform, there weren't that many outward indicators of their backgrounds. Except sneakers. That I remember. Growing up, I wasn't used to sneakers being an indicator of anything. All my friends in the Gifted and Talented program wore scruffy New Balances or whatever their parents happened to buy them. But Jaquan and Marquise were both obsessed with Air Jordans, devoting endless energy to keeping their rotation of crisp black-and-white shoes spotlessly clean. I assumed, naïvely I guess, that their backgrounds were like mine: lower middle class perhaps, but not poor.

That changed when Jaquan invited me over to play basketball at his home at Webster. The Webster Houses are one of the toughest housing projects in the Bronx, and I'm not ashamed to admit that the first time I visited him there, I was scared. Although I was thirteen and grew up in the Bronx I had never set foot in the projects before. The apartment buildings I lived in always had carpet in the hallways, plaster on the walls, and succulent plants in the lobby. They were part of the community. But where Jaquan lived, in Section 8 of the New York City Housing Authority, the projects—or whatever you want to call them—looked like warehouses, not homes. They were huge and sprawling, set apart from the world by their sheer mass. One of the first things I noticed about Webster were the surfaces. They were hard: concrete and brick and metal, scuffed linoleum floors and blue-tiled hallways. I wasn't used to it, to how loud it was, how sound ricocheted from surface to surface.

I tried to play it cool, but in our school uniforms Jaquan and I were easy targets. Or at least I was. Walking through the courtyard—really just a dusty grassy area—I noticed a guy staring me down near the entrance to the building. He was wearing black jeans, a black jeans jacket, and a red flat-brimmed New York Yankees cap, with thick gold chains hanging around his neck. I was looking at him because, well, he was interesting to me. As I got closer, I saw that his pupils were brown, with bloodshot whites around them. His skin was light brown and taut against his bones, and a thin scar ran along his cheek. Tattoos snuck up over his collar and out of his sleeves onto his hands. He looked like such a bad motherfucker he should have come with a theme song.

Looking at people had never seemed a problem to me before,

but when we were a few feet away from him and my eye contact had lasted more than a millisecond, he growled, "What the fuck you looking at, man?"

I didn't know the right answer. "You, because you have a very interesting face and also because I'm intrigued about that scar, and, finally, I'm curious about your tattoos. Did they hurt?" didn't seem to be the right answer. So instead I just mumbled, "Nothing, man" and looked away as fast as I could. I didn't want to get messed up before we even made it to Jaquan's place.

Thankfully, the guy knew Jaquan. "Urkel, tell your boy to stop looking at me!"

We made it into the lobby. It smelled like old piss, and a sign over the elevator bank reminded everyone that assault was a felony punishable by up to seven years in prison. Jaquan didn't bat an eye. This was, after all, home. And I didn't want to betray my shock or insult him, so I didn't say anything one way or the other. He lived on the fifth floor with his mother, Ms. Peggy, and his grandmother, Grandma, who teetered on the edge of dementia. His father had died when he was three years old, so it was just the three of them in the large apartment. Ms. Peggy was home the afternoon we arrived, but since she worked the night shift as a nurse at a nursing home nearby, she was on her way out. In my memory she was always wearing scrubs with cheery prints on them, like bunnies or rabbits wearing shower caps. I wondered if it made the old dying folks she cared for any happier.

Jaquan's place was much bigger than anywhere I had lived. The sprawling apartment was full of heavy wooden armoires, plush sofas, and framed photos. And the kitchen was full of food. Always. Before Ms. Peggy went to work every evening, she'd make plates of ribs, corn bread, mac and cheese, and yellow rice, cover them with Saran wrap, and leave them on the counter for me and Jaquan and his grandmother. That was a welcome shock to me, a warm, well-stocked pantry in the middle of the projects. These were the years of cheap sandwiches and hunger at my mother's house. My mom made just enough money to be ineligible for the Supplemental Nutrition Assistance Program (SNAP) and she refused to apply for NYCHA housing. Though I never asked her exactly why, I knew my mom well enough to know that she was enormously proud, and I think she saw relying on the government in any way as an admission of defeat, proof that we were actually poor. However, what that meant in practice was that whereas Jaquan's mom was paying $200 a month for rent, we were paying $2,200. Add to that, tuition at Spellman, a Metrocard, and all the other living expenses for me and my sister, and we were struggling to cover basics like heat, electricity, and food.

That wasn't the only difference between my life and Jaquan's. When I was growing up, the N-word was strictly forbidden in my house. That word was a cudgel, a lash, a curse. Even worse than the f-word, it was *the* taboo. I had, of course, heard it in music and from the kids I hung out with just before I'd gone to Africa. I even used it when I was with them. But at home it was literally the worst word you could say. Since I had returned from Nigeria, I had stopped using the N-word at all. I was proud to be black, proud to carry the name Kwame Onwuachi, an African name, a black name. I was nobody's Negro and I was nobody's nigga.

But one day, over at Jaquan's, just as he and I and Marquise were heading outside to play basketball, Jaquan's mom called out, "Put on a sweater!" Jaquan, like most teenagers would, ignored her. Ms. Peggy yelled again, this time a little louder, "Nigga, put on a sweater." I remember that moment clearly. I had heard the word said by people my own age. I had heard it thousands of times, in songs and movies, whatever. But I had never heard a middle-aged woman shout it at her son. I'm not on some self-loathing trip or a holier-than-thou soapbox, and I know how much Ms. Peggy loved Jaquan, but in that moment I just felt sad. Sad for Jaquan. Sad for his mom. Sad that this word, even though it had been "reclaimed," still stuck in our backs like a dagger and in our minds like a poison.

Just like the noise bouncing around the hallways, there was an undercurrent of violence at Webster. The Webster Houses are actually made up of the 1200, 1300, and 1400 blocks. Like most of the Bronx these blocks are Blood-affiliated, but especially between the 1300 and 1400, which are controlled by rival crews. The 1300 block, where Jaquan lived, is controlled by a crew called B.A.B.Y. I never found out what it stood for.

Even though I didn't live there, I had spent enough time at Webster that I knew that opting out of gang involvement just wasn't an option. It's unavoidable, like income tax, and whether I laid my head down there or not, I spent at least 51 percent of my time there. Jaquan was naturally cautious and risk-averse, not prime gang material. And I, I wasn't even from Webster, I was just passing through. Nevertheless, it was inevitable that he and I would get sucked in. For me it started when I was sixteen. I had gotten kicked out of Spellman after one prank too many. I had shown up on the first day of twelfth grade, fresh-pressed khakis and laundered shirt, only to be asked by the dean what I was doing there.

"Um, going to school?" I said, like a smartass.

The dean hotfooted me to his office. "Did you not get our letter?"

"What letter?" I asked.

"You weren't invited back," he said. "You need to leave."

"But my grades are fine!" I protested, because they were.

"Doesn't matter. You'll never change," he said. "You need to leave. Now."

I was confused and humiliated. I was actually looking forward to this year. But the dean was adamant.

"You need to go," he said, pushing me out of his office. And that was that. The Bronx Leadership Academy, a public charter school a few blocks from Webster, was the only place that would take me on at such short notice, and so I began my senior year in a new school, with no friends but the people I knew from the projects.

I had been around long enough to know a few guys from B.A.B.Y. indirectly. Plus, I was cool with Jaquan and Jaquan was cool with B.A.B.Y., and, therefore I was cool with them too. B.A.B.Y. may have been a Blood-affiliated crew, but it was pretty small. The guy who ran it was named Cyrus; he was the guy I had seen the first day at Webster. The other main character was a quiet guy named Barshawn. His dad wasn't in the picture, and we used to joke that his mom met a guy at a bar named Shawn. Barshawn had nothing to lose and everything to prove, and was, therefore, crazy. We'd all be hanging out at Webster and Barshawn would just snap. "Watch this!" he'd say, then he'd hop off the fence he was sitting on and start beating on whoever was walking by. It didn't matter if he knew them or not. Then, after they scampered away, he'd come back over and pretend like nothing had happened. It was crazy to watch and scary too.

Besides Barshawn, the main enforcer of B.A.B.Y. was a big kid called Ruger, named after the Ruger pistol he always carried tucked in his waistband. Finally there was Mikey, the runt of the B.A.B.Y crew. He was small and even poorer than everyone else.

I officially joined B.A.B.Y. after two fights: one I lost, the other I won. The first fight was with a kid from my new school. A few months before this all went down, when I was the new kid and still mysterious, I had slept with his girlfriend. We had sex at my mom's house and it was great, for the two seconds it lasted. At any rate, this guy found out, and naturally he wanted to beat me up. We met a few blocks from Webster at a public park in early October. The fight was to start at 4:00 p.m. I remember, because it felt like an old Western.

The kid was tall and skinny, with arms like ropes. I was not as tall and just as skinny, but game. Anyway, there was no getting out of it even if I wanted to. Had I been wiser, I might have brought Jaquan or Marquise with me. But I rolled up to that park alone and found my adversary standing with a group of kids from our school.

"You fucking ready?" he asked.

"Yeah," I said, trying to sound confident, "let's go." This was the first actual fistfight I'd ever been in. I had, just so we're all clear, absolutely no clue how to fight.

The circle of kids screamed in anticipation, holding up their phones to record whatever went down and post it to YouTube or WorldStarHipHop or whatever.

Because the other guy was taller than I was, with at least a five-inch reach advantage, I didn't want to stay on the outside. It was a sloppy fight: no jabs, no level changes, no grappling, just wild haymakers. To my surprise, I was acquitting myself well. I caught him with a looping overhand right that stunned him. I heard someone yell, and briefly contemplated what victory would look like. But the kid came back hard and caught me with a hook. It was a glancing blow but put me off balance. I tripped over a tree root and landed on my back. I expected him to pummel me with punches, but instead he started kicking me hard, first in my chest and then my head. I curled up in a ball to protect myself as best I could, but it was no use. The rest of his friends, who had been lurking in the crowd, began kicking me too, and the last thing I remember before losing consciousness was seeing the bottom of a sneaker as it came down on my face.

What I didn't know at the time was that Mikey from B.A.B.Y. was watching the whole thing. I wasn't a member of B.A.B.Y. back then, but I spent so much time with Jaquan that I was an honorary resident of the 1300 block of Webster. I was entitled to some defense. That Mikey was in the park during the fight and neither stepped in nor called for help was a serious violation of gang etiquette. By the time I stumbled back to Webster, my shirt bloodied and ripped, two things had already been widely shared. The first is that I had been jumped, and the second was that Mikey did nothing.

I knew Cyrus only tangentially at this point, but as I was walking to Jaquan's apartment, he stopped me from his perch in the lobby. "Oh, you're Kwame, right?" he said. "Mikey told us, like, you were getting jumped."

"How did Mikey know?" I asked.

"He was there the whole time," said Cyrus.

"And he didn't do shit?" I asked.

"Nah," said Cyrus, "he didn't, the little bitch." Then he paused and said, "Now you gotta fight Mikey."

Getting into another brawl, especially over something that felt like a technical violation with someone with whom I had no personal beef, made no sense to me at all.

"It's fine," I said. "I don't want to fight him. I get why I should be upset but I'm not."

Cyrus looked at me hard for what felt like an hour.

"Nigga," he said, "either you fight Mikey or I'll fuck you up right now. And after I'm done fucking you up, I'm gonna fuck up Mikey, out of respect for you. And I'm gonna fuck him up every single day. So you choose what you want to do."

"I guess I'm fighting Mikey," I said unenthusiastically.

Cyrus gave me the night to recover but said my fight with Mikey had to go down the next morning. Jaquan and I stayed up talking over my options. Of which there was only one. I told him I didn't want to fight Mikey, but as he explained it, it was no longer a personal issue. "There's a system, man. You look out for each other. Mikey fucked with the system and he has to be punished." I went to sleep that night full of dread and with a terrible headache.

I found Mikey at Webster the next morning looking just as miserable as I was.

"Hey, Mikey," I said in a not unfriendly way. "I guess we gotta fight. Look," I started to explain, "I'm upset with you, but not that upset. I don't want to fight you but . . ."

"I get it, I get it," he said. "Let's get it over with."

We took the elevator up to the fourth floor, where Cyrus hung out. There were a bunch of B.A.B.Y. kids already there, Jaquan and Ruger and a guy named Boobie, and, of course Cyrus, plus a few other guys I didn't recognize. As we stepped out of the elevator, they immediately formed a tight circle around us. "Fuck him up," said Cyrus. Jaquan watched but didn't say anything.

There was no escaping it. I had to fight Mikey, and the sooner I did the sooner it would be over. I stepped back to give myself space and put up my hands. I could see his face through my guard. Although his hands were up too, he was just waiting to get hit. Pathetic, I thought, and even I was annoyed. I didn't want to fight him either, but at least I was making a good show of it. He was already beaten and I hadn't thrown a punch. I made a fist with my right hand and decked him with a heavy cross to his chin. His head shot back and his chin raised up, so I followed that with a left hook. Mikey's head spun to the side, blood streaming from his lip. That sparked something in him, and he came back with a wild haymaker that caught me square on the nose. Now I was bleeding too. I could feel the warmth of the blood as it ran down the back of my throat. Cyrus and the rest of the crew were closely packed around us in front of the elevators, but they were quiet. In fact, unlike the fight the day before, this whole thing felt somehow solemn and more serious. I wiped the blood from my nose and squared up again. My heart was racing, and I could see that Mikey was jacked up too. I wondered how this was going to end and who was going to end it. I feinted a few times with my left and backed Mikey up to the tile wall. I didn't know what he would do once he got there or, for that matter, what I would do. Blood was dripping from his mouth and my nose onto the linoleum floor. Any sympathy I had once had for the kid had been drowned out by adrenaline. If he had been smarter he would have pivoted out of the way, but he didn't. He just kept backing up until his back hit the wall. When he turned to see what he'd hit, I took advantage of his distraction and smashed him across the cheek with a straight left. I felt first cheekbone and then his head as it bounced off the wall. His body went slack for a moment and he began to slide down. He turtled, trying to protect his head, but I didn't stop hitting him. I wasn't even hitting Mikey anymore. He didn't exist to me. My knuckles were swollen and split. I would have killed the kid if I hadn't heard Cyrus behind me.

"That's enough, man," he said.

I kept raining punches down on Mikey.

"That's enough!" he said again, louder and with menace.

I turned around to see that Cyrus had his arm out and his hand up. He grabbed my hand to shake it.

"Welcome, man," he said.

"To what?" I asked.

"To B.A.B.Y., nigga," said Cyrus. "You're one of us now."

After that I spent more and more time on the block. That fight had awakened something in me, namely power. In a way I had never felt before, I could finally control my world, and the mechanism to do that was violence. I fought often. With disputes between the 1300 block crew and the 1400 block crew ongoing, there always seemed to be a brawl to get a piece of.

Violence became part of my everyday life. Sometimes it was harrowing, sometimes it was exhilarating, but it was always real. You could always test your mettle; you knew your place. Just about every other day we'd get jumped coming back from school in the afternoon. I learned to walk with my hands free, headphones off, just in case. I learned to pack two pairs of shoes, nice ones for school and other ones for walking home. I learned which blocks to walk down and which ones to avoid, and to pack my Marmot jacket in my backpack, no matter how cold it was, so it wouldn't get lifted. But just as often as we were jumped, Jaquan and I and the rest of the B.A.B.Y. crew jumped other kids. We were constantly fighting, and I came to view this violence as natural as air. As Jaquan told me, "This is just practice."

Unlike most of the other kids who lived at Webster, I had another home to go to. The other thing is that I could slide from B.A.B.Y. Kwame to bourgeois Kwame with ease. I have always cared about how I look. For as long as I've dressed myself, I've been the best-dressed kid in my class. (Even at Spellman, I was the kid with the designer shoes.) I'd do anything I had to to afford the clothes I wanted, to look how I wanted to look. When I was younger, after my mom taught me how to wash her hair, wrap it in curlers, and blow-dry it, I turned around and charged her $20. "It's same as around the corner at the beauty salon," I told her. On snowy days, I took the subway up to Pelham and shoveled driveways for $15 apiece. I squirreled my lunch money, my allowance, until I had enough to take the train down to Century 21. While other kids were wearing Air Jordans and Air Max and Pèpè and Enyce, I rocked Prada shoes and Seven7 jeans and Ralph Lauren glasses. I didn't look street and I didn't sound street when I didn't want to. And what this meant is that to the NYPD, a constant if lazy presence at Webster, I wasn't a suspect. In all my time on the block, I was never patted down, never arrested, never even viewed with suspicion. Looking good made me invisible, damn near invincible.

So I could do anything. I bought my first gun, for instance, when I was sixteen years old. It was an old 9mm pistol that I got in a crumpled-up brown paper bag from a varsity football player at Spellman who moonlighted as the coke dealer for the teachers there. He was a bad dude. The gun was shockingly cheap and easy to come by; $60 with a magazine full of bullets thrown in for free. I didn't plan on using it per se, but it was good insurance. When we'd roll up at parties in different neighborhoods there'd almost always be a problem. Having a piece was an instant confidence booster. Talk about power—this was power. And it immediately upped my cachet with the crew. It was a good thing I never had to use it, because the thing always jammed, though even that turned out to be fortunate. One night after we'd all been partying pretty hard, Boobie grabbed the gun and pointed it at my chest. I have no idea whether he thought it wasn't loaded or just didn't care. But he pulled the trigger. *Click*. He pulled it again. *Click*. And again. *Click*. He started laughing, and I did too, but I had never felt death so close. I didn't know what to make of it.

Violence, actual violence and the threat of it, permeated Webster. I saw my first murder when I was sixteen. I was up in Jaquan's crib, smoking a joint and blowing the smoke out the window at two in the morning or something, when I saw a couple of guys arguing on the stoop across the street. I thought they were playing dice or just drunk, or both. That wouldn't have been unusual. All of a sudden, one of the guys just pulled a gun on the other and shot him point-blank in the chest. The guy ran into the building and I put out the joint as fast as I could. I didn't need to be a witness. After a few minutes I cautiously crept back to the window to watch the parade of police, then EMTs, then forensic photographers, and gradually a crowd of onlookers. I went to sleep and by morning the scene had been cleaned up, like nothing had happened. Then a few days later, as I was buying a Vanilla Dutch before school, I saw the guy who did it at the bodega. I was terrified he had somehow seen me see him. But he just gave me a nod, I gave him one back, and that was that.

Another time, I was watching *Friday* at Jaquan's when Barshawn banged at the door.

"Kwame, open the door," Barshawn shouted.

He ran inside holding a black .45-caliber gun.

"Did you just shoot someone?" I asked.

"Nah, man," he said. "These niggas from the 1200 side ran up on us. Everyone is brawling downstairs. I need to scare them away and air this shit out."

I don't know why, but suddenly I had an urge to air it out myself.

"Can I do it?" I asked.

Barshawn looked at me strangely for a second, then said, "Yeah, take the ratchet quick. Go, man!"

I ran to the window and looked out. Below us, true to Barshawn's word, an all-out war was under way. I held the gun out of the window, pointing upward. I didn't want to hit anyone on the other side.

BANG. BANG. BANG. BANG. BANG.

Five quick shots. Five flashes of light. The figures on the ground paused for a second, then scattered. I was shaken. I had wanted to take the gun, I had wanted to shoot, and yet I couldn't believe that this was somehow normal.

I heard Barshawn laughing behind me.

"Man," he said, giggling, "give me my gun back. You look shook."

I was. I couldn't stop wondering where those bullets had landed.

M y ability to slide through two different worlds was my greatest asset in those years. It made me invisible when I had to be and visible when I wanted to be. And it landed me jobs. The neighborhood's biggest employer was the McDonald's at 173rd and Claremont Parkway. But the pay was embarrassingly low, of course, and having to serve your friends—and worse, your enemies—$1 Big Macs was humiliating. Especially with the corny-ass visor you had to wear. I did eventually spend some time working there, but first I got a job at the McDonald's inside the Macy's on Thirty-Fourth Street, far away from the projects, away from the possibility of running into anyone I knew. It was a chance not only to make some money but to get out of the Bronx, away from the battlefield, out of my mental armor, a few times a week.

One summer I answered a job on Craigslist to work at Calexico, a Mexican street food cart started by three brothers. I got a job for Barshawn there too. He had dropped out of school that year and was clearly flailing. He had never had the respect of the guys on the block, and didn't have anything to offer, like I did with my cop-friendly elocution and tight jeans. He was getting pushed to commit increasingly violent crimes—robbing people outside of Webster, that kind of thing. For whatever reason, probably because I didn't live at Webster, Barshawn opened up to me. A year or so before, I asked him why he was dropping out. He said to me quietly, his long dark face looking down, "I'm not shit. I'm never going to be shit." It was heartbreaking at the time to hear it and heartbreaking to see it play out. I thought I had gotten him a ticket out of Webster with this Calexico gig. The job was great for me. I learned how to grill chicken and steak, how to roll burritos and make quesadillas. Everything we made was from scratch, from the guacamole to the famously addictive "crack sauce," and so between this and McDonald's, I was exposed to two very different models of fast food. Calexico was the first time I had worked in a kitchen, even though in this case there was no literal kitchen.

I don't think Barshawn shared my passion for cooking, but it was at least a job, and the spirit of Soho was so different from Webster I thought it would open his eyes, give him some hope. To get to Prince and Wooster we'd embark on a public transit odyssey: first the Bx41 bus to Third Avenue, then the 5 train to Fifty-Ninth Street, before transfering to the downtown R to Prince Street. It was a shlep.

I had spent plenty of time in Manhattan, as a kid going to parties with my parents in Chelsea and as a family as we passed through a series of apartments in Harlem. But Barshawn had never left the Bronx. He had never made it to Manhattan. Of course I didn't know this at the time. It hadn't occurred to me that you could be so close yet so far away. The first couple of days we spent in training, so we took the journey together. He sat on the train with his eyes wide open, and by the time we got to Soho, with its cobblestone streets, expensive boutiques, and tourists, he was gobbling everything up.

But because our shifts didn't always overlap, about the second week he had to do it on his own. I could tell he was scared, so I carefully drew him a map of where to go and how to get there. But it didn't help. He couldn't do it. After a few days showing up late or not showing up at all, he got fired. The next time I saw him on the block he said, "Sorry, Kwame. But I told you, I ain't shit."

Back then McDonald's paid about \$7.25 an hour, which barely covered the subway fare to get there and back. Luckily, there were other jobs—an entire economy, in fact—that were much more lucrative and easier to enter: drugs. Saying you sell drugs is like saying you sell cars. There's a world of difference between selling Maseratis and selling used Hondas, just like there is between moving a few grams of weed and selling massive amounts of cocaine or heroin or pills. Everyone has to come to their own conclusion—as I did. But from where I stand, saying something is bad because it's illegal and good because it's legal breaks down when the color of your skin pretty much makes you a criminal to begin with. The guys at Webster had all been in and out of lockup. I was in fact the only one who hadn't seen the inside of a jail cell. Even when they weren't serving time, the guys from Webster were constantly hassled by cops. This was at the height of Mayor Bloomberg's stop-and-frisk years, so it wasn't uncommon to be thrown against a wall and searched a few times a week. And even when they weren't being pushed into the backs of cars or holding cells, they were still in the prison of no opportunity. The projects are like a social science experiment to see which crabs could crawl out of a bucket. It's a feedback loop for hopelessness. The guys from Webster see only other guys from Webster, so they end up looking up to the drug dealers and gang leaders. And since so many of those guys, people like Cyrus and Boobie and Ruger, end up either dead or in jail, they lose hope. The world outside doesn't want them. The market outside doesn't need them. They're on their own, trying to build a life on the (literal) black market.

Although I had options I was still enamored with the bling of the dealers. And I have to give credit where it's due. Denzel Washington was really my drug-dealing godfather. I, like a lot of my friends, fell in love with his character in *American Gangster,* who outfoxed or outright bought the cops. I wouldn't say the movie made me start dealing drugs. I was definitely already thinking about it, but *American Gangster* pushed me over the edge.

Drugs were not hard to come by at Webster, but I wasn't about to mess with heroin or crack. I wasn't trying to do twenty years for a Class D felony. I basically just wanted to subsidize my own habit. Man, I loved Kush and Purple Haze. The market was just there waiting. Everyone smoked weed. I mean *everyone:* kids, their parents, their grandparents, uncles, aunts, teachers, security guards. As the lowest-level dealer on the block, I moved small amounts of product. I bought weed for $70 an ounce, which I'd divide up into smaller bags and sell for $5 a gram. All I had to do to stay cool with the gang was give them a nic, or a nickel bag, a week. It wasn't even a rev-share, so it was a good deal. Soon I was turning that initial $70 investment into nearly $140—that's one gram per bag—and using that profit to reinvest in buying more product.

By this time I was a senior in high school, and the prospect of college loomed. In my family, this wasn't optional. My grandfather had been an academic and taught at historically black colleges and universities. My father was a college-educated architect. Before she became a caterer, my mother was an accountant. And Tatiana went to school at the Fashion Institute of Technology. Even when the pull of the block was strongest, there was a part of me that knew I would end up at college. It was the thing I had that others didn't, and it would have been foolish not to take advantage of it.

It was different for Jaquan. Very few people in his family or that he knew had gone on to higher education. He wasn't sure he should, either. This isn't to say that Jaquan wasn't ambitious or was in any way lazy. But his ambition was to survive. He didn't struggle like Mikey did or like Barshawn did. His approach, as he told me thousands of times, was to "stay in his lane." It was both an effective and savvy strategy. He kept his head down with his mom, at school, with B.A.B.Y. He wasn't a pushover or a wallflower, but he was always a wary watcher. By the time we were teenagers, he had long outgrown the rambunctiousness that had first drawn us together. By sixteen, he had learned not to draw any attention to himself. The problem with that, as I told him, was that you can stay in the lane if you want to, but you can't ignore the road, either. Was a life of not being noticed in Webster really what he wanted? Evidently not. We both applied to the University of Bridgeport, a small liberal arts college just over the Connecticut border whose student body is made up of a lot of city kids like us. It wasn't a prestigious school at all. It wasn't an Ivy League or even a bush league school, but it was college, and an affordable one at that, and for us it meant an escape from the Bronx.

That summer I was living large. I had bought a beautiful

white 1992 Coupe de Ville with a rich brown top from Jaquan's cousin for $2,000, the most money I had ever held in my hand, and I rode around Webster, windows open and Lil Wayne's *Tha Carter III* playing so loud it set off alarms on parked cars. Even Cyrus seemed to finally take me seriously and would toss me the occasional nod of respect. When I thought of how scared I'd been when I first arrived at Webster versus now, when I was about to leave, I was proud of myself. I'd been thrown into a world I didn't know. I could have sunk or swum. From the low-slung seat of my Caddy, I knew I had swum.

N ow it was on to the next challenge, the next world, a new deep end: Bridgeport. My tuition was only partially covered with scholarships and the rest was paid for with my savings from selling weed. I had a place to stay—a dormitory whose small double bedroom I shared with Jaquan—but no money for food. Thankfully, Jaquan's mom used to send him care packages full of Hawaiian Punch and Gushers and Snickers. We both waited for that shipment like prisoners do their mail. One day, as we were tearing open the weekly box, I had an idea.

Back in the Bronx, during the summer, there were two things you would always see on the street. Fire hydrants pried open, letting loose torrents of water to the delight of kids, and someone pushing around a shopping cart with a cooler in it, calling out, "Nutcrackers! Nutcrackers!" A Nutcracker is the hustler's cocktail, usually a mix of rum and some juice. They're sweet and potent and always homemade. They're the summer drink in the Bronx. I couldn't believe no one had thought to export Nutcrackers north of the New York border, but as far as I could tell, there was no one selling them in Bridgeport. Jaquan and I were sitting on a potential gold mine. Although I was only seventeen at the time, the good folks at the local grocery store didn't seem to care, and I returned to the dorm room having spent my last $20 on a handle of Bacardi.

Immediately we got to work, pouring out half the Hawaiian Punch and replacing it with an equal amount of liquor. Now all I had to do was sell my latest experiment in mixology. The University of Bridgeport has a diverse student body with a lot of African Americans, many of whom were as familiar as I was with Nutcrackers. And the appeal of Nutcrackers, I quickly learned, crossed international lines. In the Bronx, a bottle typically goes for $5, though this increases with demand and can soar to double that on hot days. This was Connecticut, so I figured $10 was a good starting price. And I was right. Working my way down the dorm hallway, I quickly sold out my stock without having to leave my floor. That night, I returned to the grocery store and bought $50 worth of Bacardi and more Hawaiian Punch. Kwame's Nutcrackers were born.

I didn't rest on my laurels. I experimented with Bacardi Dragon Berry, Bacardi Black Razz, Bacardi Limón, and with the entire flavor range of Hawaiian Punch. It was the closest I came to cooking.

Officially I was studying business administration at the University of Bridgeport, but I seldom attended classes, and anyway, I was administering business just fine on my own. And I was still in start-up mode. After a week or two selling Nutcrackers, Jaquan—who with his donation of Hawaiian Punch had become an angel investor—and I had made $500, enough money to move on to the harder stuff. I headed down to the city to the 1400 block of Webster and used that money to buy two ounces of the highest quality Kush I could find. Still inspired by Frank Lucas, Denzel Washington's character in *American Gangster*, I focused on marketing. After I picked up the weed, I bought the biggest baggies I could find. I was packaging only about an ounce into each dime bag, but the surface area made it look like much more. Back in Bridgeport, I was cleaning up. I'd go door to door in the dormitory, offloading product so fast that in three days I returned to the Bronx to re-up. This time, I needed more, so I drove across the Harlem River to Washington Heights. Back then weed grew like wildflowers in the Heights. I drove down 181st Street with my window open, asking guys who was selling.

"Who got that Loud?" I asked. We called the best weed Loud because it spoke for itself. A guy on the corner jerked his head to the right, so I followed him.

He leaned through the window. "Go see Zappos."

"Where's he at?" I asked.

The man pointed down the block to a rowhouse with a few guys hanging out on the stoop. "That's his crib," he said.

I parked the car and walked up the stairs to meet Zappos. For a kingpin, he looked like a schlub. A middle-aged Dominican guy wearing a tank top, he sat in his small and cramped kitchen. In the living room there was a plastic Playskool set.

That day I bought four ounces, what we called a QP, or quarter pound. Driving back to Bridgeport, the windows of my Caddy open, I felt I was finally living the life I deserved. The QP in Saran wrap hidden underneath my seat, I was an American Gangster.

Back in our dorm room, Jaquan and I set up a full-scale operation cutting and parceling out the weed into nickel and dime bags. We were in business. Because we established ourselves so early in the year, we became the one-room party supply store for the whole university. Acceding to demand, I added pills—Ecstasy, mostly—to my inventory while Jaquan grew our weed operation. We recruited a friend from the dorm, a big bear of a kid named Gianni (we called him G), who despite the Italian name was a six-foot-tall black dude from Miami with a goofy smile and a nose for trouble, to help move product. Everyone knew that Room 204 was the recreational pharmacy. By the end of the first semester we were doing nearly $3,000 in revenue in weed and pills a week. It was the first time I never had to worry about money.

We had everything we wanted, could buy anything we wanted, could eat at Burger King three times a day every day. I could afford all the Prada I could possibly wear but I tried to keep a low profile. Nevertheless, it didn't take long for the school authorities to suspect our extracurricular operation. There were a lot of close calls.

I had learned about lookouts from Web and the guys in B.A.B.Y., and because I knew campus security was already suspicious about the foot traffic in and out of the room, I paid G a few hundred dollars to switch rooms with me. I paid his roommate too to find another place. Soon enough I had turned G's room into a full-scale operation, with stacks of cash, glassine bags, and product on all surfaces. In one close call, I was bagging up in G's room when I saw campus security head straight for mine. I threw a couple thousand dollars into my backpack and the QP of inventory I had, and ran down the back stairs.

Despite the close calls, I, who should have been extremely cautious in calling any attention to myself, felt invincible. I smoked weed all the time and everywhere. I'd be sitting in an Intro to Macroeconomics class, receive a text message asking me to meet for a sale, duck out, come back ten minutes later, then my phone would buzz and out I'd go again. It was a busy time. Besides arranging for product, traveling down to Zappos' now on a weekly basis for a half a pound, I had to manage the division and packaging of the product and also, when I had to, the collection of payment in arrears. When a customer stiffs you, you have to collect, otherwise you just keep on getting rolled. It's the same reason I had to beat up Mikey. There are codes, and those codes need to be enforced. So when money was owed to me, I collected. And if that meant cornering a guy in an elevator and telling him I'd beat him up if he didn't pay, so be it. If it meant following him back to his dorm room and taking every single cent he had and all the food his mama had sent him, I'd do it. If it meant stalking two guys through campus in my Cadillac until they were alone, then jumping out and stomping them both—here I had help from G—I was going to do it. Who were they going to complain to, the campus cops, the real cops, their moms in Riverdale? What were they going to say, my drug dealer beat me up?

Darting in and out of class, high all the time and pocketing $3,000 a week, not caring was part of my persona. But it was only a matter of time before I was caught.

When the undergraduate dean called me in to talk, I knew it wasn't going to be good news. And it wasn't. Walking into his office on the afternoon of our appointment, I saw a nasty, dangerous smile plastered on his face.

"Good afternoon, Kwame," he said. "How's your semester going?"

"It's great," I said, affectless.

"Are you enjoying yourself?" he purred.

"Bridgeport is a blast," I dead-toned.

"Kwame, do you remember what you were doing last Thursday night, by chance?" He said this with a fake casualness that sent alarm bells ringing in my head.

"Studying, of course," I told him. "I have Intro to Accounting on Friday morning."

"That's interesting," he said, turning to his computer, "because this certainly looks like you."

And true enough, there I was on the screen, standing outside our dormitory beside Jaquan and Gianni. A grainy spark of flame flared as I lit up a blunt and took a deep inhale. Soon our heads were encased in a cloud of smoke. The dean paused the video and looked back at me.

At that moment I knew there was nowhere to run and nothing I could do to wriggle out of trouble. That was me in the video, and I knew I had to play my hand right. Here was a guy who had probably seen hundreds of kids like me, a guy who, stuck in his role as an administrator, clearly delighted in playing detective. However, after getting into and getting out of trouble my whole life, I knew how to handle his kind: Appeal to his mercy in the most pathetic way possible. Flatter his power.

"Oh my God," I said, burying my head in my hands, "I'm so ashamed." I kept my head hidden and made quiet simpering sounds. "I'm so ashamed," I repeated. "My mom is gonna kill me if she saw I was smoking weed."

I raised my head and near tears said, "I promised her before I left for college—you know, I'm the first one in my family to go—that I would stay away from the drugs!" Again I buried my face in my hands.

The dean was wavering. "Kwame—" he said, his tone gentler now.

"No, no, no," I cried, "I've tried so hard to make something of myself, and I let you down." I lifted my head, wiped away nonexistent tears, and gave him the five-star deluxe treatment. I told him about my father. I told him about poverty. I told him I had nothing but the projects if I got kicked out, that where I came from you don't get second chances. I painted a pitiful portrait. Who wouldn't feel charitable after seeing my display?

Finally, after a half-hour monologue, he relented and said,

"Kwame, I know you're a good kid. If it's true what you say, I'll let you stay enrolled, but you have to pass a drug test." I thanked him profusely and promised I wouldn't let him down. I had survived Round 1. Now all I had to do was find a way to cheat on the test.

It turns out I was the last of the three of us to be called in. Jaquan and Gianni had denied everything, which, as I had anticipated, did not go over well with the dean. They were in deeper trouble than I was, but regardless, we all had to report for a drug test that Monday. Thus began three days of drinking water and peeing in constant rotation. But we knew it wasn't enough. We had a virtual pharmacopeia in our systems. Jaquan and I went to GNC and bought a detox kit that promised clean piss in twenty-four hours. Gianni, on the other hand, ordered a device called the Whizzinator online. At $139, the Whizzinator, a realistic veiny rubber dick, came with a few ounces of synthetic urine called "Golden Shower," a cotton belt, discreet leg straps, and a few heating pads to give the fake pee the right body temp. I had to admit I was jealous of Gianni's plan. I wish I had thought of it.

The Whizzinator arrived the morning before we had to report to the medical center for the urine test. Well, it was a dick all right. But perhaps G should have read the online description more carefully. The Whizzinator comes in white, tan, Latino, brown, and black. Gianni was black and the dick he held up was the whitest I'd ever seen. I don't even think white dudes' dicks are that white. Now he was stuck with a dick as white as James Van Der Beek's. We all cracked up, but there was no question: G was in trouble.

The next morning the three of us showed up at the medical center like men condemned. Jaquan went in first for his test. He was escorted to the men's room by an unenthusiastic middle-aged female nurse. When he emerged a few minutes later it was with a grim look on his face. I didn't have a chance to say anything to him before I was summoned. The same nurse led me into the men's room, handed me a plastic cup and, to my surprise, entered the stall with me. "What are you doing?" I said. "I'm watching," she said. "Why?" I asked. "It's protocol. I have to see your penis as you pee." I shrugged and began to pee. As I did, I understood why Jaquan had been so glum. My urine was the bright green color of antifreeze, a telltale side effect of the kit that I hadn't anticipated. The nurse looked at me, looked at the pee, and rolled her eyes. I was caught, red-handed and green-peed.

"G," I whispered, when I made it back to the lobby, "she's going to watch you pee." I had only a moment to glimpse his face before he was called inside; it was white as a sheet. G was in there for much longer than Jaquan and me. Perhaps the Whizzinator was malfunctioning, I thought, giggling at the idea of him fumbling with the rubber dick. Yet when he emerged it was with a big grin on his goofy face. He flashed Jaquan and me a thumbs-up and waved a jolly goodbye to the staff as we left.

"What happened?" we wanted to know as soon as we got back to the dorm.

"Well," he told us, "the nurse did follow me into the bathroom stall. But I said, 'What are you doing?' and when she said, 'I'm going to watch you pee,' I told her, 'You can't. I'm too embarrassed.' I told her that, even though I didn't seem like it, I was actually half black and half white. But the only part of me that was white was my dick. She gave me a look like I was full of shit. I said, 'No, I'm serious. I've been made fun of for it in the past, so I'm sensitive about it.' She promised me she wouldn't laugh, and so I pulled out my fake white dick and she almost cried. She said, 'Oh my god. I'm so sorry I didn't believe you.

It *is* white!" The Whizzinator, despite the mixup, had been his salvation. G was jubilant, but Jaquan's and my fates were sealed. Sure enough, as soon as the test came back positive for marijuana, Jaquan and I received letters informing us that we were officially no longer students at the University of Bridgeport.

What should have been a wake-up call wasn't. I had gotten letters like this my entire life, warnings and warnings and warnings, then I was gone. And yet I was fine, or so I thought. My life was heading down a dangerous path, but at that point I didn't care. G stayed at Bridgeport while Jaquan returned to Webster.

For me the party continued. I was making too much money to give it up. Plus, my mother had moved to Baton Rouge, and I no longer had a place to land in the city. So I simply moved my drug-dealing operation to a two-story house I rented off-campus. I had always dipped into my own inventory—that was part of the initial appeal of dealing. But when I didn't have to bother with classes, I started hard into Ecstasy. Alone in my new apartment, I ate almost nothing but pills. I dropped from 165 pounds to 120. With Jaquan gone and G pretty much out of the picture—we were warned not to interact—I surrounded myself with new friends. And when you're a dealer, your friends are fiends. I hardly remember the names of that small, transient crew, only that they would never say no when I dumped a bagful of pills on the table and said, "Let's party." We'd smoke as much weed as we could, sitting around until smoke filled the house and the ceiling fan just pushed the haze around. I pictured myself as a benevolent king, ruling over a debauched court. In some ways I did act like a lord. The binge party would start around eleven one morning and not finish until the next. After smoking a few grams of weed and ingesting a handful of pills, I felt immortal. I was the best rapper in the world. I was a brilliant mind. My feelings were deeper than a river. I was as baller as a gangster. I had cash. I had girls. The world was mine. I was fucking girls one at a time, two at a time, names I don't remember, in poses I had only seen on the internet.

Then, one morning, a cold cloudy day in November, I awoke from yet another binge with a stranger in my bed and a headache the size of a tree. I emerged from my room to find the apartment in absolute chaos. What furniture I had—futons and beat-up tables—was toppled. Empty liquor bottles rolled on the floor. A bong had spilled, leaving a puddle of water and ash on the carpet. Everything stank of weed and old smoke. The kitchen sink was filled with trash and ashes. I found a few of my "friends" passed out in the hallway and another nestled in a pile of dirty laundry behind the couch. Someone had left the television on in the living room and I foggily remember pushing a bunch of empty red cups to the floor and sitting down to watch it. It was right after the 2008 election, and on CNN some commentator was talking about how historic the victory was. The commentary was cut with footage of Obama, all smiles and hope and change.

I had never felt so alone or so rootless. I was hungover, strung out, and depressed. When I looked at what my life had become, at who I had become, I felt a total estrangement. Something about seeing Obama on the television and, when I turned the set off, seeing myself in the reflection, brought my situation into clear focus. I felt the world was moving forward without me.

For the past year the closest I had come to cooking was mixing the Nutcrackers in my dorm room. That morning, though, I felt an irresistible need to make something, I didn't care what. I raided my kitchen to see what, if anything, I had. The truth was, not much. A few dried herbs, a bag of basmati rice. I threw on a coat and a pair of boots and stumbled to the grocery store around the corner. It was around eight; I hadn't been outside this early for months, and I marveled at all the people I saw. I grabbed a cart and squinted at the harshly lit aisles. I bought five pounds of chicken breasts, ginger, Scotch bonnets, curry powder, a head of garlic, a few onions, a bunch of scallions, and oil. It was a strange time to make chicken curry, but that's what I wanted. It reminded me of home all those years ago, when my mom stood next to me at the counter, teaching me how to chop and slice, onion tears rolling down our cheeks. I had made this recipe hundreds of times before with her and with her stepdad Papa Winston, who had taught it to her, and it reminded me of real love, not the chemical highs of Ecstasy. I came back to the house, cleared a space in the kitchen, and began to work. The old rhythms of cooking came back to me. The click of the gas stove and the purr of the flame, the sizzle of the oil and the chicken as it browned. The comforting softening of onions and garlic as they released their sweet aromas into the apartment. Everything was predictable; everything made sense. I wasn't just cooking a recipe, I was regaining my sanity.

The smells of home filled the house. The kids passed out in the hallway and behind the sofa woke up and like groggy zombies came into the kitchen. "Kwame," they said, "that smells delicious. What is that?" We cleared the table, just shoving all the cups and bottles into a trash can, and sat down. It was the first time I hadn't started the day with a handful of pills in a very long time. It was the first real meal I'd had in a very long time. Sitting around, spooning the chicken and mounds of rice, it was the first time these strangers I called my friends and I actually talked. When they stumbled out into the sunlight I was left, finally, alone, I knew what I had to do. I called my mother down in Baton Rouge. "Mom," I said, "can I come stay with you? I gotta get out of here."

It was as if I had wakened from a dream. It was as if I realized I was drowning. When I looked at what I had surrounded myself with, I felt like an idiot. I made a reservation to fly from JFK to Baton Rouge as soon as I could. I didn't even stick around long enough to offload my inventory. Thousands of dollars of pills went down the toilet. There was at least a pound of weed hidden in the bedroom closet, a farewell to my so-called friends if they found it. I left that afternoon with two duffle bags and nothing else. And when I closed the door on the apartment, I hoped I had left my habits and my addictions behind.

Chicken Curry

YIELD: 2–3 servings

¼ cup minced celery

¼ cup ginger,
roughly chopped

¼ cup garlic,
roughly chopped

½ cup yellow onion,
roughly chopped
(approximately half a
large onion)

½ cup scallions,
roughly chopped

½ cup cilantro, roughly
chopped

1 Scotch bonnet pepper,
chopped

3 tablespoons fresh thyme
leaves

⅓ cup canola oil

2 tablespoons curry
powder

2 teaspoons turmeric

2 pounds chicken,
cut into pieces

1 quart chicken stock

Juice of 1 lime

Kosher salt

---

1. Place the celery, ginger, garlic, onion, scallions, cilantro, Scotch bonnet, thyme, and canola oil into a blender and puree until smooth.

2. Transfer this mixture to a small bowl, add the curry powder and turmeric, and marinate the chicken in mixture overnight.

3. Sear the chicken pieces on both sides over high heat for approximately 3 minutes on each side. Remove the chicken and add the chicken stock to the pan. Place the chicken and all of the prepared marinade back into the pot and simmer for 30 minutes, letting the broth reduce until thick.

4. Season with the lime juice and salt to taste. Serve with a rice of your choice.

Gulf State

Fifty years earlier, my grandmother had left her husband and home behind in Louisiana and headed to Chicago with her children in tow, part of a tide of African Americans trying to outrun the hot toxic breath of Jim Crow. After hitting rock bottom in Bridgeport, I made the reverse commute. Like Grandma Cassie, I was looking for escape. Unlike Grandma Cassie, it was myself I was running from.

During my lowest lows in Bridgeport, my mom was living in Baton Rouge, working as an executive chef at a catering company. She never knew what I was really getting into, so was spared the details of my drug dealing. All she knew, when I called looking for a new beginning, was that I needed a place to stay.

I'd thought about going back to New York. Jaquan's couch was always waiting back at Webster, but to have to be seen by the same people, to become again the same Kwame from the corner, a junior member of the B.A.B.Y. crew, to be reminded that I'd dreamt of college but had fallen back to the projects, would have been too humiliating. If others saw me as a failure, I feared that whatever future I had imagined for myself when I left for college would permanently evaporate.

And there was no way I was going back to my father's house, even though it would have made financial sense. The wounds he had inflicted were what I had been trying to paper over with the money and the drugs and the violence. The wounds I had seen him inflict on others, watching him beat his girlfriends mercilessly while I tried to stop him, still haunt me today.

But my mom, she'd stood where I was standing, caught between here and there, many times before. She was an expert in the art of the skedaddle, something that had affected me in both positive and negative ways. From her relationship with my dad, with Tatiana in tow, to a series of ever-shrinking apartments; from one tight situation after another; and finally from New York City altogether, she had cleared out with ease. How it made me feel depended on whether she took me with her. Sometimes she did, sometimes she didn't. But from her I learned perhaps the most important lesson in my life: Always keep moving.

For as long as I can remember, I've been able to move back and forth, uptown and downtown, between the black and white worlds and in between. Going to school in the Gifted and Talented program, I'd been exposed to well-to-do culture, to the world of the Gallaghers. But unlike the Gallaghers, I knew the streets too. And unlike some of my friends from the streets, I'd been to Chelsea, where I'd been surrounded by black people full of pride about who they were and where they came from. I still carried the pride of bringing kola nuts to my grandfather across the dusty paths of his compound, his pride in his ancestors, our ancestors, and me. I knew how to be black in Nigeria, black in Soho, black in Harlem and the Bronx. But I didn't know how to be black in the South.

When I stepped off the airplane into the humid air of the Baton Rouge airport, the first thing I noticed was how the world seemed settled into black and white—with white at the top, black at the bottom. Every janitor I saw sweeping the terminal, every cashier working at a retail kiosk, every porter with red cap and trembling hands, every cabbie driving a beat-up Chevy, every unlicensed hustler trying to score a fare, was black. In New York, you can be black and rich, black and educated, black and a boss. I'd seen men my skin color in positions of power, as principals and coaches and businessmen and academics. I'd also seen them sweeping the hallways or spearing trash along Frederick Douglass Boulevard in the bright blue uniforms of the Doe Fund. But beside them were Hispanics doing the same thing, and Southeast Asians and Asians and whites as well. No one can deny that America is built on the backs of black and brown people. But at least in New York you can kid yourself.

But from the very first moment I arrived in Louisiana, I saw that down there, the world was black and white. On one side were the whites, on the other were people like me, who had skin so dark they seemed invisible. I was struck by how the white people in their pastel polo shirts and diaper-bottomed khakis glided by the man buffing the floor as if he was furniture. As if he didn't even cast a shadow. I'd never seen people who looked like me so openly overlooked. Or, if I did, it didn't matter, because everyone in New York City is equally overlooked. We're not a city full of people who say, "Good day, y'all!" But here in Baton Rouge, the cradle of the famous southern hospitality, the difference between friendliness and nada was pronounced. This would be the perfect place to reinvent myself. No one saw me as a failure because no one saw me at all.

My mother said she could get me some work at the catering company, but it wasn't enough to live on, even if I was staying with her rent-free. She lived in a small one-story brick house on Pecan Tree Drive, a street with neat lawns and houses that all looked the same. Bridgeport wasn't exactly the center of the universe, but the corner of Baton Rouge I landed in was on the back side of nowhere. I spent most days stoned on her couch, watching reruns of *Iron Chef*. One night, after my mom came home bone-tired from working an event and found me watching television, she said, "Kwame, you need to get your ass a job."

She was right, but I felt paralyzed. In Connecticut I had been making $3,000 a week selling drugs tax-free. The idea of working a minimum wage gig in Baton Rouge was just too humiliating. Better not to do anything than to accept this total and utter failure.

"I know, Mom," I said. "It's just hard."

My mom fixed me with a look like a bayonet. "Of course it's hard, Kwame. What did you think? Life is gonna be easy?" she said, her voice rising in anger. "You think success is handed to you? You think it was handed to me?"

"Mom," I said, "chill out. I'll go tomorrow."

"Don't tell me to chill out, Kwame," she said, using that tone of voice I knew meant I was in trouble "I get it. You're scared. You're sad. You think you deserve better. But I'm going to tell you this right now, though it's something you should have learned already: No one *deserves* anything. You get what you work for."

My mom's love is like a mama bird's. She cared for me and fed me and sacrificed for me for years. But eventually she was gonna push me out of the nest—or, more accurately, off the couch. Her expectation wasn't that I would fly, because I had tried and failed at that before. But she wanted to teach me a lesson about what to do when you hit the ground feeling broken.

"I love you, Kwame," she said, "but either you get a job or you get out of my house." And with that, she left the living room, turning off the light and leaving me to contemplate the future by the glow of the television set.

What followed was a sad-ass parade of short-lived menial jobs with a special southern flair. At my first gig, a high-end rib shop called Zea's, they had me take an aptitude test. I knew I did well but they wouldn't let me see the results. They threw me on the dish pit as a porter. I asked if I'd ever work the line and the manager just laughed at me. After six months dismantling huge towers of dirty dishes that rose like columns from the sink, I quit. I made a tour of Baton Rouge's crummiest restaurants, but the only thing I got was a good weed connect and a couple of friends to smoke with.

I even tried working with my mom, prepping at her catering company and later, when she got a job as the executive chef at a local hotel, doing what she called "the bitch work," like cutting the tops off eight cases of strawberries. Living with your boss and working with your mother are both bad ideas.

Whatever joy I had found in the past in cooking was gone. It wasn't a career for me; it was just a way to get my mom off my back. To her credit, she never bawled me out or made me feel terrible about it. The important thing to her was that I wasn't idle, that I kept moving.

One morning she dropped me off in the parking lot of a nearby restaurant called TJ's Ribs. TJ's was founded in the 1980s by a guy who had the novel idea of serving barbecued baby back ribs when everyone else still served spareribs. The place is the local hangout for Louisiana State University sports fans, called Tigers, and the walls were crammed with LSU memorabilia. Before I walked in the door looking for work, I had never been inside the place.

I knew better than to go back home without a job. Luckily for me—I guess—a place like TJ's is always hiring. Turnover is high, which isn't surprising when the pay is so low. I walked in and asked the hostess to see a manager. She looked at me a little sideways but picked up the phone to call someone. A few minutes later a white lady in her forties with her blond hair teased up and her eyelids covered in purple mascara, sidled out of the dining room.

"Hello," I said, sticking out my hand for an eager handshake and assuming a professional tone of voice, "my name is Kwame Onwuachi. I was wondering if you are hiring."

"You worked in restaurants before, Kwame?" said Janice.

"Yes, ma'am," I said, lying through my teeth, "in New York, where I'm from."

Janice greeted the news by raising her penciled-on eyebrows. "From New York, huh?" she said suspiciously. "I didn't think you was from around here. What brought you to Baton Rouge?"

I could have told her the truth. That I was trying to start somewhere new from somewhere bad, that I had decided to abandon my burgeoning career as a drug kingpin because I'd had a moment of self-reflection and realized I had become a stranger to myself.

"Uh," I said, "my mom lives down here. She's an executive chef."

Judging from Janice's arched eyebrows, the answer surprised her. "An executive chef?" she asked, as if pondering the impossible. "Where?"

"Yes, ma'am, an executive chef," I said evenly, "at the Radisson Hotel."

She was clearly doubtful, trying to ascertain whether I was a liar, which I was, but not about this. She didn't even try to hide the appraisal. In fact, I think she wanted me to know that she was a cool customer, nobody's fool. Was I a hard worker or would I give her trouble? The answer, I silently responded, was yes to both. I held her gaze and refused to look away. The moment was a tiny tug-of-war that hinted at a larger battle raging just under the surface.

But I needed a job and Janice could offer me one. So when she nodded to a back section in the dining room and said, "You can be a server if you want; we're a man down," I said, "Oh, thank you very much, ma'am. When can I start?"

When I arrived for my first shift the next morning, there was an LSU game at the nearby stadium so the place was packed. The dining room was a sea of white faces and purple-and-gold jerseys. A good number of people wore purple-and-gold face paint on which barbecue sauce was smeared into Joker-like smiles. This wasn't a normal lunch crowd. This was a tribe, and I was an outsider.

Though nearly the entire back-of-house staff was black, I was the only nonwhite server. When Janice led me to my section for the first time, the far corner of the restaurant near the restrooms, I noticed that all my customers had one thing in common: they were black. At first I thought it was a coincidence. But after the third party walked in and sat down, I understood that it was not. This was a revelation only to me. Everyone, including my customers, knew the game already.

The most difficult part of working at TJ's wasn't that the pay was pennies compared to my dealing days, and it wasn't the endless sidework, and it wasn't leaving every day smelling like a fry station. I actually loved being a waiter, and in the South, it *is* true that people are friendlier. Some people. The hardest part was enduring all the eyes that were turned on me.

So many of the eyes I met at TJ's didn't so much see me as look through me. Like the black men and women I saw in the airport or by the sides of the road, I was, to Janice, to most of the other waiters, to many of the patrons, a thing. An object. The eyes of my customers were even harder to take. Those whose money was just as green as the white patrons' but who were led back to my section. Was it rage I read? No, though there was anger. It was resignation born from enduring indignities that I could never fully comprehend, among which being led to the back section of a rib restaurant was more than likely the most benign. What they sought in my eyes, in the unscripted moments before I launched into my welcome spiel, before we settled into the familiar patter of server and customer, was recognition and brotherhood. We're in this together, their eyes said. I felt their claim on me and I shied from it. I regarded them as things too. "No," I said to myself, "I'm not in this together with you. I'm just passing through."

But the front-of-house looks were nothing compared to those in the kitchen. The kitchen staff were, almost to a man, black men my father's and even my grandfather's age, who worked twelve- to fifteen-hour shifts for $6 an hour. Hair hidden under bandanas, chickeny arms extending from white short-sleeved uniforms, aprons spotted and splattered with barbecue sauce and fry oil. The kitchen was hot as hell and poorly ventilated. The wheezing hood above the racks of ribs did little to clear the smoke. When I came in to pick up my orders, I'd catch the line cooks' eyes as they hefted the meat-laden plates to the pass. This is what it looks like, I thought, to be bone-tired and beaten.

Periodically, the GM would crash into the kitchen to yell abuse at the men who worked there. Even the shoutiest chefs on television didn't shout with this level of malice. This wasn't tough love or motivation. The managers verbally lashed the staff for no other purpose than to demean and dehumanize them.

"There are so many people who need a job!" I remember one GM yelling, a kid just out of college whose pale pimply cheeks were flushed with anger. "You guys are fucking disgusting! You're scum." When Janice came back, she tossed "your kind" and "you people" into her tirades. "You people are so lazy!" she'd rail. "Your kind just don't know how to work!"

Behind the window of the pass, the cooks bowed their heads in silence and continued working. They moved not like men but like machines running on fumes. I think Janice humiliated them on purpose in front of me, as a cudgel and a caution, and as a wedge. It worked. One time, a few minutes after I had witnessed one of Janice's rages, I came back to pick up a plate of brisket. The cook behind the pass, a guy around fifty, I'd say, looked out at me.

"Order up!" he shouted angrily, even though I was standing in front of him. When I looked at him, he was staring at me hard. An expression met me behind the metal pass, a look full of anger and animosity I couldn't figure out. As I ran the brisket out to the dining room, the look haunted me. Was it that he saw me seeing him be humiliated? Was it that he thought I wasn't just on the other side of the pass, but that I was *really* on the other side, Janice's side? The fury of that man's look still smolders in my memory all these years later.

I used to call Jaquan after work sometimes, just to check in. He was still selling, and it was nice to hear his voice. Jaquan was now on a different track than me, for better or worse. Certainly he was living larger than I was. I remember his uncontrollable laughter when I told him I was making $20 a shift.

"Kwame," he said, "you're crazy. Just come back up here. I made four grand, dude, and that was just today."

"I can't," I'd say. "I can't go back to selling. It's gonna be all right down here."

I tried to sound upbeat and certain, but the truth was I had no idea. I worried that I had made a terrible mistake, that I had driven myself into a dead end and thrown away the keys. As days turned to months I grew to dread waking up, I grew to dread every shift at TJ's.

When my mother decided to move to New Orleans to work as an executive chef for a catering company called Fleur de Lis, I decided it was time to get out of Baton Rouge too. Without knowing quite what I'd do next, I marched into TJ's to resign. I wish I could say my last shift was dramatic, that I cut Janice down to size with a speech about the equality of men and the dignity of work. I wish I could say anyone noticed at all. But the truth is, when I quit, Janice nodded like she'd expected it all along. After all, she thought all my people were lazy. As far as the kitchen staff went, they saw me as a transient anyway. This was their reality, for days, months, years, decades, lifetimes, generations. But I could get out, so I did.

Shortly after my mom left, she introduced me to a chef at her new catering company. It turned out the guy had worked on a cleanup ship for the Deepwater Horizon spill that had happened a few months earlier. When he told me how much he made working as a cook there, I couldn't believe it: $1,900 a week. I wanted in, and he assured me that because there were so many crews—and so many ships—in the Gulf, they weren't picky at all. I was excited about the opportunity and to get out of the minimum-wage rut. I had no idea whether I could hack it, but I'd get paid $1,900 a week regardless, so I had nothing to lose.

When I told my mom the plans, she was less cocksure. "This is going to make you or break you as a cook," she told me, "and you're not going to have cell phone service or anything."

"I know, Mom," I said. "I'm not *that* addicted to my phone."

"It's not that, Kwame," she said "You can't look on the internet for anything, no recipes, nothing. You just got to cook from the heart."

Sure enough, the contractors responsible for staffing the cleanup ships weren't picky at all. I filled out an online application form, had a five-minute chat on the phone with a human resources coordinator about nothing in particular and barely touching on my cooking experience (which was a good thing), and at the end she asked, "Can you start tomorrow?"

I was so anxious I could hardly sleep that night. I'd never really been on a ship before, save for a few visits to see my grandfather, who had also been a ship's cook, and his vessel was docked the whole time. I had never been responsible for ordering, planning, or executing meals for a group, let alone thirty exhausted guys cooped up with no other options. I was excited but also scared. It occurred to me that just because an opportunity was offered didn't mean it was a good idea to take it. But it was too late to reconsider. They were expecting me on the ship the next night. I threw a week's worth of clothes and a few books including *The Autobiography of Malcolm X*—which was ultimately responsible for me giving up the N-word—in a duffel bag and I was ready.

The next day my mom picked me up midmorning and we began the journey, arriving in Houma, Louisiana, in late afternoon. The city was an old Cajun outpost of fishermen, shrimpers, and oystermen, but due to the oil spill it had become a hive of industrial activity. We made our way to the Port of Terrebonne, past the towering rigs of shrimping boats, barges, and drydocks to the tiny office to which I was told to report. I gave my mom a quick hug in the car, grabbed my bag, and headed inside.

I'd be working on the *Maine Responder,* an oil spill response vessel that was capable of skimming and recovering up to 444,000 gallons of oil and water a day. To get out to the ship where I'd be cooking, I had to take a series of ever smaller crafts, and I seriously questioned what the hell I was doing more than once on that bumpy ride into the unknown. The trip took about three hours, and it was after nightfall when we arrived.

The *Maine Responder* was a massive ship, 210 feet long, weighing 1,300 tons, with nearly forty workers on board, a helipad on the back, and four tanks, each capable of holding 1,000 barrels of oil. In the dead of night, it just looked like a constellation of red and blue lights in the sky. A rope ladder was flung down and the gruff captain on the boat I was leaving just nodded and said, "Good luck." That night I was so tired I stumbled sleepily into my bunk, not noticing much beyond the strong smell of gasoline and the constant hum. I slept in a cabin on the lowest deck. There were two of us in a space smaller than the closet I had grown up in.

In the morning I put on my clean white chef's coat, black pants, and clogs and made my way to the deck. The sky was beautiful, pink around the edges. But the water all around us was jet black. I had never seen an oil spill before, and the sheer volume of it was shocking. The smell was overpowering.

There were two chefs on a ship this big: a lead and the assistant. I was going to be the assistant. The guy I'd be assisting was standing in the cramped space when I walked in, pouring an industrial-size bag of frozen hash browns into a fry basket. He looked like he was in his fifties, with thick stubble and no chin, and was wearing an apron with only a tank top and boxers underneath. He had a belly, but his spindly legs and arms stuck out like a bug's.

"Hello," I said, "I'm Kwame, I'm the new sous."

"I'm Tex," he said with a strong Texan drawl.

"What can I help with?" I asked.

"I need to ask you a question," Tex replied, looking up at me for a sec before turning again to the fryer. "Can you fucking read? That's all I need to know."

I looked at him, speechless with anger. I wanted to tell him off. Had I just consigned myself to the same treatment I'd endured in Baton Rouge but in the middle of the Gulf of Mexico, where I couldn't walk out? I stood there silently for a long enough time that it became even more uncomfortable in the small hot kitchen.

Finally I said, "Yeah, I can fucking read."

"I didn't mean it like that," said Tex, spinning around, trying to backpedal. "You're clearly educated. I just see a lot of these people not knowing how to read. I didn't know if I had to teach you everything from scratch. I was just trying to help out."

My temper wasn't assuaged, and it only got worse from there. The way the work was set up, Tex would plan and dictate the menu and I would help execute it. Though I hadn't really worked in a kitchen before, the extent of Tex's cooking was essentially dumping Sysco ingredients either into deep fryers or spilling them, still frozen, onto a flat-top. I don't think I saw the man use salt or pepper, let alone any other spice, the entire time I was there.

The boat and senior staff came from Maine and ate in a separate kitchen. But the thirty or so guys I would be cooking for, the guys who actually did the grunt work of skimming the oil, were deep-country Louisiana boys. They were all young, all white, and all poor. I began to see why Tex had asked whether I could read. It had less to do with my being black and more to do with the simple fact that many of these guys probably couldn't. Watching them crowd into the mess hall, their faces covered in grime, their teeth yellowed and rotting, I was, I have to admit, terrified. I was the only black guy on the ship— well, there were two black engineers, but they didn't eat at the same mess hall—and this seemed straight out of *Deliverance*. These men called themselves "coonasses," a word, like the N-word, that had been used against them and that some of them had reclaimed as a badge of pride. When I first glimpsed them, every stereotype I harbored came to mind. I thought by default they'd be dumb racists.

Life on the ship was rough. For the two weeks on board, they worked nonstop. Shifts stretched twelve to fifteen hours and the labor was backbreaking. They made good money and had perks. For each week off, we'd get helicoptered back to Houma and given free airfare anywhere in the country.

At first Tex and I tried to work together, but the man didn't make food. He made fuel, tasteless bland slop meant only to keep the workers fed enough that they could continue working. It didn't have to be this way. If he had given just the tiniest of shits, these self-described "coonasses" could have found a taste of home, a bit of love, in the mess hall. Unlike in the kitchens of Baton Rouge, it was just me and Tex in the middle of the Gulf. If I wanted to take a stand, here was a good place to do it. Plus, since BP was picking up the tab for all of this, we could order whatever ingredients we wanted. Strangely enough, sitting hundreds of miles from land, the world was our oyster. So one day I said, "Look, man, why don't you let me order this week?"

"Fine," he said, shrugging, "less work for me."

On the next helicopter drop I rushed excitedly to the kitchen to unpack the boxes I had ordered. I thought of the food that had given me the most comfort when I was a kid. It had to be something I knew so well I could cook without a recipe. So I decided to make the guys something I had grown up with, my mom's shrimp étouffée. I spent all day preparing the shrimp stock, peeling the shrimp, and perfectly chopping the onions, celery, and bell peppers. I must have tasted it a million times, wanting to make sure it was perfect. This was, after all, the first meal I had ever made, not as a cook but as a chef. I wasn't following any recipe other than my own. As the kitchen filled with the aromas of my childhood, guys kept on peeking into the kitchen with funny looks on their faces.

"Damn, that smells good!" said one guy.

"It's like I'm back home," said another.

I felt the same way.

By dinnertime word had gotten out that I was making shrimp étouffée, and the guys weren't shy about expressing their excitement or ratcheting up the pressure. One of the men yelled out, "It had better be good, 'cause I've been eating this my whole life!"

They carried their bowls back to the mess hall. I waited. The dining room went silent, which is always a good sign. One guy came back to the pass-through where I served the food and announced, "The next time we get to shore and I go home, I'm gonna smack my mama for what she's been feeding me my whole life, 'cause your étouffée is ridiculous!"

Tex, meanwhile, didn't take kindly to being upstaged, and the animosity between us grew. I was constantly trying out new recipes, doing whatever I could to make the lives of these guys easier. I baked cupcakes between meals, which I'd carry up to the main deck and pass out to the crew. I started plating their meals instead of just slopping the food on a plate as they passed by. I don't think those boys had ever eaten as well as they had with me. This all, naturally, infuriated Tex. He started cursing me out regularly and sabotaging my plans.

"Look," I said one day, "you cook your food. I'll cook my food." For the rest of our time, I cooked breakfast and lunch, and he'd cook dinner. Then we'd rotate and he'd do breakfast and lunch and I'd do dinner. The only time I saw the man was at night. He slept on the bunk below me, although I wouldn't call what he did sleep. Tex was an inveterate sleepwalker and sleeptalker. As for what he said, it's too obscene even to write here. Suffice to say, he was a man stuck on a ship with a bunch of other men and craved the company of women, and this craving came out at night. But he'd also just wander around the ship. One night they found him wearing nothing but his boxers and a life jacket, standing on the railing, about to jump into the Gulf. It would have been the end of Tex, and that would have suited me fine.

As it turned out, *I* was the end of Tex. Because I cared, because I actually tasted what I made, because I treated these "coonasses" not as animals but as people who deserve food made with care, I quickly became their favorite. So when Tex went on his one-week break, the captain told the contractor and the contracting company to make me the lead cook. Tex wasn't invited back, and his replacement became my sous. And that was that.

Not just in the kitchen but out of it too, I bonded with these backcountry guys. In our downtime, we'd crowd into a cabin and play Nintendo Wii or just bullshit with each other. I found myself thinking they'd get on pretty well with my friends back in the Bronx. I listened to their stories of home, of the gumbo and red beans and rice, jambalayas, crawfish boils and fried catfish their mamas made. Then I tried to re-create those recipes for them, drawing from my memory and from their descriptions. Seeing their crooked raggedy smiles beyond the pass was one of the greatest feelings I'd ever had.

That time on the *Maine* made me a chef. Granted, my kitchen was small and my staff only one other person, but that's not what mattered. I learned to see beyond my own biases, to see that when it came to eating, these guys, who looked nothing like me, just wanted something that reminded them of home, something made with love. And I learned that I could be the guy who could give them that. I had the skills, the palate, the recipes, the heart.

Grandma Cassie's Shrimp Étoufée

YIELD: 6 servings

½ cup unsalted butter

½ cup all-purpose flour

1 medium onion,
small diced

2 large ribs of celery,
small diced

1 large green pepper,
small diced

5 garlic cloves,
coarsely chopped

1 tablespoon Cajun spice

1 bay leaf

4 sprigs fresh thyme

1 quart shrimp stock

2 pounds shrimp,
peeled and deveined

Kosher salt

---

1. In a large, heavy-bottomed pot, melt the butter over medium-high heat until foaming. Add the flour, reduce heat to medium-low, and whisk into a smooth paste until a blonde roux forms: approximately 2 to 3 minutes.

2. Add the onion, celery, pepper, and garlic and cook, stirring until vegetables have softened, approximately 6 minutes. Add Cajun spice, bay leaf, and thyme and cook for 1 minute.

3. Add shrimp stock in thirds, and simmer for 30 minutes.

4. Add shrimp to the stock and cook for approximately 3 minutes. Be careful not to overcook shrimp.

5. Season to taste with salt and serve with rice.

Finding My Craft

Like the rest of the crew, I worked on the *Maine* on a two-weeks-on, one-week-off schedule. I could have used the free flight I got on every week off to see the country, but instead I mostly headed back to New York to blow everything I had on food and clothes.

I've always cared a lot about how I look. It's one of the few ways I can really control how I'm perceived. So I worked hard to save up enough money, then I'd head down to Century 21 to get my Gucci and Prada on. But that summer I was a straight-up Fifth Avenue cat. Walking proudly past the suspicious guards, I'd emerge with slim-fitting blazers by Christian Lacroix and sneakers by Yves Saint Laurent and crisp dress shirts from Maison Martin Margiela, all thanks to the sweaty hours I'd spent in the Gulf.

I'd go home, or rather to my sister Tatiana's apartment in the Bronx where she let me crash, and Google "best restaurant in New York," then meet a girl and ask her to dinner. We'd eat white truffles at SD26, Tony May's Italian restaurant in the Flatiron, and salty tongues of sea urchin at Marea, and seasonal salads so beautiful they looked like paintings at Gramercy Tavern. I'd pore over the menus and the plates, enthralled by ingredients I'd never heard of, from puffed barley to ramps to guanciale, miso, kombu, and thumbelina carrots; proteins I had never tasted, like guinea hen and sweetbreads and squab; preparations I hadn't imagined, from sous-vide to pickled to confited. It was a peek into the upper reaches of food I had never tasted. And it wasn't just the food that was blowing my mind. It was the entire experience: the solicitous way the servers asked whether we wanted sparkling or still water, the way they recited the long nightly specials from memory, the way they referred to the chef as if he or she were the wizard from *The Wizard of Oz*. It was sitting on the same banquet as an old man in a nice suit trying to seduce a much younger woman who kept looking at me like I was the shit—because, frankly, I was. But mostly it was how eating in these restaurants made me feel: like I was taken care of, like there was a guy in the back very concerned that I was having a wonderful time, very concerned that everything that was put before me was to my liking, that my liking it mattered.

I'd fly back to Houma-Terrebonne well fed and well dressed, with a mind full of recipes and techniques to try out on the boys. Without Tex there to give me the stink eye, the kitchen galley of the *Maine Responder* became the Gulf of Mexico's best floating restaurant.

When my contract ended at the end of the summer, I headed back home. Between eating in New York and cooking on the boat, the thought had wormed its way into my head that I could and should pursue cooking seriously. Before that summer, I had thought of working in a kitchen as simply a job. It was a job I knew well, but it was still just a job. What I gained that summer was passion. I realized that being a cook wasn't only about providing people with food, but rather about providing them with the feeling that they were cared for. As soon as I got back to New York, I started looking for ways to get involved in a more serious way with food.

My first thought was catering. Of all the kitchens I had worked in, other than my own on the *Responder,* the catering kitchen seemed like the best setup. I was so scarred from working in those miserable restaurants in Baton Rouge, I didn't want to be demeaned. As a caterer, I wouldn't have to deal with the bullshit of a professional kitchen. Plus, I had watched my mom cater for as long as I could remember. Even though the income was unpredictable, I liked the idea that I could land gigs by hustling on my own terms and set my own schedule. In addition, working on the *Responder* wasn't all that different from catering. I didn't have to worry about orders coming in. I decided the menu and I served everything at once.

But as I so often did, I found myself broke yet again. Although my closet was bursting with thousands of dollars' worth of clothing, my pockets were empty. If I wanted to become a caterer, I knew I'd need some funds. Running a catering company wouldn't be cheap, something I knew well from watching my mom. The tools, spatulas, whisks, knives, chafing trays, serving plates, cutting boards, stockpots, side tables, and piping bags, not to mention side towels, uniforms, and aprons, would cost thousands of dollars. And that didn't include a commercial kitchen space to rent, cash for ingredients to float before the checks came in, employees to hire and transportation to provide.

Also, I was a kid with no track record and no access to capital. How was I going to bankroll myself? The answer came to me one day on the subway.

"Ladies and gentlemen, good evening." It was a kid no more than twelve years old—way too late for him to be out, I thought. "I'm not here selling candy for my basketball team," he began, "I'm just trying to make some money to stay out of trouble." He carried with him a case of Peanut M&M's. I could tell from his bulging backpack he had plenty more. "I've got Peanut M&Ms, Welch's Fruit Snacks, and Starbursts. Only one dollar a bar."

I'd heard his soliloquy a thousand times. There are a few phrases anyone who's ridden New York City's subways knows by heart. There are the official kinds that crackle to life over the intercom: "Stand clear of the closing doors please." "If you see something, say something." Then there are panhandlers, who tug at your empathy, or at least try to, with calculated tales of woe, some of which might actually be true. Then there are the acrobatic pole dancers, the Norteño bands who don't miss a note through the trains' stops and starts, and the doo-wop quartets who sadly sing "Stand by Me" while shuffling through the car, the last man jangling a small bag with a few coins inside.

The candy racket, on the other hand, is neither straight-up panhandling nor pure performance. It's a bit of both. It's commerce, literally the underground marketplace in action. People have sold stuff on the subways since there *were* subways, from paperback books to penknives to batteries. But no one needs that stuff anymore. What they want is candy, and the market is happy to oblige.

As I watched this kid manage to move five or six bars in a pretty dead car, the candy game all of a sudden made a lot of sense to me. If I wanted to start a catering company, like any small-business owner I needed money. Sometimes capital comes in the form of a candy bar. I did some simple math. Say I bought a box of forty-eight bags of peanut M&M's at Costco for $25. If I could sell through my inventory at $1 a bag, that's an easy $23 in pure profit. It's cash, so no taxes or withholding. If I sold three bars per subway car, spent three minutes in each, I could clear a box in under an hour. And hell, if a twelve-year-old kid could do it, so could I.

By the time I got off my mind was set, visions of Butterfingers dancing in my head.

E xcuse me, ladies and gentlemen, I'm here selling my candy in order to launch my own catering company." A few days later I stood in front of the mirror in Tatiana's living room where I was still living. On my bed I had laid out my haul from a recent trip to BJ's Wholesale Club. "I have Butterfingers, Peanut M&M's, regular M&M's, Nutter Butters, Oreos, Snickers, Nutri-Grain Bars, honey roasted cashews, honey roasted peanuts, gum." I was nothing if not exhaustive. If I was going to do this candy thing, I was going to crush the competition. I worked on my cadence to emphasize the absurd abundance of choices I offered. I taped together eight boxes into what I called a Frankenbox, with all the labels pasted on the outside, and I was ready to go.

At first it felt strange entering the subway as a candy man. After years of being on the other side of the equation, of conditioning myself to block out the noise, now *I* was the one trying to get everyone's attention. I couldn't help but see myself through the eyes of the other passengers: "Just another kid selling candy to stay out of trouble." But I knew it wasn't trouble I was looking to stay out of but a new world I was looking to enter. Some of us have banks. Some of us have savings. Some of us have Snickers.

I stood with my back against a pole: "Excuse me, ladies and gentlemen . . ." Most people ignored me. Some glanced up and quickly dismissed me. A few women chuckled as I recited the almost endless selection. "If you'd like to buy, please let me know," I said. "I would greatly appreciate it." I began pacing down the car, rotating side to side to better entice the passengers.

My spiel worked. It wasn't as if people threw their money at me, but it also wasn't *not* like that. "You're starting a business, brother?" said one man. "Here you go." He pressed a dollar into my hand. "I got student loans too," said a woman buying a Snickers bar. "Good luck." Groups of middle-school kids getting out around 3:00 p.m. were my sweet spot. A dollar wasn't too much for them, and they loved candy. It was perfect for me. I got on the downtown train in the Bronx a little after rush hour. By the time I arrived at Fulton Street in Brooklyn, the Frankenbox was nearly empty and my pockets were full of cash.

I was quickly accumulating enough money to cover at least some of the supplies I needed to launch a catering company. The first thing I did was buy a chef's jacket, crisp and white. Before anyone would hire me, I knew I needed to look the part. Then I needed a name for my business. I decided on Coterie Catering. A coterie, I learned, was "a small group of people with shared interests or tastes." That sounded about right. I chose a logo—a hand holding a cloche—from a uniform website and ordered a coat with that embroidered on the chest. I might not have had any clients, but I looked like a chef.

I re-upped my Frankenbox and headed back underground. This time, just as I was beginning my run in the Bronx, another candy-selling kid entered the car I was in. I guess this was inevitable, but I hadn't counted on it happening so early. He stood on one side of the car and I stood on the other.

"Yo, man," he said, "where you from?"

I didn't know how to answer, but I figured the best response would be the one that instilled in my rival the most fear possible.

"Web," I said, using the street name for the Webster Houses. Immediately the kid's demeanor changed. It was as if I had used a safe word.

"Oh, shit," he said, turning meek. "I'm sorry, man." He turned to face the door and got off at the next stop.

I thought this was interesting but chalked up the incident to the fearsome reputation Webster had in the city, especially in the Bronx. So I went back to selling and didn't think much about it at the time. Meanwhile, using the money I had earned, I went about establishing my first-ever aboveboard small business. Unlike dealing, starting a small business entails lots of paperwork and forms. Thankfully, soon Coterie Catering LLC was born. And not a moment too soon.

The upside of selling candy on the subways is that it was a good excuse to explore the city. After I sold through my box, I'd fold it up, stash it in my bag, and just walk the streets. I spent a lot of time in the cookbook section at the Barnes & Noble on Fourteenth Street, and I spent a lot of time just on the sidewalk. One day, wandering in Soho, I came across a small fashion boutique near Prince Street. For some reason, mostly because I had nothing else to do, I wandered in. I asked the sales clerk, a black woman about my age, how long they'd been open. She told me they'd just opened, she was actually the owner, and that in fact she was planning a party to celebrate the opening.

My ears pricked up and my hustler sense began to tingle. "I'm a caterer," I told her. "Do you need one for the party?"

She looked at me, at my baby face, surprised. "How old are you?"

"Ma'am," I said, acting offended, "that's irrelevant."

"What can you make?" she asked.

"Anything you want," I told her. "How do cheesecakes sound?"

I don't know why I picked cheesecakes, which I had no idea

how to make, but I guess I remembered the mini-cheesecakes my mom sometimes made in little graham cracker crusts for her Catering by Jewel gigs.

"You know how to make cheesecakes?" said the woman.

"Ma'am," I said again, "I'm a chef. Don't disrespect my knowledge."

My haughty attitude paid off. She suggested we set up a tasting for the next day, and I agreed. I walked out with my first client within reach. I spent the rest of the day—and all of the night—in the kitchen. I planned out a menu for the tasting, channeling some of the ingredients and techniques I had tasted during my fine-dining adventures back when I had cash. I used what remained of my candy money to buy enough product for one tasting at the supermarket. The menu had four courses: a crostini made with shaved filet mignon with a bleu cheese foam; butternut squash wontons; chicken and waffles with maple butter; and, of course, the miniature cheesecakes. All of it was really straightforward but time-consuming to make. After I was done searing the filet and slicing it, frying the chicken, making the squash filling, and hand-whipping the cheese, it was already 8:00 p.m.

Now it was time for the miniature cheesecakes. The thing about cheesecake is you don't know if the consistency is right until the whole thing is cool. So you have a good two hours per batch. I had to make only six miniature ones, but I just couldn't get it right. No matter how many recipes I consulted, my filling was either too liquidy or too firm. The night stretched on, and I worked feverishly through it. For the first time in my life, I was completely laser-focused. No phone. No music. No texting. No jerking off. Nothing. The tasting was at nine in the morning, but it wasn't until six that six small cheesecakes set perfectly in their graham cracker crusts. I had done it. I went to bed for a few hours, to the sound of birds and bus hydraulics, knowing that this would be the first step in a career.

To my delight, I got the gig. It wasn't a big party but it was *my* party, even if no one else knew it. And it marked my first official job as an independent caterer. Unfortunately, I had agreed to cater the party at cost, so although it built my résumé and boosted my confidence, I was no richer for it. Soon I went back to selling candy.

For a few days I was back in business, clearing $400 every day as I traipsed through the city underground. One morning I got on the A with my box. Things were going normally until I hit Jay Street–Metrotech in Brooklyn and was about halfway done and ready to head back up to the Bronx.

"Excuse me, ladies and gentlemen," I began. The doors opened and two kids got on sporting Giuseppe sneakers and designer jeans. They were older than me but not by much. They were holding boxes of candy too.

"Excuse me ladies and gentlemen," started the shorter kid.

I looked at him in disbelief. What was he doing?

"What the fuck are you doing?" I called from my post a few feet away.

The taller kid made a beeline for me. "What the fuck are *you* doing?" he growled, his face an inch from mine.

"I'm selling candy, what the fuck does it look like I'm doing?" I responded.

"This is our cypher, motherfucker," he said.

"Cypher?"

"Yeah," he said, "it's our territory, our route." He took a step back and looked hard at me. "Where the fuck you from?"

It occurred to me to try the same trick from last time. Glowering at the kid, I said, "I'm from Web."

I expected him to back off but he didn't. In fact, he seemed more suspicious. "Oh yeah? You're from Web? Nah, man. *I'm* from Web. Cliff put you on this cypher?"

I didn't know who Cliff was, but I said, "Yeah, Cliff gave me this cypher." I've never been so full of shit in my life.

By this time the entire car was looking at us, cellphones out, ready to throw this up on WorldStarHipHop if it went south.

The other kid came up to see what was going on. "I haven't seen you on the block," he said. "You said you were from Web?"

"Thirteen hundred block."

"Oh yeah, who you hang with there?"

"Urkel's my boy," I said. "I've known him for years."

Their eyes lit up. "You know Urkel?" They were on the cusp of believing me but didn't fully. "Okay, who's Urkel's best friend?"

That was easy. It was Ruger from B.A.B.Y.

"Ruger," I said. That did the trick. Any trace of malice left their faces, replaced with a huge smile of recognition.

"Shit, he *is* from Web!" said the shorter one.

After that the three of us got off at the next stop and these two kids explained everything to me. The whole city's candy game, it turns out, was run out of Webster, but in the 1400 block, where a guy named Cliff controlled the entire operation. It occurred to me that I had actually met this guy before, a slightly older dude who came into the McDonald's I worked at near the projects. I remember him because he wore an expensive gold watch and because his arms were covered in tattoos of M&M's and Skittles. Cliff set kids up on predetermined routes called cyphers, and took a cut—a large cut—of their sales. I had no idea the thing was so organized, but looking back, it makes sense. How did all the kids know the same script by heart? How come there weren't more candy-selling turf wars? Cliff was, according to Jaquan, not a guy to mess with. He was connected and ruled his boys with the threat of violence. He took most of their money and paid them hourly and beat the bejeesus out of any that complained. Freelancing, like what I was doing, was the worst crime you could commit in Cliff's eyes.

Looking over my box the tall kid said, "That's at least a four-hundred-dollar flip. You're lucky we know Urkel," they said. "But you gotta be careful."

I wasn't looking to get killed over Butterfingers. I took the rest of my candy bars, stashed them in my backpack, and tossed the Frankenbox in the trash. I had dodged a bullet, it turns out. That was the last time I ever sold candy on the subway, but man, was I grateful now for the time I had spent at Webster.

Without that revenue stream and with Coterie still just a side hustle, I needed a job fast and figured I may as well look for work in a restaurant. One day I found myself in Union Square, walking north on Broadway. I peered down the cross streets looking for opportunities. Close to Park Avenue on the north side of the street, I caught sight of the warm glow of Edison bulbs shining through large plate-glass windows. I crossed the street hoping it was a restaurant and not a high-end interior design store. The space was awash with earth tones, warm leathers, and wood. There was no sign on the window but there was a menu, illuminated in a glass box mounted on the wall.

I remember thinking it had to be a good restaurant because the paper stock for the menu was so thick. The dishes were listed in plain English. The offerings were divided by techniques— braised, grilled, and roasted—and under each were proteins, from rabbit and sirloin to monkfish, with only a few accompanying ingredients listed. Amish chicken, I thought, that's funny. They don't say Jewish lamb or Episcopalian pork loin.

Then I came to the bottom of the menu: Chef / Owner: Tom Colicchio.

Beside the door was a buzzer for deliveries. I pressed it, and a woman's voice crackled through, "How can I help you?"

"I'm looking for a job. Can I fill out an application?"

"Come on up to the office," said the voice, and the door clicked open.

I walked past the coat check, past a massive floral arrangement, and peered into the dining room. I clambered up a flight of stairs into the restaurant's office, where I found Renée sititng behind a desk.

"Hello," I said, "I'm Kwame Onwuachi."

"Hello, Kwame," Renée said in a friendly, businesslike way, "Do you have a résumé?"

I handed her one of the crisply folded copies I'd been carrying around with me all day and she gave me a form.

"We ask all our potential new hires to fill it out," she said.

It was a standard application, but aside from biographical information—name, address, age—the last question was, "If there was one dish you could eat right now, what would it be?" Two things about the question checked me. First, I was excited that this was an important enough question that they put it on the job application. Clearly, they cared about food here. That was a good sign. But I also knew it was a loaded question. What *did* I want to eat, and how honest did I want to be about it? What I really wanted was the comforting warmth of my mom's gumbo. The last time she cooked for me was a farewell feast the night before I left Louisiana. Her small apartment kitchen in New Orleans was filled with the pepper-tinged seafood smell of gumbo, the faintly chlorinated scent of shrimp, and the spicy meatiness of andouille. But that's not what I wrote.

Instead, I came up with the most sophisticated and fancy-sounding combination of ingredients I could. Drawing on the knowledge gleaned from years of watching cooking shows and reading food magazines, from the menus of the places I had been that summer, I wrote "Foie gras crostini with white truffle and black garlic."

When I handed Renée the form, I saw her eyes toggle between my address—Bronx, NY—at the top and my answer at the bottom.

"How do you know about this dish?" she asked obviously impressed.

I explained that my mother was a chef—which was true— and that I had always been interested in fine dining—which was vaguely true. But I left unsaid, of course, that I had never acted on this interest.

"Wow," she said, "you're hired!"

I was hired as a server. But at Craft even front-of-house staff trail for a day in the kitchen since it was important for us to understand what we were serving.

Craft was totally different from any other kitchen I'd been in. Unlike at TJ's, all the chefs were young white tattooed guys intently focused on what they were doing. They moved with an intensity that might have had to do with youth but was likely to do with passion. These guys *wanted* to be there, you could feel it. They listened carefully to the chef, James Tracey, responding to everything he said with a quick "Oui, chef." In the kitchens I had been in before, the ranges were coated in grime and the hoods practically fossilized. Here everything was spotless, from the tidy work areas to the small saucepans and bains-marie. There were tools I'd never seen in real life before, like offset spatulas and long tweezers. The crew wrapped and rewrapped foie gras torchons, carefully made rabbit ballotines, and seared off steak, and I stood there transfixed. Only reluctantly did I leave to learn about the sidework for which I'd be responsible as a server.

There was a real camaraderie between front of house and back of house that I had never felt before. It was the first restaurant job I had where everyone wanted to be there, from the hostess to the chef to the servers to the porters. Craft was, and is, one of the best restaurants in New York. And we all took a lot of pride in the food we put out and the atmosphere in which it was served. We were a team, and though Tom rarely showed up, he was our leader.

For the first time I was happy to be part of a group. For the first time on a job, I showed up early and stayed late. I rushed through my own sidework, rolling up silverware, carefully polishing thin-stemmed wine glasses, setting tables, so I could help out the others. I listened intently to every preshift meeting, attended every optional workshop on wines, and looked forward to our family meal every day. As long as the restaurant was open and I was working, I was happy. But after we closed and locked the doors, switched off the lights, and the team disbanded, that happiness began to fade. My life was a lot different, a lot farther away, than the comfort of Craft and the people there. I wasn't content to be just a server; that wouldn't be enough to drastically alter my life circumstance. I needed to be in control. I needed to get Coterie off the ground.

I hustled any way I could. This was in 2011, and Steve Stoute's book *The Tanning of America* had just come out. Stoute is a prominent black businessman who is legendary in the music world, having worked with everyone from Jay-Z to Nas. I thought he'd help a brother out. So one day I went to a reading of his at Barnes & Noble. Afterward, I bought a book, waited in line for him to sign it, and when I got up there I told him I was a caterer and that he should let me cater one of his parties. "I know you have a lot of parties," I said.

Stoute laughed and said, "Sure, man. You have a card?"

I actually did, having invested a few hundred dollars in my first business card: "Kwame Onwuachi, Chef," it read. I handed one to him and he said he'd get in touch. Naïve as I was, I held him to it. In the next few weeks I waited in vain for an email from Stoute or one of his people to set up what would be essentially the launch of Coterie. But no call or email came, and I was furious.

I found out he was having another reading in a few weeks, so I went to that one, bought the book again, and waited in line. This time when I reached Stoute, I said, "Yo, man, It's me, Kwame, the chef. Remember you said you'd get in touch? Well, you haven't. What's up with that?"

Stoute didn't remember me, and, even if he did, was pissed off that I was so aggressive.

"Get the fuck outta here," he said. "What the fuck's your problem?"

I stormed out angrily and was about to toss his book when I heard someone say, "Excuse me."

I turned around and saw a beautiful woman with light brown skin and nice hair. "I was standing behind you in the line. I couldn't help but overhear you. Did you say you were a chef?"

"Yeah, I did," I said. "I mean, I am."

"I'm Liz," said the woman, offering me her hand to shake, "and I think I have an opportunity that's a perfect fit for you."

Liz Bacelar was the executive producer, she told me, of the Singularity Summit, a conference of global thought leaders that was taking place that October in New York. She was looking for a caterer for the entire summit. That consisted of 1,600 people over the course of the four nights. I have no idea why she would ever take a chance on me, but she did. When she asked if I was interested in preparing a tasting for the gig, I said of course I was. I was terrified, but I didn't—couldn't—let on. I told her I'd email her with details of the tasting, the location, and time. She seemed pleased and said it would have to be soon. The summit was the next month.

I was so excited about the opportunity I didn't think about all the challenges I'd face. For instance, where to meet my potential clients. When you're a caterer, it's common practice to cook a sample meal. Sometimes, as I did for the boutique gig, it can be at a store or a venue, but for this, I felt like I needed a show kitchen of my own. It's an audition not just of your kitchen chops but of whether or not the two parties get along. I was confident in my skills as a chef and a schmoozer but I had nowhere to entertain. I couldn't very well invite these prospective clients to River Park Towers, the dank sprawl of building and flickering fluorescent lights where I still lived with Tatiana, her boyfriend, and her baby. Nothing is a turnoff like a New York City Housing Authority kitchen. People want to hear about that once you're successful, not when you're living it.

Luckily, my mother came through as she had so many times before. She called up a couple of old friends of hers in the music business who lived in a brownstone on Striver's Row, a group of elegant nineteenth-century town houses on 139th Street in Harlem that has long been home to black luminaries from Adam Clayton Powell Jr. to W. C. Handy. She explained that I was looking for a kitchen to call my own, at least for an evening and they were only too happy to help out. They said they'd stay upstairs and that I could use the ground floor.

I emailed Liz the address and said to meet me at my home the following night. When she and her business partner arrived,

I welcomed them to the town house like it was my own. I led them through the living room, past the crowded bookshelves, original art, and family photographs, desperately hoping they wouldn't ask who the smiling faces in the frames were. I could tell they were impressed with the place and with me as lord of the manor. I was like the black Count of Monte Cristo, and I wanted to keep it that way. For the entire night I was on a high frequency tuned to the charming Kwame station, unleashing a constant flow of words to forestall any uncomfortable questions.

I led them back to the spacious kitchen, with its marble-top counters and an eight-burner range. I opened up a bottle of $50 cab franc, worth a hundred candy bars of profit. I told stories about my mother, about my time spent in Africa and New Orleans, carefully leaving out the untoward parts. As I spoke, I prepared the dinner: tagliatelle with pesto and marinated tomato, roast chicken with a pomegranate gastrique, a vinegar-laced reduction sauce. Liz and her partner ate it up. Not just the food, but the whole scene: me, my chef's coat, the kitchen. When I led them to the door later that night, I had landed my biggest gig. It was going to be a trial by fire for sure, to make 1,600 meals over four days. I didn't even have staff, let alone a kitchen to cook in. But I'd figure all that out. I was a legit caterer now, that's what mattered. The hustle was working.

The conference took place over four days at the 92nd Street Y. I was responsible for dinner each night for four hundred people. It's fair to say I had no idea what to do. The first thing I did was fly my mom and a few of her crew from New Orleans up to New York. She came straight from the airport to meet me at a restaurant downtown and I showed her the menu I had in mind, a version of which I had cooked during my audition.

With her help, we calculated quantities and broke everything down into a prep list.

"Always trust the prep list," my mom said to me. "You've made it in your sanest moment. In the kitchen you'll be crazy."

On a few sheets of paper she scribbled down how and what we'd need to do in the next few days in order for me not to crash and burn. She converted each dish into ounces and portions, then multiplied that by four hundred. I was shocked by the sheer amount of food we'd need: Twenty-five pounds of pistachio pesto. Four cases of zucchini. *Five hundred whole chickens.*

We took a car out to Restaurant Depot, a huge warehouse of a store on Hamilton Avenue in Brooklyn. Walking down the aisles, pushing a flatbed cart like you'd get at IKEA, I couldn't believe the size of the products: Ten-gallon drums of ketchup, barrels of soy sauce, every type of food you could imagine. We picked up some supplies there and returned to Tatiana's with a trunkload of stuff.

So I had chefs; now I needed a kitchen. There was no way I could prep from Tatiana's tiny apartment. Traveling from Manhattan to the Bronx, I frequently passed a place called Hot Bread Kitchen, on Park and 113th Street. Hot Bread is a culinary incubator for start-up businesses with an emphasis on those that are minority owned. Sounds perfect, I thought.

I called them up and said, "Hey, I'm a small business. I see you have an incubator program for small businesses. How can I get in there?"

It turned out that their application process would take a few weeks at the very least. I needed to get in that day. I explained that I had a $30,000 job feeding 1,200 people—exaggerating, but just a bit.

"Well," said the woman I spoke to, "you can definitely turn a profit."

I asked how much it cost to get in. She said I'd need a $2,000 deposit, then I'd pay hourly. I told her I'd be there in fifteen minutes with a check, and I was.

I don't know how many guys roll into an incubator kitchen with ten chefs and $17,000, but it felt pretty good for me. Fifteen minutes after I hung up, I was there with a check and my crew. For four days we worked, heads down, methodically crossing off tasks from the pages-long prep list. And almost magically, the meal began to take form. On the first night of the summit, I was quaking with fear but tried not to let on. We transported sheet tray after sheet tray to the venue, each covered in reams of plastic wrap. We set up a line in the back of the banquet space and began to plate in batches. We were all hard at work. My mom and I and the other guys, sweating it out together. When there was a question, I was the one who answered. I was the chef. Finally.

Before my mom returned to New Orleans, I took her out for breakfast to thank her. Chatting over pancakes and coffee, we were both exhausted and spent but happy. My mom isn't one to dole out praise, but I could tell she was proud of me. The little bird she had pushed from the nest had finally learned how to fly.

Admittedly Tatiana's Cheesecake

YIELD: One 9-inch cheesecake

FOR THE CRUST

1 cup cinnamon graham cracker crumbs

½ cup gingersnap cracker crumbs

½ cup sugar

1 tablespoon ground cinnamon

¾ cup butter softened

1 teaspoon vanilla

½ teaspoon Kosher salt

FOR THE FILLING

4 cups Philadelphia cream cheese, softened

1½ cups sugar

¼ cup sour cream

Juice of 2 lemons

2 large eggs

1 tablespoon vanilla

1 vanilla bean, scraped

---

1. **Make the crust** Preheat oven to 350° F. Combine all the ingredients for the crust in a mixing bowl. Mix well. Spray a 9-inch round springform pan with cooking spray and spread crust mixture in an even layer at the bottom of the pan. Bake crust for 10 minutes, remove from oven, and allow to cool.

2. **Make the filling** Meanwhile, in a stand mixer with a paddle attachment, whip the softened cream cheese until smooth. Add the sugar and sour cream and mix until the sugar has dissolved. Add the rest of the ingredients and mix until well incorporated.

3. Pour the filling into the cooled crust and place springform in a shallow baking dish. Add water to the baking dish to reach at least half way up the springform pan.

4. Bake the cheesecake for 50 minutes. The filling should not look entirely set in the center. Be mindful of your crust not overbaking. If necessary, cover crust with strips of aluminum foil.

5. Remove the cheesecake from the oven, and set it on a rack to cool. Once cooled, refrigerate it, covered, until you're ready to serve. For best results, allow to chill overnight.

CIA Man

———————

When the definitive history of modern American chefs is finally written, it'll be full of names we all recognize. But there's one name that I'm almost sure will be missing: Bruce Mattel.

Bruce Mattel has no Michelin stars. He's not on television and is barely known even to Google. He doesn't have a fancy restaurant in Manhattan or Los Angeles. Hell, he doesn't even have a fancy restaurant. He's in his fifties, wide, gray-haired, and my hero.

As soon as I got the Singularity gig, I hustled to pull it off. My mom came up from New Orleans with a few of her own chefs. I found space at Hot Bread kitchen, an incubator in Harlem for food start-ups, and worked for a week straight to get those meals out of the kitchen.

After the event I realized that a) I could do this catering thing, and b) I couldn't do it while still working at Craft. So I quit and devoted myself fully to Coterie Catering. As the gigs became bigger, tougher, and more frequent, however, I quickly came to realize I was in over my head, trying to plan and execute jobs with no help. That is until one day, wandering around the aisles of the cookbook section in the Barnes & Noble on Fourteenth

Street, I came across a hardcover entitled *Catering: A Guide to Managing a Successful Business Operation*. It was written by Bruce Mattel, who smiled out at me a little awkwardly from the back cover. The book isn't filled with sparkling prose or gauzy memories of catering gigs gone swimmingly. It's a book of diagrams and prep lists, basic staffing requirements, equipment needs, pitfalls to avoid, and best practices to adhere to. It covers everything from how to price per portion to how to deal with a drunk customer (ignore and stall). As a twenty-year-old with no business background or managerial expertise, let alone food safety training, it was exactly what I needed. I bought that book and for the next few months clung to it. Mattel's down-to-earth guidance continuously saved my ass.

At the same time, although no clients were complaining, I was butting up against the limits of my own skill. Having seen how Chef James and his line operated at Craft, I began looking at my own prep work and execution with a more critical eye. There's no other way of putting it: I was good but not great. I could sear and braise and dice and cube but didn't know *why* I was doing what I was doing. So when I read that Mattel was an instructor at the Culinary Institute of America, I decided to make a pilgrimage an hour and a half north to the campus.

In 1946 an attorney named Frances Roth, the first woman to enter the Connecticut Bar Association, and Katharine Angell, the wife of Yale University's president, founded what is now the Culinary Institute of America in an old house in New Haven, Connecticut. There was nothing fancy about the institute, then called the New Haven Restaurant Institute, and nothing particularly glamorous about the profession. The school was started to help returning World War II veterans reenter the workforce. Because Americans were eating out in ever growing numbers, professional cooking seemed like a good way for these men—in the first class, of the forty-four students, forty-three were male—to support their families. At that time being a chef was still a vocation, a blue-collar trade not unlike that of welder or electrician. Chefs were not seen as artists. It took nearly fifty years for cooking to become the exalted career it is today.

By the time I passed through the gates of the Culinary Institute of America, the profession of chef was a thing to be and the campus of the CIA had grown in scope, ambition, and grandeur. In 1970 the school exchanged its New Haven home for a majestic decommissioned Jesuit novitiate on the banks of the Hudson River in Hyde Park, a town previously best known as FDR's familial home. Everyone who is anyone in food service had passed through the two-year culinary program there, though some stayed for the full four years to earn a bachelor's degree. The camera-ready personalities I had watched on television while growing up, like Rocco DiSpirito and Cat Cora, badasses like Tony Bourdain and Roy Choi, world-class chefs like Grant Achatz and Alfred Portale, were all CIA graduates.

Arriving on campus felt like being transported to another universe—the universe, to be exact, whose creator is a blond English woman named J. K. Rowling, where Quidditch is a varsity sport, where Gryffindors hate Slytherins, and wizarding is totally cool, not dorky at all. For a Harry Potter superfan like me, who had waited in line at midnight for every new book to drop at the only Barnes & Noble in the Bronx, my only frame of reference for the campus was Hogwarts. The institute's picturesque brick-and-marble buildings sat on a well-kept campus. Maple and elm trees lined the school's meandering paths. An impressive circular water fountain shot plumes high into the air just because fountains are dope. The old Jesuit buildings are accompanied by modern ones named after wealthy hospitality figures like Conrad Hilton and J. Willard Marriott, old white dudes in seventies suits who peer out of bronze reliefs in the lobbies that bear their names.

Like their Hogwartian brethren, CIA students wear smart uniforms and carry thick textbooks that look like volumes full of spells. In a way, they are. The recipes and techniques laid forth in those books and in the syllabus, the promise goes, can magically transform whoever walks through the gates of the campus from a muggle into a chef. Magic, a lot of hard work, and, I would find, frustration, burnout, money, debt, and doubt.

As I often did when trying to make a strong first impression, I wore the best suit I had, an Italian merino wool suit I had used too much of the Singularity profit on, and carried a black leather briefcase. Appearances, I knew, mattered.

When I arrived at the school, I met with Michael Brown, an assistant admissions officer. Michael, a handsome middle-aged guy with wavy black hair, a broad smile, and tanned skin, asked where I was from. I told him the Bronx. It turns out that as an admissions outreach counselor, he had spent a lot of time there too. He'd even been to my old school, Mount Saint Michael, though I may have been cutting class that day. We made small talk. He was impressed by my suit. I was impressed by his office and his willingness to engage. I mentioned that I was there on a Bruce Mattel pilgrimage. He smiled and said, "Do you want to meet him?" I couldn't believe it. I considered myself pretty chill, but Bruce Mattel? *Damn.*

Michael led me from the quiet, carpeted admissions office around the corner to Bruce's office, a small, windowless room, more of an antechamber to a kitchen attached on the far side. But there, behind the desk, sat Bruce—the man, the myth, the legend—Mattel. I love Bruce but he's not much to look at, just another wide white guy, midfifties, with pink skin and gray hair. But he seemed to exude an impressive logistical competence. His appeal was halfway between that of Yoda and General MacArthur. Here was a man who faced defeat armed with prep lists, chafing trays, and a brilliant strategic mind. I was totally intimidated. Bruce stepped from behind his desk and warmly shook my hand.

He asked me about myself and I gave him the five-star bells-and-whistles Kwame story. It was a narrative I had perfected during dozens of catering pitch meetings, fine-tuning the balance between rags and riches. I cast myself partly as a lost wretch who had been saved (glossing over the exact nature of my transgressions at Bridgeport), partly as a one-man show of the black diasporic experience, and totally as a hustler. I grew up in the Bronx, I told him. My mother was a caterer, I lived in Nigeria, I cooked in Louisiana, I worked at Craft, then I started my own catering company—guided by his book—and now I wanted to take it to the next level. If that wasn't enough to charm him, it turned out Bruce was from the Bronx too. He grew up on 241st and White Plains, so we quickly fell into conversation over the great culinary unifier of the borough: Arthur Avenue. We compared and contrasted notes on the great Italian bakeries there, whose biscotti crumbled with just the right amount of hardness. We both agreed that Madonia Brothers' cannoli is the best in the world. After we had been chatting for a half hour or so, he said, "You need to come to this school. Apply. We'll push your application through." Thanks to his book, when Bruce Mattel says something, I was in the habit of listening.

"Yes, sir," I told him. "I will."

"Then I'll see you in the fall," he said.

Walking out of his office, I was naturally elated. But on the ride home, watching the trees turn back into the bricks of the city until the train rattled above Park Avenue, there was only one problem. At $33,000 a year, the Culinary Institute tuition was way above anything I could afford. I wanted to be there; they wanted me there; but between us stood the Grand Canyon of insufficient funds. I just couldn't see a bridge to get from where I was to being in a position where I had that kind of money lying around. I wasn't slinging dope anymore, and my cash flow was slow. Though Coterie was a money-making operation, all the money went straight back into growing the business. I wasn't turning a profit, and if I cashed out, I'd be slaughtering my best chance at ever making a living cooking, whether I got into the CIA or not.

After speaking further with my new friends Michael and Bruce, we agreed that I needed only $4,000 to begin. But I would have to come up with another $2,000 every month if I wanted to stay.

I had already given Bruce the Kwame pitch, now I gave it to myself. But I found it wasn't so easy to convince myself anymore. It used to work like a charm, like poppers of self-esteem. I had total confidence in my abilities, that I was the one who could do what others couldn't. I could get rich, be famous. I would get out of the projects. I could tackle all projects and I would emerge victorious. It was an attitude with no shortage of self-confidence, I knew, but I thought I could adjust that on the back end. The goal for now was to achieve, to get there. Where? Somewhere. The destination was almost immaterial. It was just somewhere different from where I was.

But I was increasingly aware by now of the danger of thinking I could do anything I wanted. It had gone quickly from empowering to self-sabotaging. I saw that the opportunities I had squandered were a result of thinking I didn't have to follow the rules. To be honest, I'm still wavering on this one. If I had followed the rules, the guidelines and parameters that had been set for me—as a young black man in America—would have ground me down by now, legs cut off, subservient to someone. Obedience is not an option when the system is aligned against you.

Taken to the other extreme, though, in the red zone high revs of rule-breaking, bucking the system quickly turns to screwing yourself over. I had been running at 7,000 RPM: juggling too much, taking shortcuts where I could and risks all the time, feeling invincible and realizing I was not. Those were the hangovers of rule-breaking of which I'd grown weary. Just once more, I told myself, tell yourself you can do anything. "This is your chance. This is what you've been working toward. You've hustled, now hustle harder."

The Culinary Institute of America represented a way to both redeem myself and to gain a foothold in the professional world that I had not yet found. It might be one of the last chances I had to change, in a meaningful and immediate way, the direction in which my life was headed. I was determined to make it work. I'd been kicked out of more schools than most people ever attended. I'd gotten into college but then gotten expelled because I couldn't kick my ambition to be a drug kingpin. Growing up I'd had near misses with violence, near misses with the law, near misses with almost everything that moved. Some friends had been shot, others had died, many had ended up in jail, not just because they were black or poor—which is close to an indictable crime in America—but because they had gotten themselves into the types of hairy situations that end in lengthy sentences or full stops. To escape, perhaps, I had always kept pushing forward, applying constant pressure to the future in the hope that some avenue would open up. So far it had worked, which is why I found myself at the CIA. Eventually, though, I knew I wouldn't be able to find an exit in time.

When I got back to the Bronx, I was unabashed about asking for help from my family. Sometimes when people talk about hitting up their parents, it's as if mom and dad could spare the money, as if they had it on hand. That's not how it was for me. There's a huge difference between asking someone who has money for help and someone who is, like you, struggling. By this point in time, I was on my own, but my mother and Westley still struggled financially. They were living in New Orleans, my mother still working as an executive chef at a catering company and Westley, much to her consternation, not working at all. Mom didn't struggle with spending; she struggled with earning enough income to cover the costs of having a family. Even with me and my sister gone, it was hard. I knew this when I called her. I caught her coming off an event and she listened happily as I told her about my trip to Hyde Park and my meeting with Bruce. I told her what he had said, that I had to go to the CIA. Then came the hard part. "Mom," I said, "I'm going to need some help." Could she, I wondered, possibly help me scrape together enough money for tuition? I knew every dollar from her had a real, very tangible cost. It was a zero-sum game. Every dollar she gave to me would be a dollar she didn't have, not just for retirement, but for rent and groceries.

"Kwame," she said, "this is your chance. I wish I had been given it, because if I had, my life would have looked very different and your life would have looked very different too."

I knew what she meant. My mother had been worn down by the bare-bones years of worrying and making do. "I'm helping you not just to help you because I love you. I'm helping you to help your children someday too." She gave me what little savings she had, about $2,000.

With my mother's money and support behind me, I made the much more difficult trip uptown to ask my father. It was an uncomfortable task, to say the least. Though we had not yet stopped talking entirely, we were not close. He lived only a few blocks from where I was living, but it might as well have been another country, I saw him so rarely. This was both my choice and his. As a young man I tried to insulate myself from his anger; as an older man he tried to insulate himself from my rage. But my dad, by now working as an architect for a construction company, had money, and I wasn't in a position to be picky about who I asked.

He welcomed me into his house with the wary air of a person who knows they're going to be asked for something. It was kind of obvious, since I didn't make social calls on him anymore. When I sat down in his living room and explained the situation, much the same way I had to my mom, he looked confused and didn't say anything for a while. What he said next shook me.

"Why don't you just start dealing again? You made a thousand dollars a week back at Bridgeport."

First of all, I made $3,000 a week at Bridgeport. Second, I couldn't believe what my father was saying. What kind of father actually suggests to his son, a son who is asking him for money to pursue his education, that he go back to dealing drugs? That he return to perhaps the worst thing he had done in his young life?

"Yeah," he continued, shrugging like it was no big deal. "I can get you weed, and Marist College is right there. You'll make more than enough to pay for school."

I couldn't tell if he was trolling me or what. What did he

mean, he could get me weed? Since when did my dad have a connect? Since when did he ever want to go in with me on something? And when he did, it was this, selling drugs to kids at a small liberal arts college? I couldn't believe it. I stared at my father's face, a face not unlike mine but older and leaner and harder. It was clear to me then that he, who had always seen the worst in me, would continue to define me by my worst moments. When I was a boy, it was dropping glasses. When I was a man, it was selling drugs.

I couldn't believe I had to explain to my dad why I didn't want to go back to selling drugs. It was humiliating and hurtful.

"Where will I be in five years, ten years? How am I going to raise a family as a dealer? What kind of life is that?" I asked him.

My dad didn't say anything, and I thought for a moment that perhaps he was embarrassed or ashamed.

"I want to be a chef," I continued. "But I need to go to the CIA to do that, and I need your help."

In the end the man agreed to give me a few hundred bucks and his old Jeep so I could get to and from school from the city. But for all intents and purposes, our relationship ended that day. For so long I had carried with me the suffering of his emotional and physical beatings. I still do. But that day some of it evaporated. One of the heaviest burdens of walking through life with the scars of abuse is loving your abuser, respecting them, trusting them. Because if you do, it means you deserve their scorn, their blows, their insults. But when I left that day, I took with me a check for $200 and a set of car keys, and what I left behind was my father, my pathetic father with his half-assed offer to hook me up with weed, with his distorted view of who I was and what I could become, with all his poisonous anger.

Ironically, my next stop was at a drug dealer's. Though I had left slinging behind ever since my misadventures at Bridgeport, Jaquan hadn't stopped selling drugs. As he had since we were little kids, he had stayed modest, in his lane, with his head down. He sold only weed, never moving on to pills or cocaine or anything harder. He had limited his market to the Webster Houses and the 1400 block within them, never seeking to expand his territory. And he sold only to people he knew. He had stupid money, kept under his mattress tightly rolled in $100 stacks kept together by rubber bands. Because these were the proceeds of criminal activity, Jaquan couldn't invest his savings in the standard economy. And it was doing little under his bed except, perhaps, mildewing. Jaquan was a naturally prudent small-business owner. He didn't drive flashy cars or dress in designer clothes like me. More importantly, he was my friend.

Sitting on the couch of his mother's house where he still lived, he peeled off a thousand dollars in twenties and handed them to me. "Kwame," he said, "you know this means I eat for free, forever, wherever you are." "Yeah," I said, grinning and giving him a hug, "it's a deal."

I accepted that $1,000 from Jaquan with nothing but love and gratitude. I don't care how he got it. I don't care where he got it. That money was clean. I accepted the $200 from my dad with nothing but resentment and pain. I don't care if he paid taxes or how he earned it. That money was dirty.

With enough cash finally in hand, I filled out the application online and wrote an essay version of the Kwame story. I also immediately started scouring scholarship opportunities. I had the first month covered but I knew the pressure would be on as soon as I arrived. Michael Brown and Bruce both helped by directing me toward grants both big and small. For the Honeybee Association, I wrote recipes using honey—like burnt honey meringue tarts and honey-glazed salmon roulad— for a few grand. I agreed to start the semester on a less popular rotation in order to receive the stipends the school administration used to even out attendance. I agreed to become a resident advisor, or RA, to offset housing costs, a real change up from my drug-dealing days at Bridgeport. And I wrote additional essays on everything from the wonders of milk to the health benefits of fungi in an attempt to get industry-backed scholarships. Still, by the time I was accepted and began classes— acceptance at the CIA is all but a given if you can pay—none of the scholarship money had come through. I decided to chance it anyway. If everything went south, at least I'd have made it a month.

That first morning on campus, I arrived hopelessly awestruck and excited, hoping I'd find my people in the kitchens and classrooms too. Together, we'd become a SEAL Team 6, the Magnificent 7, the Wu-Tang of the passe. I followed a chirpy clipboard-wielding sophomore into the dorm, which felt dully familiar. I had gone through the same hopeful rituals when I first arrived at the University of Bridgeport. This time, I vowed I would not be leaving so soon.

After I deposited my stuff and met my roommate, a big kid from Jersey named Mike, I followed the rest of the students to Roth Hall, the former chapel that now served as both dining hall and gathering space. The incoming class was about a hundred strong. We were soon broken up into groups of fifteen to twenty student with whom we'd stay for the ensuing two years. We clumped together, a bunch of giddy, apprehensive kids. There were some adults among us, which reflected the changing student body due to the fact that by 2011 being a chef represented a second-career goal for a lot of folks. But most of my fellow students were younger than I was, straight out of high school. I was a little different from the rest of the class. Most obviously, I was black, a fact that stood out as we gathered in the dining hall. There were only three other black kids in the class.

Less obviously, I was already a seasoned cook. Most of the incoming class had some restaurant experience but few had come fresh from the trenches. As excited as I was to be there, being in the kitchen was nothing new for me. I knew I could handle the pressure.

Behind the podium stood a mild-looking dude, the school's president, Tim Ryan. Ryan had taken over in 2001 and had delivered scores of welcoming addresses I was sure were just like this one. "It's not the destination," he began. "The journey is the reward." I zoned out. Staring at the faces of my classmates as the multihued sunlight streamed through the stained glass, I thought that if my time here was to be fleeting, I'd make the best of it. When Tim asked for one of the students to sing the alma mater, I raised my hand. I popped up and, staring down at a sheet of lyrics, began in a thin falsetto: *"Culinary Institute of America . . ."* When I finished, the whole class exploded in laughter and applause. "Nice job, man," said the kid next to me, who introduced himself as David Paz-Grusin. "Everybody calls me Paz." Paz and I became fast friends, and he's still my best friend today.

Then we headed back to the dorms and prepared for classes the next day. I could barely sleep, I was so happy to be there. I was excited that the skills I had been honing through trial by fire with my own catering company would be professionalized. After hustling like a mother for two years, I was excited to have a chance to take a beat and then, perhaps, to grow, as a man and as a chef. Coterie had been going well and growing, but I knew the pace wasn't sustainable and that without proper training even that growth would have a limit. More to the point, growing up I had seen my mother struggle with the unpredictability and seasonality that ruled the life of a professional caterer. I had felt it firsthand. Culinary school represented a way out of that unpredictability, an entry into the world of professional restaurants and fine-dining kitchens.

As part of the curriculum, after the first six-month semester I would extern at one of the most prestigious restaurants in the world. Then, back at Hyde Park, I would be instructed by professors with deep ties in the industry and develop friendships with classmates that would, I hoped, prove fruitful once we graduated. Like most centers of higher education, the Culinary Institute is only partially about the knowledge one gains. The rest concerns what rooms it allows you to enter and who shakes your hand once you get inside.

Lying in my bed that night, I was worried. The money stashed in the glove compartment of the Jeep in the parking lot was all I had. And if I didn't figure out a way to get more, my dreams of higher culinary education would be a nonstarter. I'd go back to the grind. So even as I unfolded the school uniform and laid out the white chef's jacket and houndstooth pants, I felt like an interloper.

Each incoming student is given a set of knives. This set, delivered without fanfare in a soft black case, contains a chef's knife, a filet knife, a serrated bread knife, a paring knife, and a peeler. Though humble, they would be the tools of my trade; a toolkit to change my world. If I survived. I held on to those knives as tightly as a Marine does his rifle. Part of it was just the thrill of holding them; part of it was also because I was terrified they'd be taken away. A few days into orientation Andrew, one of the few black kids in the class, walked in on me crying over my knife roll on my bed. "I can't afford to go here," I said. "I can't afford to go here." Andrew, to his credit, was nice about it, but he couldn't do anything about it so he slowly backed out of the room. (Years later he confessed to me that he struggled with the same worries I did, crying alone in his room too.) I called my mom, distraught. "Don't worry, we'll find a way," she said. "You need this education."

With the precariousness of my situation ever present in my mind, I threw myself into life at Hyde Park. Thousands of hours of prep had made me adept at wielding a knife or searing off proteins, but I had never been exposed to the theory behind what I did, or had rigor imposed on me as I did at the Culinary Institute. The first glimpse I had, and that any first-time student has, is the Culinary Fundamentals Course, an intensive semester-long class designed to give us, as the title suggests, the basic skills on which to build a career as a chef. Here we learned the basic vegetable cuts, how to turn carrots, onions, and celery into a neat dice, or a mince, or a cube. How to julienne and how to batonnet. We were taught the basic mechanics of why a raw piece of meat becomes a richly flavored steak—the holy Maillard reaction. We were introduced to the five mother sauces as devised by Marie-Antoine Carême—the velouté, sauce Espagnole, Béchamel, Hollandaise, and Tomato—as well as their derivative daughters, the Bordelaise, Lyonnaise, Ravigote, Soubise, and Béarnaise. We were taught basic kitchen etiquette and best practices. We burned through hundreds of pounds of produce, dicing until the correct dimensions and physical knowledge were in our bones.

Some of these skills I knew. Some I didn't. But the chance to practice them, for no other reason than to get better, was entirely novel for me. It wasn't as if we were wasting what we made—everything was served in the dining hall—but I had never before had the luxury to just practice. I was always moving forward, cooking as if my life depended on it—because it did—and I had never paused to learn proper technique.

My teacher was a tall mustachioed guy named Jeff Klug who had begun his career at the CIA back in 1982. Klug had worked in various hotels in New York, Miami, and Lausanne, Switzerland. Looking back on it now, he may not have been the most innovative chef at the CIA, but he had technique on lock. He knew a high-volume, high-quality, traditional kitchen like the back of his hairy, scarred hand. Klug was patient but stern, a throwback to the early days of the CIA, when being a chef was less about personal expression and more about getting a job done. He was, in short, the perfect professor for fundamentals.

What stuck with me most from that course were stocks. Stocks, Klug explained, are at their essence meat-infused water. Heating bones or meat, or a combination of the two, in water, releases the proteins and flavors of the meat and diffuses them into the liquid. The heat unwinds the collagen inside the bones into water-soluble strands of gelatin, which are like little flavor diplomats that travel beyond the borders of bone, bringing flavor with them. Growing up I thought of gelatin only as the carnival-colored Jell-O my friends' mothers would serve for dessert. But here gelatin is a necessary tool to turn sauces silky and give stock its fulsome mouth feel. It is gelatin that boiling bones releases, gelatin that forms the stock. As a classically trained chef, knowing how to make stock allows you to build sturdy flavors going forward. With a good stock, anything is possible. With a weak stock, nothing is.

The most important and difficult task we had in Klug's class was how to make a consommé, and this consumed my first months in Hyde Park. At its heart, a consommé is a double stock, which means that after the initial stock is made, a secondary process is still needed. A consommé is a much more elusive and difficult thing than a stock. What makes a consommé a consommé is its crystal clarity and deep flavor. It's actually a pretty ingenious process. As Klug showed us the first or second week, every consommé begins as a basic broth. This broth can either be white, meaning made with uncooked bones, or brown, in which case the bones have been seared to a dark rich color prior to being heated. To the cold stock you add finely chopped meat, mirepoix, and a couple of egg whites shaped into a loaf, and acid in the form of tomatoes. As the liquid begins to heat up, the egg whites create a "raft" that floats to the top. As the meat releases its proteins and impurities into the liquid, the larger particles float to the surface, where they are caught in this raft. As more and more of the fats and proteins are released, the raft grows and grows. Over the course of a couple of hours, the meat releases its flavors into the liquid. If you do it right, by the end of the process you can neatly remove the raft, strain the liquid one more time, and are left with a brilliantly clear, extremely flavorful liquid, the consommé.

Because I had a leg up on most of the other students, I quickly became a leader in the classroom. It also didn't hurt that instead of a backpack I carried all my things in a briefcase. Mostly, though, it was because I finished everything sooner than everyone else. I had a few years' experience busting my ass in the kitchen. Whereas most of the other students had to learn not just what to do but how to do it with a fire under their ass, I'd been in the weeds before. So I started printing out the station assignments for the entire class and writing up the tasks on the whiteboard before each session started. Even though there is no formal brigade in a culinary school classroom, I began to act like the chef (except when the real chef, Klug, was there). I admonished my fellow students to keep their stations clean, encouraged them when I saw them doing well, and provided support when they were struggling. I drew a diagram for our knife tray when the other students kept forgetting what they had to do. To my surprise, my classmates started treating me as their leader. Mine was the door they knocked on in the dorm room after a long day. And unlike at Bridgeport, it wasn't Ecstasy or weed they were looking to score but knowledge.

Unfortunately, I was hardly ever on campus at night. To help pay for school, I'd gotten a job in town as a sous chef at a Mexican place called Cesar's Bistro. So after I grabbed dinner at school, I quickly changed out of my crisp CIA uniform, slipped on an old chef's jacket, and drove into Hyde Park for a night shift. Daytime was for consommé and braising; nighttime was for quesadillas, tacos, and espazotes. My routine was to grab a cup of coffee from 7-Eleven on my way to work for a shift that started at 5:00 p.m.

The kitchen at Cesar's was definitely not up to CIA standards, but it was a much better representation of what a working restaurant kitchen looks like. It was a small and cramped space, not much larger than the kitchen on the *Maine,* and there were three of us on the line at any given time, me plus two cooks. In a kitchen so small, we were all equal. No one was there to learn; we were there to work. I knew the guys I saw beside me would likely never make it the few blocks to the Culinary Institute. During my time there I worked with a rotating cast of exhausted-looking cooks from Ecuador and Mexico. They were, though I never asked, here illegally. They were exploited by Cesar, who rarely paid them—or me—on time, and suffered so silently I was sure they had no legal recourse. For me, the gig was to help pay my tuition. For them, the backbreaking labor was the work of their lives. Not that I really blamed Cesar. He was just an old guy in way over his head. A cook, not a chef or a restaurateur. He was hungry for my knowledge, so when I showed the guys in the kitchen how, by using a mirepoix, you standardize cooking times or when I helped Cesar sear off his carne asada, he greeted this knowledge with gratitude and wonder. There I was, a freshman at the CIA, and I was teaching this old man who runs a restaurant how to cook. Tired as I was, I still felt fortunate to return to the dorm every night, to wake up and fail again at making consommé.

Not only was I working at Cesar's, I was also commuting back to New York nearly every weekend for catering gigs. Despite my being in school, Coterie was still going full bore. In fact, it was going better than ever. By this point I had access to a nearly unlimited pool of talent in the form of my classmates. They were all hungry for experience, worked hard, and loved food. Nonetheless, running a business is exhausting. During the day, when the other students took smoke breaks or just relaxed for a moment before sweating again on the stoves, I was working my phone, arranging new gigs, scrawling prep lists and menus on three- by five-inch cards and recruiting my friends to come down to the city to work with me. That's how I meet Greg Vakiner, a round-faced, moon-eyed kid from Pittsburgh who became one of my best friends. Greg's got a mellow demeanor and a country accent but he's a deeply ambitious guy. One day he overheard me talking to a client and asked if he could help me out. I was drowning at this point and needed someone to handle things like transportation, picking the crew of students who could work, and coordinating scheduling with the industrial kitchen in Harlem that served as my base of operations. All this Greg did with an easy smile. He quickly became my operations guy.

Catering on the weekends, I was able to save some money for tuition. After paying my crew I didn't have enough to accumulate any savings, but it did cover the $2,000 I needed each month. Together with the scholarship money that came through, it was enough to build a fragile sense of security.

But that sense of safety, for me, is always illusory. One Friday evening I was driving home after my shift, which after the kitchen was cleaned for the night put me on the road at around two in the morning. I was at the gates of the campus when I saw police lights flashing a menacing red-and-blue behind me. *Careful, Kwame,* I said to myself, pulling the Jeep over. Don't get shot by some country-ass cop for nothing. I waited, hands on the wheel, peering in the rearview.

As the cop approached the driver's side, I notice his hand was already on the butt of his pistol. It looked so comedically goonish, I momentarily forgot to be scared and angry. He seemed like the kind of guy who wanders around with his hands down his pants, making sure his dick is still there.

I wanted to roll down the window, since I knew he'd ask me to do so, but I didn't want to get shot for suspicious reaching. When he got to my side, he rapped on the glass. "Lower your window, sir," he said, annoyed that it wasn't open but also seemingly happy for the chance to be annoyed.

Before asking me for my driver's license and registration he asked if I had any weapons in the car. I could tell he wasn't used to seeing a black kid in his town. The fear came off him like stink from roadkill. Black male. Early morning. Suspected perp, natch. That I was returning from a night shift didn't cross his mind.

"No, sir, I sure don't."

He finally asked for my documents.

"Are you aware you have a taillight out?"

"No sir, I'm sorry, sir. I'll get it fixed right away."

I keep my anger on a tight leash. But it's infuriating and pathetic that I'm the latest generation of black kids who have to soft-shoe their way around authority with this deferential bullshit. Yes, sir. No, sir. I felt like screaming "Don't you have anything else better to do than pull me over for a broken tail-light at two in the morning?" On the other hand, I wasn't going to give this guy an excuse to beat me up or worse on the side of a backcountry road.

The cop went back to his car for what felt like hours but was actually minutes. When he came back with a self-satisfied saunter, he said, "Sir, you have a number of outstanding parking tickets." He waited a beat, then went on: "I tell you what I'm going to do: I'm going to take you down to the station until we can sort this out." At first I didn't realize he was arresting me. He said "Tell you what I'm going to do" with a tone like "I'm cutting you a break, kid." And anyway, since when are parking tickets an arrestable offense? But this was the first time I'd been pulled over upstate. Every town has its own local form of petty punitive policing. Up here, maybe that I was from the city and black was just too much for him to get over.

The officer told me to get out of the car and to turn around, placing my hands behind my back. The cold metal of his hand-cuffs closed around my wrists. With the click of the cuffs closing I was completely helpless as a human being. My liberty gone. That click, that loss of freedom, set off a chain of thought. What got me here? I started thinking of all the bad deeds I'd done, about Bridgeport and back in the Bronx. Nearly every sin I'd committed rushed into my mind. Did I deserve it? I'd done some bad things in my life; maybe this was my penance. The thought festered. So simple was the action of cuffing me, so matter-of-fact was the cop, it was just another collar, but for me it was a profound experience. I understood what it meant not just to have your body in chains but your mind as well. The cop treated me like I was a criminal, and without wanting to, I began to think of myself as one too.

As the cop cuffed me I went quiet on the outside. As I've done all my life, I cut the signals from my brain to my face and my hands and my voice. The cop searched first my pockets and then the car. Then he put me in the back of his squad car, called a tow truck for my Jeep, and booked me at the Hyde Park police station. Somewhere there's my mugshot out there, wearing a silently angry expression and a white chef's coat.

Luckily, this all went down very early on a Saturday morning, which means that I didn't have class in the morning and also that I'd just been paid. I spent only a few hours in jail, kept company by a toothless old man in the can for public drunkenness who cried in his sleep and woke up in a pool of piss. At daybreak I bailed myself out. I was free, but my car wasn't. I realized I had to call my dad, since the Jeep was in his name. I didn't want to, but it had to be done. It was a short conversation that ended with his snapping that he knew I'd find a way to fail at culinary school and hanging up. I guess he picked up the car because I never did, and we never really talked after that.

It was late fall and the foliage was brilliantly orange. By this point in the semester I'd become a master of consommé. All morning I kept an eye on the simmer, noting with pleasure the formation of a sturdy seeming egg-white raft on the surface. The way the egg whites form a natural filter, removing impurities from the stock, felt like a metaphor for where I was in my own life.

I thought about how so many of my earlier struggles had come to help me now. How being left on my own as a teenager gave me a leg up when it came to being a self-starter; how building a business, first with Nutcrackers and then with weed, translated quite easily into catering; how those sweaty claustro-phobic nights on the *Maine* equipped me to deal with pressure. I wouldn't change any of it.

But as I gently skimmed off my egg-white raft and strained the liquid through cheesecloth I was reminded of the necessity of removing those elements that didn't serve me in my life. I never wanted to struggle again because I saw the awful choices it forces. I never wanted to be seen as a failure again, not by my father, not by anyone. I never wanted to feel powerless again—pulled over, hands behind my back, for no good reason. I resolved that I would become someone not to be messed with, not through fear but through talent, someone who couldn't be seen through and dismissed. And when I poured out the con-sommé, slightly amber, steaming and fragrant, the liquid wasn't the only thing that had become clarified.

Chicken Consommé with Charred Vegetables, Verde, and Feta

YIELD: 4 servings

FOR THE CONSOMMÉ

8 egg whites

1 onion, chopped

1 tomato, chopped

1 celery stalk, chopped

1 carrot, chopped

1 pound ground chicken

8 cups roasted chicken stock

1 coffee filter

Kosher salt

FOR THE CHARRED VEGETABLES

1 onion, thinly sliced

10 garlic cloves, sliced

1 zucchini, cut and scored

5 florets broccoli

5 florets cauliflower

5 florets broccolini

2 tablespoons white balsamic vinegar

½ teaspoon red chili flakes

¼ cup feta cheese

Parsley for garnish

FOR THE VERDE

1 bunch cilantro (with stems)

1 bunch parsley (with stems)

2 tablespoons honey

1 cup olive oil

½ teaspoon salt

½ teaspoon chili flakes

1 tablespoon sherry vinegar

---

1. **To make the consommé** In a large bowl whisk together the egg whites, onion, tomato, celery, carrot, and ground chicken. Place the stock in a large saucepot and whisk in the ground meat mixture. Place the pot on medium-high heat, stirring constantly until the liquid comes to a boil, taking care not to let the ground

meat mixture stick to the bottom of the pot. Once the broth has reached a boil—do not stir—a raft should form. Puncture a hole in the raft so the broth can circulate and clarify through it. Reduce the heat and simmer gently for 30 minutes. Remove from the heat and gently extract the liquid from the pot using a ladle, making sure not to break the raft. Strain the broth through a coffee filter (to remove excess grease) and season with salt to taste. Reserve.

2. **To make the charred vegetables** Preheat the broiler. Meanwhile, in a cast-iron pan sweat the onion and garlic. Add the remaining ingredients except for the feta and parsley, and sauté for 5 minutes. Place cast-iron pan with contents under the broiler and allow to char on top but not to burn—about 5 minutes. Remove and reserve.

3. **To make the verde** Place all verde ingredients in a blender and puree until smooth.

4. In a wide-rimmed bowl, arrange the charred vegetables and top with crumbled feta, parsley, and verde. Pour the broth around the vegetables when ready to serve.

Blood on the Eggshells

I n the military, basic training is meant to weed out the weak from the strong, those who cave under pressure from those who rise to the challenge. A fresh-eyed, soft-bellied grunt heads to Camp Lejeune or Fort Benning and emerges as a hard-bodied, steel-willed soldier. The runts wash out.

For chefs, at least for those like me who enter the profession through culinary school, basic training—in the "break you down to build you up" kind of way—doesn't start until the second semester. For the first few months of our education, we were tested by demanding professors who did not tolerate an improperly turned turnip or a broken sauce. But this was not hell, or even heck. Our lessons took place at a leisurely pace, during daylight hours, on a scenic campus, and, importantly, without the pressure of paying customers. In fact, the only ones paying were us, coughing up $2,000 a month for the privilege of learning how to concassé, consommé, batonnet, braise, broil, and reduce. If something went sideways in the kitchen class-room, it wasn't great but at least you could contemplate your failure sitting on a bench overlooking the Hudson, without hellfire coming down on your head from an angry guest.

But eventually, every student is required to get an externship, a word that seems like it should be the opposite of an internship but is really just the same thing. The position has existed in the form of apprenticeships in craft guilds since the Middle Ages. The idea of an externship is not only that we enter into the hustle and flow of a working kitchen, but that the knowledge we've been handed in the classroom is burned into us by the pressures of nightly service. We are in the weeds for fifteen weeks of toil with live ammo and real danger. Most of us will return to the Hudson Valley campus for the third and fourth semesters. But some will wash out—the weak, the wilted, the runts.

The difference between an amateur and a professional chef isn't always a matter of skill or knowledge, and it's rarely one of taste. What makes a professional chef is that he or she has had technique imprinted onto them with the permanence of a tattoo and that they have withstood the pain of the process.

For much of the first semester, the talk in the dining hall, the dorm rooms, and the classrooms was about where we might land for our externships. The institute has relationships with hundreds of restaurants around the world. Chefs from some of the most famous establishments, from L'Arpège in Paris to Pujol in Mexico City and all points in between, let the school know they are accepting externs, and a steady stream of applicants—supplicants, really—arrive like the faithful on a culinary pilgrimage. For restaurants, the appeal of an extern is clear. He or she is a body in a kitchen, one with some degree of training and a reverence for the industry. An extern will work to exhaustion over the course of four months. At the time I did mine and for centuries before that, before schools like the CIA monetized the educational process, and still in many other places today, externs aren't paid. The belief was that experience was wage enough. Today externs make from minimum wage to $15 an hour but they are still ridden hell-for-leather for it. Even good chefs run externs like sprinters while they treat their employees like marathoners. The margins of a fine-dining restaurant are so narrow that chefs have come to rely on working externs until exhaustion, each one sinking after a brief moment of support.

Many of my classmates who were more interested in becoming banquet or institutional chefs found extern positions in respectable restaurants at big hotels and resorts, the kind of workhorse business that does a thousand covers a night with efficiency, competency, and at least a whiff of ambition. Others, the second-careerists and the easygoing, who viewed the CIA as something between a lark and a day camp, found work in smaller, less famous though often very good kitchens in the hinterlands. Neither route appealed to me. I swung for the fences.

Since I bought my first pair of Prada sneakers, I've always been someone who found the shiniest, flashiest, hardest-to-get thing and gone for it. When the best thing—doesn't matter what it is, shoe, restaurant, accolade—is out there staring you in the face, I've never understood how someone could settle for less. Surround yourself with the subpar, and you can't blame anyone for thinking you are too. Surround yourself with the best, and the best rubs off. My motto has always been to do better every single year. Don't settle for a step down. So I saw my externship as a chance to move a level up.

For anyone, or at least any student with ambitions as high as mine, there were only a few kitchens worth externing in. Then as now, there was a simple way to find out which ones they were. For the past sixteen years an obscure trade publication in the UK sponsored by San Pellegrino, an Italian water company has been issuing what it claims to be a definitive restaurant ranking, *The World's 50 Best Restaurants.*

The year I was externing, the top ten restaurants were, in

descending order: elBulli in Spain; the Fat Duck in the UK; noma in Copenhagen; Mugaritz and El Celler de Can Roca, both in Spain; Per Se in New York; Bras in France; Arzak, also in Spain; Pierre Gagnaire in France; and Alinea in Chicago. To me and my cohort, these were the only ten restaurants that mattered, and by the time the second semester came around, we were determined to be on the line at one of them.

Would I have liked to spend four months in Europe? Sure. But choosing an externship provided me with a lesson in balancing my ambition with the necessity to make money on the weekends. I was tethered to the city, to the real world, to the reality of having to hustle to survive. I still depended on Coterie Catering gigs to make enough money to pay tuition. Virtually all my clients were in New York so *I* needed to be near New York. There was, therefore, only one option for me: Per Se.

Since it opened in 2004 on the fourth floor of the Time Warner Center at the southwest corner of Central Park, Thomas Keller's Per Se has become synonymous with the most extravagant, most ambitious, and most luxurious meal in New York City. Keller, a tall handsome guy with a cowboy lope and an air of quiet intensity, opened the restaurant after building his reputation as the undisputed champion of American cuisine at the French Laundry in Northern California. Per Se is his East Coast outpost, and there is nothing like it in New York. For starters, it is one of the spendiest places in the city. Back then, a seven-course dinner cost $300. That's without wine, tax, or tip. A typical two-top doesn't get out of there for less than a grand. For that price, diners can expect an hours-long feast presented with all the accoutrements of fine dining, from elaborate flower arrangements to exquisitely trained servers to, of course, brilliant and refined food. Over the course of a few hours, Keller pairs technical perfection with culinary imagination. He uses some of the most expensive ingredients in the world, from caviar to gold leaf. Even if Keller is using a humble beet, you can be damn sure it is the best, most perfectly formed, delicately flavored, most recently picked beet you can find. Keller knows the name of the farmer and probably his mother's too.

Per Se isn't a Rolex restaurant. It's an Audemars Piguet, a luxury product at its most swaggering, inch-from-the-ground bravado. And the luxury isn't restricted to the jewels and platinum. It's in the way Keller and his team treat every ingredient as if it were precious, and by so doing *make* it precious. As I would discover, from the time a product enters the kitchen, it's treated with reverence.

Many diners are so besotted by the views of Central Park that stretch beyond the floor-to-ceiling windows and the unbelievably luxury of the meal—foie gras from whole flocks of geese; enormous quantities of shaved truffles, black and white; caviar up the wazoo—that they don't realize how ambitious and brilliant every dish is. But to a chef, Keller's appeal is squarely that what he puts on the plate is not to be found anywhere else. Not in terms of imagination. Not at his level of execution. He and his team have inscribed their names among those of the greats by devoting intense scrutiny to every element on every plate, not to mention the plates themselves.

Keller's reputation as a demanding, no-nonsense grinder was already well known to us in Hyde Park. The campus was deconsecrated, so Keller was the closest thing to a god we had, the savior of America's bounty. Aside from Grant Achatz, the spritely chef of Alinea—a CIA grad himself and a Keller protegé—Keller was the only one of the top ten chefs in the world with an American accent.

Landing an externship at one of the best restaurants in the world was, naturally, a fiercely competitive process. The kitchens receive thousands of applicants yet select only a handful. By complete happenstance, I had an in. A former pastry chef at Per Se had taken over as head baker at Hot Bread Kitchen. We were never that close but we knew each other enough to share cigarettes and had kept in touch over the years. Knowing that I had to work as many angles as I could if I hoped to land a spot at Per Se, I shot him a text asking if he could hook me up. He offered to introduce me to the chef de cuisine, a brash guy from Brooklyn named Eli Kamieh, himself a CIA graduate. This is, by the way, how most jobs in kitchens are filled. It is relatively easy to get a space on the line to stage (in other words, to try out) or at least to trail (observe) when a trusted cook vouches for you. The presumption of basic competence is often given since, if you flame out, you'll flame out quickly and publicly and be fired so fast your head will spin. I mailed off my résumé, and a few days later, word came down. Eli said I could come in for a stage, a day-long trail that served as an audition.

So one crisp morning in the fall, I took the train from Hyde Park down to Grand Central, then the A train to the Shops at Columbus Circle. Per Se is perhaps the world's best restaurant in a mall. I entered the shimmering glass shopping center full of things I could never afford and passed Colombian sculptor Fernando Botero's large bronze statue of a naked man whose penis has turned shiny from all the lucky rubs. I walked past the Williams Sonoma, with its displays of dry rubs, selvedge denim aprons, and expensive shiny pans, and ascended a series of elevators, gliding past mannequins of handsome headless men in merino wool suits and windows full of sweet-smelling moisturizers. Though employees entered through the back, I wanted to check out the front of this hallowed restaurant. Turning northward, I followed the signs to Per Se until I reached what looked like a beautiful blue wooden door with a large brass knob in the center. I strode up to it and pulled on the knob. It was stuck. *So much,* I thought, *for Keller's famous attention to detail.* I waited for a few moments, then somewhat sheepishly realized that the two glass windows on each side of the door were automatic sliding doors. I slunk away, happy no one had seen me, descended in the elevator, walked out, and reentered through the much more straightforward employees' entrance around the corner.

If the stutter-step of the blue door, the florist shop's worth of flower arrangements, and the hushed dining room are meant to inspire awe for the diner at Per Se, the massive scale of the kitchen did the same for me. I hadn't imagined anything could be more impressive than the one at Craft, but this was way beyond anything I had ever seen. And compared to the other kitchens—TJ's Ribs, the galley of the *Maine*—this was another species entirely: a quantum leap in evolution, the ideal form of a kitchen. There are actually three kitchens in the back of house: the prep kitchen, the main kitchen, and the private dining room (or PDR) kitchen. On the morning of my arrival, morning prep was in full gear in the five-thousand-square-foot main kitchen, which was a symphony of gleaming stainless-steel hardware and immaculate white plastic working surfaces. Despite the constant bustle there were no spills or messy stations, no errant tongs or even sprigs of herbs left carelessly on the workspace. There was no shouting, just a murmur of activity. At each pristine station, butcher paper held in place by blue tape, a cook stood with his or her head bowed over their *mise en place.* Sleeves smartly rolled up, towel neatly tucked in their apron strings, they were as silent and focused as I had ever seen chefs be. In front of them sunchokes were turned into pints of perfect brunoise. A bunch of radishes, fresh from the farmer, were lovingly trimmed and cleaned until they were reduced to one single, almost cartoonishly beautiful radish. On one wall, a large television screen displayed a live video feed of the kitchen at the French Laundry, across the country, equally pristine.

The day of my stage, Eli supervised me. I didn't know much about him at the time, and he didn't say more than two words to me. One of the sous chefs put me on prep. Since none of the chefs knew (or trusted) me, the work was menial. No foie gras or, for that matter, proteins of any kind. I didn't get anywhere close to a plate. Mostly Eli observed my kitchen demeanor from afar. Did I lean on the wall when I had nothing to do? When I finished one task did I hungrily seek out another? How did I move in the kitchen? Was I in control? Did I hold my knife right and say "Corner" when I turned a corner to avoid colliding with anyone coming the other way? Did I get the fuck out of the way when someone said, "Get the fuck out of the way!"? Could I hustle? Of course I could hustle. I was no stranger to busting my ass, and that turned out to be the most important qualification. At the end of the day, just before dinner service began, Eli nodded to me and said, "You're okay, man." And thus I was officially an extern at Per Se.

That April, with a few duffel bags of clothes, a winter coat, and my knife roll, I landed back in the Bronx, ready to start the next stage of my career. The next fifteen weeks would, I was sure, be some of the most intense of my life. I was eager to return to the city from Hyde Park, which while beautiful was maddeningly quiet. I moved in with Tatiana, crashing on the couch in her apartment in the River Park Towers, a sprawling housing project. In a weird way, it was comforting to be back among the bricks and courtyards and playgrounds, the hard surfaces of my youth. The apartment was an hour and a half away from Columbus Circle but rent was a few hundred bucks, so I wasn't complaining.

For most of my classmates, their externship was the single most important thing in their lives, and they devoted themselves wholly to it. I, however, had to eat, and to do so I had to make money, so I was still booking Coterie Catering gigs on the side. By this time I had a pretty solid crew of guys from the CIA who helped me out. During my externship I deputized Greg Vakiner to handle the events while I was in the kitchen at Per Se and recruited Paz; Andrew; and a kid named Nick Molinos to be my prep cooks. When we had events in the city, they'd come down to my sister's apartment and prep with me during the very early morning. My sister would wake up, with her toddler daughter Trinity, to find a crew of guys hunched over her little two-burner stove, brining chickens or passing purees through chinoises and tamises. Then I'd head to Per Se while they finished up behind me. For the actual event, I left everything to Greg. I had to. The only eye I could keep on things was to occasionally sneak into the bathroom to text him. But my man never dropped the ball once in the handful of gigs we had during my externship.

Besides catering and cooking, the last third of my time was spent waiting for my fifteen minutes of fame. Let me explain. Because I had grown up watching *Iron Chef,* and because a $10,000 cash prize was for obvious reasons appealing, that spring I had signed on as an understudy for *Chopped,* a reality show on the Food Network. Even before I went to culinary school, I had applied a score of times. With each rejection came another excuse from the casting director—"You're not the right fit" or "We're looking for a different demographic"—but eventually the producers took pity on me. As a consolation, that spring they offered me an understudy role. Just like on Broadway, it would be my job to step in if someone hurt themselves too severely to continue. Catastrophe wasn't an unheard of occurrence. There's a lot of dashing around on the show, and injuries were fairly common. Under time constraints and with the addition of adrenaline and a new kitchen, chefs do crazy stupid stuff they'd never do on their own. They run with knives. They grab burning-hot pan handles without a towel. They reach into still whirring food processors.

Being an alternate was a pretty cushy gig. All I had to do was show up at the Food Network studio in Chelsea Market in Manhattan at 6:00 a.m. a few times a week during production and sit in the green room waiting to be called. Barring any kitchen TKO on behalf of the contestants, I'd be out of there by 8:30. I had just enough time to hop on the A train and make it up to Per Se by 9, that is, if there were no delays or track fires or sick passengers. For this I got $100 two times a week. That was enough to cover rent at my sister's.

I had no idea what I'd do if someone *had* been injured. It would have been the end of my time at Per Se for sure. Flaking on a shift with notice is pretty bad; ghosting the day of that shift earns immediate termination. Still, I prayed that Marc Forgione, who was a contestant that season, would accidentally amputate his thumb and that Cat Cora, whisking egg whites to stiff peaks, would dislocate her shoulder. Thankfully (unfortunately) it was an injury-free season. So I never made it onto TV but I did keep my job at Per Se.

As an employee, of course, my approach to Per Se was much different. Employees enter through a nondescript door on the south side of Fifty-Ninth Street. There are no fancy retail opportunities, just a warren of linoleum-and-cinder-block offices and hallways with industrial-strength lighting. On my first day I made my way along the corridors behind the Shops at Columbus Circle, wending my way through the unglamorous guts of the luxury retail experience, until I passed through a plain white door into the Per Se locker room. Like everything else within Thomas Keller's orbit, it is kept spick-and-span. Somewhere between a gym changing room and a sacristy, the narrow space was lined with rows of gun-metal-gray lockers with a communal bench between them. Silence greeted my arrival. I found an empty locker, threw in my backpack, and unrolled my newly laundered chef's coat. As I was buttoning it up, a young guy, all bones and nerves and burns on his arms, walked in to grab a pack of smokes. He glanced over at me. "Is that the fucking face you're going to walk into Per Se with?" he asked. Apparently, jittery and scared was not the preferred facial expression here. I stared back at him, wondering which Kwame would respond. On the one hand, I thought, if this was some alpha-dog show of dominance, he'd picked the wrong dog to tangle with.

On the other hand, his tone was hard to read. Perhaps this was an incognito pep talk? Maybe this is what friendship looked like at Per Se? I didn't know. This wasn't the vibe on the line at Craft, from what I had seen. And a macho pissing contest certainly wasn't the norm at the CIA. On the other hand, this dude looked like he'd stepped out of Anthony Bourdain's *Kitchen Confidential* or sprung from the loins of shouty chef Gordon Ramsay. I knew Angry Hard-Ass Chef was a thing, and usually they had a heart of gold somewhere under their shell. But still, what a weird come-on. I just narrowed my eyes and contorted my face into an exaggerated grimace, pantomiming determined bad-assery. He seemed satisfied. "All right," he said, "let's go."

Having learned the basic workings of a kitchen, at least in theory, at the CIA, I knew what to expect at Per Se. As an extern—or an apprentice, as the restaurant chooses to call its interns—I occupied the lowliest position in the complicated and extremely regimented kitchen hierarchy. This hierarchy, called the *brigade de cuisine* system, had been around for more than a century, first developed in 1890 by the legendary French chef Georges Auguste Escoffier. Escoffier was looking for a way to ease the chaos, waste, and inefficiency of the traditional kitchen, which had stayed pretty much unchanged since the Middle Ages. That system—in which one cook was responsible for an entire dish from start to finish—may have worked in a castle, but it sure didn't work in a restaurant. Escoffier, who had served as a military chef, based his new system on that of the French army, and it is as structured as you'd expect from a soldier. The first innovation was a division of labor. Turning out hundreds of dishes a night, each with multiple components, in a timely fashion and upon request, would be impossible if each plate were thought of as a whole. Instead, Escoffier saw the professional kitchen as an assembly line, in much the same way Henry Ford did with the automobile a quarter century later. In the new brigade, the tasks of preparing a meal are divided up between workers, each specialized in their own discipline and concerned solely with the task before them. This increased not just efficiency but expertise. It's a high-stakes system, since if one cook fails, the entire system fails, but if every component in the kitchen works as it is meant to, a perfectly plated dish appears at the pass minutes after the order comes in.

The second feature of the brigade, and a direct requirement of the first, is an iron-clad chain of command. Like the military, a kitchen is set up to function as one brain with many hands. The chef is the brain and the cooks are the body. Messages must be relayed precisely, with no room for individual ideation and certainly none for insubordination. Any and all measures will be taken to maintain this system.

The general of the kitchen is, naturally, the chef. Although Thomas Keller was the boss, the guy who had absolute control of the day-to-day was the chef de cuisine, Eli. Eli had graduated from the CIA in 2000 and had joined Per Se shortly after it opened, moving quickly up the ranks. Like his mentor Keller, he was famously demanding. But unlike Keller himself, who is famously soft-spoken, Kamieh had a volcanic rage.

Reporting to Eli were three sous chefs, each of whom led a team of their own: a morning, an afternoon, and a prep team. That two of those teams—the prep and morning team—were devoted solely to preservice preparation gives an idea of the sheer amount of labor needed to present the seven to nine courses, most no more than a few bites, offered to the hundred guests who dined at Per Se on an average night. Apart from those three battalions, there were two other teams, pastry and baking, headed by a chef patissier and a chef boulanger, respectively, who also reported to Eli. But they functioned largely independently from the rest of us and moved like powder-covered phantoms in our midst.

Beneath the sous chefs were the chefs de partie. While a sous chef holds overall command responsibility, he or she is not tied to a specific task. Chefs de partie, on the other hand, are assigned clearly defined areas of responsibility known in kitchen parlance as stations. At Per Se, stations include roast, which is responsible for all the sauces and meats, and is one of the most esteemed positions in the kitchen; poissonier, responsible for fish; canapé, the station devoted to the VIP appetizers;

fromagier, whose job is all things cheese; entremetier, who takes care of vegetables; and garde manger, who oversees the cold appetizers. Reporting to each of the *chefs de partie* were three or four prep cooks who serve as the infantry of the kitchen.

And the ground on which everyone walked were the apprentices. There were four of us working at a time when I was at Per Se. Through the four months, we would rotate between the morning, afternoon, and prep teams, getting a taste of each as we went through the entirety of the Per Se kitchen structure. The majority of our work took place far from the hours of service and away from the main kitchen. We were assigned the monotonous but essential labors of *mise en place*. For every gesture a line cook makes during service, there are hours of preparatory work performed by lowly staff in the commis—or prep—kitchen.

I started my time at Per Se on the morning prep team. Though impeccably kempt, that kitchen is much smaller and more cramped than the main one. There were four large stockpot burners, a walk-in freezer, a reach-in freezer, a reach-in fridge, and a couple of lowboys. It always seemed crowded in that windowless room, even if you were alone. And I never was. The standard cast in the commis kitchen consisted of a sous chef, who was my boss; two commis; and an apprentice. It fell to the apprentice to dice thousands of pounds of vegetables for stock—the Culinary Fundamentals courses finally paid off— and then strain and restrain those stocks until they ran silky smooth. It took hundreds of gallons of veal, chicken, and lamb stocks to create the richly flavored reductions that appeared as precisely placed dots and swooshes on the plate. A stock is like a toddler. It doesn't take tremendous skill to raise one, just constant attention and patience. Cooking at the scale Per Se needed—about ninety covers a night—it also took a strong back and biceps to tip the massive pots into the strainers dozens of times throughout the shift.

Veg prep, another of our main responsibilities, took more fine-motor skills and, though the cuts were basic, immense mental focus. We brunoised absolutely everything. Before our blades, rounds of parmesan and pounds of olives were turned into mounds of identically sized cubes. It could be mind-numbing work, but the temptation to let your mind wander was quickly corrected by a clean slice through the finger. Unlike on *Chopped*, there were no alternates at Per Se, and I quickly got to know where the first aid kit was.

It was up to us in the prep kitchen to prepare ingredients for the hands of the more experienced senior chefs in the main kitchen. So we cracked and peeled walnuts to reveal their brain-like kernels. We separated each petal of pearl onions, lay-ing them on parchment paper like gold leaf. Using tweezers, we picked endless sprigs of microgreens, separating from the already precious stems their perfect miniature leaves.

The work itself was by nature boring, but I was new to a kitchen operating at this level and still in awe of it. I couldn't believe I was there, so it was hard not to simply marvel every once in a while. But one of my first encounters with Eli quickly made me realize that wide-eyed wonder was not on the menu, at least in the back of house at Per Se. It was a day or so in, and I was meant to be picking rainbow lucky sorrel. I remem-ber thinking, "Ha, that's funny. I'm lucky too!" I paused for a moment—maybe it was longer—unbending my spine from my station to look around at the other chefs. Through a small window in the wall, I could see the main kitchen with its heat-lit pass, the sign over the door for which Keller is famous that reads "Sense of Urgency," and the video screen with its feed to the French Laundry. Suddenly Eli was right next to me, and he wasn't happy. His black eyes narrowed and sparkled with anger.

"What the fuck are you doing?" he hissed at me. "Your herbs are dying. You're looking around? Do you want to be here or not? I need you to fucking move! MOVE!" He screamed that last word, and the veins bulged over the collar of his chef's coat. Later I would wonder if they soundproof the walls at Per Se so that diners can enjoy their opulent evenings without hearing the screaming in the kitchen. But at the moment all I said was, "Yes, Chef."

I was humiliated, ashamed that I had so quickly foundered and been called out. Well, part of me was humiliated, the soft tissue, the part that was wilting over my rainbow sorrel with flecks of Eli's spittle lodged in my ear. But in my bones, even then I could see that this was madness. I knew it was unreasonable that such a minor offense would cause such an abrupt and angry reaction. In what other workplace would that be accepted? Perhaps Eli wasn't nuts, but he was part of a system that was. Now I was playing a role too. He yelled, and I was yelled at. Simple, really.

Perhaps then and there I should have walked out. But there was some part of me, some angry rebellious part of me, that wanted to tough it out. I wanted to beat this asshole at his own game. And at the same time this dynamic—him yelling, me being yelled at—was very familiar to me. As a kid, there was no escaping my dad and his rage, and nothing I could do to soothe it. But in the kitchen it was a different story. If I worked hard and kept my head down, if I hustled, did my prep work, listened, hustled harder, and made no mistakes, well, then there was the possibility of earning the respect of these guys. That was better than the odds I had growing up. At least it was a possibility.

After a month of morning prep, I rotated to afternoon prep. It was in the same kitchen but different tasks with a different taskmaster. The good news was that I didn't need to be there until 11:00 a.m. The bad news was that since I was up at the crack of dawn anyway, freezing my tits off in the unheated green room of the Food Network studios, it didn't really matter. The even worse news was that it was up to the afternoon apprentice to tackle the dreaded eggshells.

One of Per Se's signature dishes is a white-truffle-oil-infused custard served with a ragout of black winter truffles. It's presented about midway through the chef's tasting menu, arriving on a silver platter, a small amount of silken custard in a hollowed-out hen's egg. The custard is made from egg, Keller's thinking goes, so why not serve it in an eggshell? At Per Se, the egg is held in a silver coil, with its top neatly cut off. A translucent tuile—a play on a potato chip—juts up from the opening like a jaunty geometric feather. The wonder of the egg is meant to hit the diner on multiple levels. First of all, it's just nice to look at it. Second, the egg-in-an-egg plating is conceptually clever. Third, of course, is the taste. The softness of the custard as it dissolves on the tongue releases the fragrant truffle oil, while the black truffle in the ragout hints at earthiness. It's no wonder that Keller never takes it off the menu: it's his masterpiece. But someone has to hollow out and clean the eggs, and for a month that job fell to me.

A tower of cardboard flats awaited me every morning. These were my eggs. Unless you've ever needed to clean the inside of an egg—and there's no reason in the world you would, because it's an insane thing to do—you might not know that it isn't only eggshell, white, and yolk. Between the shell and the liquid inside, there are two thin membranes made of keratin, the same substance from which our hair and our nails are formed. In order to prepare the eggs, both membranes need to be removed. It's a tricky operation. The first step is to score a circle with a tourné knife (the smallest in a knife roll) a third of the way down the eggshell. Then score it again, to cut the top off cleanly, leaving the shell looking like a trepanned head. Then you carefully empty out the yolk and the white, separating them into bowls to be used later. To loosen the membrane, you use a mixture of vinegar and hot water that must be poured carefully into the now empty egg. It takes one minute and nine seconds. Any less and the membrane will stick. Any longer and the shell becomes fatally fragile. After pouring out the water, you have to use your finger to scrape the membrane from the shell until it peels off like a snake's skin. This is where my troubles began.

First of all, even in the best-case scenario, you lose about 30 percent of your eggs. Sometimes they crack funny, chipping at the point of incision. Some eggs are just not pretty enough to make the cut. Often, digging in to remove the membrane, you'd catch the edge of the shell and the thing would chip. And, since this was Per Se, one chip was one chip too many. Into the trash it went. The vinegar, meanwhile, is great at softening the bonds that bind the membrane to the inside of the shell but also at softening skin. The repetitive action of scraping the membrane off with the softening effects of the vinegar meant that halfway through the stack, my fingertips were pinkish and cracking. Three-quarters done, droplets of blood had begun to form. This I noticed with some alarm and, admittedly, some pride. Looking down at my perfectly clean eggshells, I saw each one speckled with blood.

Because I was on egg duty for a month, my fingerprints

vanished. I looked like a serial killer trying to escape the law. Basic training was working. Who I was before I walked into the kitchen at Per Se was gone. Even the knowledge I thought I knew, I didn't. There was the way everyone else does a task and the way it was done at Per Se. For instance, one day a tattooed Tennessean sous chef asked if I knew how to torch peppers. I said I did, of course, since torching peppers is a pretty basic skill. But when I said, "Yes, Chef" he asked if I had ever done it at Per Se. "No, Chef." His reply? "Then you don't know how to do it. Got it?"

He took me aside and showed me how to use a butane torch and a 3M scrubby to turn charred peppers perfectly soft and smoky while not losing any of the flesh. He was right. I didn't know how to torch peppers the Per Se way.

I also realized that the rhetoric of a restaurant is vastly different than what actually happens in the kitchen. When I first arrived, I took at face value the stated philosophy of only accepting the best. The anger I had witnessed, I thought, wasn't justified but could be understood in part as a sort of intensely discriminating standard of excellence. Passion for the best, perhaps, overflows into uncontrollable passion. But one morning while I was in the prep kitchen, I became painfully cognizant of how what happens in a kitchen differs from what is said about what happens in a kitchen. We had just received a shipment of mandarin oranges. We used them to make demi-sec rounds that we served as an accoutrement to a fish main. It was my job not only to take off the membranes but to peel the segments, scrape off all of the pith, and dehydrate them. Even though they'd eventually be dried, it was important to use only the ripest, most flavorful mandarins since the dehydration doesn't take away flavor, it intensifies it.

The batch I was working with that day was clearly off. The

oranges were already desiccated, their flavor paler than what I was used to. Part of my responsibility wasn't just to prepare the oranges—or whatever ingredient I was using—but to taste them too. I knew that if a diner sent back a dish, or if it made it to the pass and Eli kicked it back, it was my ass that was on the line. So when I saw these oranges and tasted them, I knew I had to say something. When the sous chef supervising the commis kitchen at the time passed by, I told him I didn't think we should use the oranges. I told him they were much drier than what we usually used.

He grabbed a mandarin and looked at it. "We can still appreciate its beauty," he said, which was a very Per Se way to say STFU.

"I just don't think it tastes good, Chef," I replied.

"What the fuck did you say?" the sous growled, his cheeks flushing with anger. "Nobody asks your fucking opinion."

"Are you going to question my taste buds?" he went on bellowing. "Nobody wants you to be here!"

By this point I had recovered enough to realize I'd just driven into crazytown.

"Why the fuck would you tell me that? I'm not your fucking friend. We don't have fucking conversations," he continued.

There were other moments too, when I felt like I was being called the N-word with no one actually saying it. No one had to and maybe they were too smart to. So it was left to me to decide whether it was because I was black or because I was just me that I was the only one greeted with a growling "Get the fuck back in the prep kitchen!" when I ran food out to chefs on the line. From that point on, I took those words to heart. I didn't have conversations. I came in and did my job, getting better and better each service, but I didn't look for friends or colleagues. I had my mask on and shield up. It was that old familiar feeling of being confused, scared, unsafe. And as I did as a boy, I did now as a man, cutting off the wires of my emotions. When the other chefs yelled at me I was no longer there. But I felt foolish to have imagined that I could ever escape the power dynamic I had first experienced at TJ's. If it was alive and well at Per Se, would I ever find a kitchen in America not poisoned by racism?

When service began in earnest, around five o'clock, the afternoon apprentices either continued prep in the commis kitchen or, if you had proven yourself, you were allowed to assist the garde manger in the main kitchen. There are seven to nine official courses at Per Se, but Chef Keller padded these out with *amuse-bouches,* small bites sent out to, as the French indicates, make the mouth happy. These are like the culinary equivalent of those first few throat-clearing bars from Jay-Z or 'Ye: half warm-up, half taste of what's to come. And totally fun. They take only one bite to eat but hours of work to make.

Ever since he opened the French Laundry, Keller has been making these salmon cornets. They're often the first bite of food a guest has, and so set the tone for the rest of the evening. The cornets are small sesame tuiles wrapped, while still warm and pliant, into tiny cones. These cones are then filled with similarly dainty scoops of salmon tartare with tiny bits of chive, to resemble ice cream cones with sprinkles. Thomas Keller, Dad Joke king of the kitchen. Having proved myself, my job during service was to man the cornet station, which was tucked right by the door to the kitchen, next to the garde manger.

For an apprentice to be on the line during service at Per Se was an honor. And to have even a small role in the flow of dinner service was a big deal. Though the hierarchy of the kitchen can be cruel, there's still a sense of togetherness on the line during service. As soon as a waiter puts in an order and a ticket is generated, we became one body. We'd brace for whoever was expediting that night—usually Eli—to call out a number, and as soon as he did the assembly line would spring into action. Me with my cornets, while at other stations other chefs began the beautiful and intricate dance of world-class cooking.

From my station on the line, I grew to understand what Keller meant by "sense of urgency" and understood why the overbearing chefs bore down so hard on all of us. If the intricate rhythms of the kitchen are interrupted by even one beat, the whole thing topples dangerously into cacophony. The sloppy *mise* of a morning commis, uneven knife cuts for instance, translates into vegetables of varying doneness at dinner. Even a moment of laziness in a line cook during service exposes the entire kitchen to disaster. Food dies under the heat lamps. Foams collapse. Meat grows cold. Yet none of this justifies the abuse.

By the time four months were up and I was approaching the end of my apprenticeship, I was ready to leave. My skin was bulletproof by this point but I hated that it had to be that way. At the end of service one evening, we were all sitting around the pass discussing the menu—well, I was standing, because as an apprentice I wasn't allowed to sit. Every single night we had to create a menu for the next day. It didn't matter what time it was or how long it took. We'd gotten to the main course and everyone was dog-tired. It was 2:00 a.m. and we had started work at 11 that morning.

Eli looked at our exhausted eyes and asked, "What are we going to do for tomorrow? No one knows? What is the fucking main course?"

I took a chance: "Why don't we do Wagyu, Chef?"

Everyone looked around to see who had spoken up. I stood

there with a blank face, no emotion, but at the same time not backing down. I had my Per Se game face on, a face I now donned automatically every day when leaving the locker room to approach the kitchen. And as the rest of the kitchen turned toward me, I noticed maybe for the first time that they were all hiding behind similar masks.

"What did you say?" Eli demanded, his voice cutting into me.

Keeping my tone as steady as I could, I responded, "Why don't we do Wagyu, roasted. With hakurei turnips, hen of the woods, and a Marsala veal jus. Maybe we can put a quail egg on it and make it like a riff on 'steak & eggs.'"

The *chefs de partie* looked at each other, shook their heads, and rolled their eyes. Everyone, including me, braced themselves for an epic verbal assault. *Which approach will he take this time?* I wondered. Maybe it would be Eli's usual riff when he got mad: "You fucking scum, you don't even get to sit down and you think you can put a dish on this menu!" Perhaps he would go with, "Do you know how hard and long I've worked to be in my position? To put my blood, sweat, and tears onto this menu? Do you really think you can spew some off-the-cuff 'dish' and think you can make it onto the menu of the best restaurant in North America?"

To my surprise, Eli stared down at his notes, scribbled something, and looked back up at me. "Sounds fucking good. We will run it tomorrow." My dish, on the menu at Per Se. I should have been overjoyed. I suppose that somewhere inside of me, I was. But by this time nothing could get through the game face. I was too afraid to smile, too exhausted to rejoice, and too beat to celebrate. I left Per Se a few days later, returning to Hyde Park and to the soft landing of the classroom. There was no teary goodbye, nor was I expecting one. The kitchen at Per Se was a clean place but hard and heartless too. The hierarchy was a necessary one but the weight of it was crushing to those on the bottom. The brigade system ensures that food gets to the plate looking pretty; it also gives free range to rage-inclined pricks to indulge their worst impulses. The anger was like black mold in the air ducts, infecting everything. As I've opened my own kitchens, at times I've certainly been guilty of regurgitating the habits I learned at Per Se. But when I grow enraged, I also try to remember how it made me feel to be yelled at on the line. From Per Se, I try to extract the sense of urgency without the poison of anger.

Steak and Eggs

YIELD: 4 servings

FOR THE PICKLED
QUAIL EGGS

½ cup white balsamic
vinegar

¼ cup sugar

⅛ cup salt

4 quail eggs

FOR THE SOUBISE

2 tablespoons canola oil

1 medium white onion,
thinly sliced

1 cup heavy cream

½ cup whole milk

Kosher salt

FOR THE STEAK

2 rib eye steaks, each
1½ inches thick

1 tablespoon canola oil

Kosher salt

1 tablespoon butter

Sprig of thyme

3 garlic cloves, smashed

---

1. **To make the quail eggs** place 1 cup water, the balsamic, sugar, and salt in a small saucepan and bring to a boil. Remove from heat and cool. Meanwhile, separate yolks from whites and reserve egg yolks. Once the pickling liquid is cool, place yolks in it for 4 hours.

2. **To make the soubise** In a large skillet, heat the canola oil over medium-high heat. Add the onion and cook until soft and translucent, 6 to 8 minutes. Stir in the cream and milk, and bring to a light simmer. Cook, stirring occasionally, until slightly thickened, 15 minutes. Transfer to a blender and purée until smooth. Season with kosher salt to taste and reserve.

3. **To make the steaks** Bring the steaks to room temperature. Meanwhile, heat a cast-iron skillet over high heat. Rub the steaks

with oil and season aggresively with salt. Place in the skillet for 5 minutes on each side. Toward the end of the second 5 minutes, add butter, thyme, and garlic and baste for the remainder of the cooking time. The internal temperature of the steak should read 132° F for medium rare. Allow steaks to rest to continue to cook and evenly distribute their juices before serving.

4. **To serve** Slice the steaks against the grain and plate. Spoon the sauce soubise in a circle and position a pickled egg yolk in the center to mimic an egg.

From Old Guard to Start-Up

You might think I'd run screaming from the high-pressure, no-fun, fine-dining kitchen at Per Se. And I did; and then I went screaming right back into it as soon as I could. After my externship ended, I had to return to the Culinary Institute, but suddenly those leisurely hours at Hyde Park in the kitchen classroom seemed like a fantasy to me, and not in a good way. The lessons felt like war games, and I yearned to get back into the trenches of a real restaurant kitchen. It wasn't that I relished getting yelled at or appreciated the specks of spittle as they landed on my face; I just missed the adrenaline rush that came with every service. If things went well and you were in your flow, the payoff was simply a nod from your chef, if you were lucky, and a sense of belonging with the other cooks. If you got stuck in the weeds or slowed down the line or messed up in some other way, you could expect cursing and yelling and being told you were a worthless speck who had no right to be in a kitchen in the first place. Don't mess up, survive. Mess up, and hellfire would rain down upon you. It was an extreme world but a simple one, easy to understand.

Even though I loved the increasingly technically complicated skills we were learning in the second year of the CIA program, the classroom just didn't have, to borrow a Thomas Keller phrase, a sense of urgency. I made do, cramming in as many Coterie Catering gigs as I could, which helped both with boredom and with money. Though the service wasn't live and to order, it was still a challenge. Yet all I wanted was to get back on the line of a real kitchen.

An opportunity presented itself that fall, as I neared graduation. For a long time I had been a fan of Eleven Madison Park, Daniel Humm and Will Guidara's ambitious restaurant in the Flatiron district. It was unapologetically luxurious, staggeringly expensive, and yet the vibe seemed a bit more playful than at Per Se. From what I knew of Humm, whom I had interviewed for a school project at the CIA, he was both a very intense guy and a very charismatic one.

That fall Greg and I took the Metro-North from Hyde Park to trail for a day at EMP, as the restaurant is sometimes known. By this time I was much more confident as a chef than I had been when I first showed up at Per Se. I had none of the jitters that shook me a year earlier.

The kitchen, gleaming and spotless, was impressive but not shocking. The silence with which the commis worked, the delicacy of their movements, and the economic intensity of their actions were all familiar. The rhythms of the fine-dining kitchen were becoming natural to me. Greg, meanwhile, had started to gravitate to the dining room. Under Will Guidara's watchful eye, EMP was nearly as lauded for its impeccable service as it was for its impressive cuisine. The plan was that Greg would get a job in the dining room and I would work in the kitchen. It was the first time either of us had worked together outside of Coterie, and we were giddy with the prospect. Daniel Humm wasn't in the kitchen the day I arrived. Instead I was greeted by James Kent, the chef de cuisine. I knew of him from a few visits he'd made to the CIA; a handsome guy who smiled out the side of his mouth. He had an informal manner and started every sentence with "Yo!" He was matter-of-fact, tough but not unfriendly. He had a warmth that I had never experienced at Per Se.

My job that day was just to work prep, brunoise a rainbow of peppers, clean sunchokes, peel down carrots, that kind of thing. I did it all with a fire under my ass, as I had learned at Per Se, and this got me the notice of the chef de cuisine, a tall clean-cut guy from Colorado named Brian Lockwood. He came over to where I was prepping and asked, "Where'd you work before?"

"Per Se," I replied.

"I could tell," he said, pleased. "I used to work at the Laundry."

Keller's famous "sense of urgency" was like a secret handshake among chefs who had been through his kitchens. Maybe, I thought, all that yelling was worth it.

I knew Brian liked me, and Chef Kent seemed like a really great guy, but if I wanted to stay in the kitchen, I'd have to prove I could cook. I knew it was coming but was still surprised when I heard Chef Kent call me from the pass.

"Come here, Kwame," he said.

"Yes, Chef," I replied, with vigor.

He nodded to a sheet pan holding four bright red, heart-shaped lamb loins. They were beautiful, pretrimmed and marbled with fat.

"There's your protein," he said. "You can use anything you want in the walk-in, except microgreens, which are expensive. Dry goods storage is fair game too. No finished sauces. Meet me in an hour with a plated dish."

There was no mistaking this. It was a test. But I felt so

at home, so instantly at ease at EMP, I wasn't nervous at all. Everyone I encountered in the kitchen was friendly. There was none of the "game face" posturing of Per Se. If I needed to know where the chervil was I could just ask and not expect a torrent of abuse as an answer. I set the meat down at a station that had been cleared for me and walked briskly into the walk-in. I grabbed a pint of cherries and a handful of fingerling potatoes. From dry goods I grabbed some cinnamon and lavender, a bottle of red wine and another of port. Then I got to work. My idea was a simple seared lamb loin with cherry jus and potato écrasé, the French term for smashed potatoes. I didn't want to do too much, no ras el hanout, no sous-vide, nothing fancy. I just wanted to, and needed to, show Chef Kent that I had a mastery of the fundamentals, that if he gave me a place on the line, I wouldn't upset the whole system. An hour gave me just enough time to reduce the wine and port, add the cherries, sweat some onions, soften some garlic, and add a bit of chicken stock, then blend and sieve for the jus. The meat wouldn't take long at all, six minutes to cook to medium rare and another six to properly rest. For the first time in my life I was completely at ease in the professional kitchen. Everyone I spoke to, or who spoke to me, was kind. There was no nervousness at all. Just excitement and attention. Fifteen minutes before the hour was up, I started plating. After letting the loin rest for a few minutes to absorb its own liquid, I placed the meat on the plate. Then I mounted the jus by adding a few cubes of butter to turn the sauce shiny, and swished a tablespoon of it in a semicircle alongside the protein. It was an elegant, if not overly complicated, attempt.

When Chef Kent approached me, he took a look at my plate and then at me. Like Brian, he was also impressed.

"Yo," he said, "you can definitely tell you were at Per Se."

He poked at the meat with his finger to gauge how well done it was, dragged a finger through the jus to taste it, and then nodded.

"When can you start?"

During my last semester of CIA I took the train to Manhattan every weekend to work as a commis. Like every new arrival in the EMP kitchen, I started in the back kitchen but was told by Chef Kent that he was putting me on the fast track. I could expect to move from commis to garde manger to working either the fish or meat station in a couple of months. During school I worked only Sundays and Mondays, getting up at the butt-crack of dawn on Sunday morning and catching the last train back after service on Monday. During the week I balanced coursework with developing recipes that I wanted to show Chef Kent. I let the Coterie gigs fall away. I wasn't partying. I wasn't drinking and I wasn't smoking. I was a man on a mission.

Greg and I graduated from CIA and moved to an apartment in Astoria, Queens. As we had planned, Greg had started as a kitchen waiter, parlaying orders from the dining room waiter back to the line. But he was so good at it, so unflappable and dependable, that in a matter of weeks he jumped a few positions and was promoted to expediter. It was a high-stress job, coordinating eighteen courses for forty tables, each with a slew of components, meanwhile juggling allergies and aversions and preferences and EMP's constant PPX—kitchen slang for VIP—treatment. For me, to look up at the pass and see a mentor in Kent and a friend in Greg made every shift that much easier.

Greg and I were all in on EMP. It was the closest to being in a cult I'd ever experienced. I was twenty-four, and being paid to cook at a restaurant with the maximum three Michelin stars.

That all changed one day in October when Chef Humm called an all-staff meeting in the dining room. Though we had shift and preservice meetings, this was a rare assembly of both kitchen and dining room staff. We met altogether only for serious or exciting news. As we stood around the dining room—a room that as a commis I rarely saw—I knew it was serious.

"Good afternoon," he began in his faint Swiss accent.

"Good afternoon, Chef," we replied in unison.

"As you know, we're always pushing the envelope here at EMP. The guy who's been integral to this is James Kent," he said, nodding to Chef Kent, who stood looking abashed beside the glass vases filled with crab-apple blossoms.

"And as you know, we've continued pushing the envelope since we opened the NoMad," the new restaurant Humm and his partner Will Guidara had opened a few months earlier. "I'm happy to announce that James will be heading the kitchen there, starting immediately. In his place, Chris Flint will be chef de cuisine at EMP."

The rest of the staff clapped and cheered. I did neither. I felt I was losing a father figure, losing a healthy sane presence in the kitchen. I loved working with Chef Kent and Chef Lockwood. Flint, meanwhile, I had seen a few times in the kitchen, a bald-headed wiry guy with lots of tattoos who didn't talk as much as he barked. I was scared of what kind of boss he would be and what that would mean for me day to day. I didn't have to wait long to find out.

Nearly immediately after he started at the pass, the vibe in the kitchen drastically changed. Under Chef Kent, the kitchen was focused and quiet, intense but not unfriendly. Most services, you could hear a pin drop. Imagine the shock we all felt when Flint began to scream at the pass.

"What the fuck is *this!*" he shouted one night when a plate of black bass landed with imperfectly placed zucchini shingles atop them. (Not, let the record show, from my station.) With one arm Flint swept the pass, sending plates clattering onto the floor. The kitchen—or at least those in the vicinity—seized up for a second in shock, frozen in fear. This was so profoundly *not* what EMP was. But after a mere moment, we all sprung back into action. The porter came to sweep up the mess. The expeditor, who happened to be Greg, had to laboriously remove the white linen that had wrapped the pass and retape a fresh sheet. And we cooks returned to our work, this time tense with fear.

Just like that, with a sweep of an arm, we readjusted ourselves to living with a tyrant. Flint was vicious and volatile, like Sergeant Gunnery from *Full Metal Jacket*. No one, that I knew of, thought to tell Chef Humm or Guidara about Flint, how he'd punch the wall next to your head, how he'd find some cook, seemingly at random, to berate and then spend the rest of the shift on him like a pitbull. We all figured they knew about his tantrums, overheard his rants, and that since he had been promoted to CDC anyway, they were okay with it.

To my credit, or to my horror, I easily accommodated myself to his stormy presence. By this time I had moved to the garde manger section, working on what was called the smoke station. Tucked into a far corner in the massive kitchen, I was pretty far from Flint. My tasks were menial. My sole responsibility was preparing the smoked sturgeon that would be served in a smoke-filled glass dome on a metal serving tray, accompanied by a tin of caviar, a jar of dill pickled cucumbers, and slices of rye toast on a metal toast rack. It was monotonous to say the least. I get it—that's what 98 percent of being a cook is about.

But as I watched other cooks rotate through the stations, my anger grew and grew. Kent's promise of a fast track faded into the past.

The whole time I was at EMP under Chef Kent, I'd hardly been conscious of the fact that I was one of the few black cooks in the kitchen. But as soon as Flint arrived, the four or five of us reflexively drew together. That's how fear works. It galvanizes and tribalizes you. Just as quickly as we had accustomed ourselves to his temper after the first outburst, we realized that we would likely be targets too. And it wasn't lost on any of us that we didn't change stations much at all. For my entire time at EMP, I worked on that smoke station, alongside a Nigerian cook, Michael Elegbide, who had been on smoke even longer than I had.

I was lucky that I had Greg, who as expediter stood at the pass and could insulate me from Flint's wrath. Flint and Greg worked well together, and Flint thought Greg was a like-minded asshole. So he was constantly sneaking little asides to Greg, who, not knowing what to do, grimly nodded and continued working. Greg didn't tell me this until later, but I didn't need to hear it from Flint's own mouth. I could feel it. The most insidious kind of racism isn't always being called the N-word. At least that's shameless enough to get you fired. It's the unspoken shit, the hard-to-prove, hard-to-pin-down, can't-go-viral day-to-day shit. It's being passed over, time and time again. It's having opportunities you know you earned never materialize. It's that no matter how hard you work, it's never good enough. It's not even seen. In the few instances when it was overt, Flint tried to frame his racism as a joke. One incident in particular sticks out. The dining room staff did a lot of tableside preparation at EMP, sometimes using a cylindrical grater called a *mouli*. As probably everyone in the kitchen knew, "mouli" is the name of the French company that has been making the device since the 1940s. But what no one else was aware of is that the word *moulie*—pronounced the same way—is also a racial slur used primarily by Italians to insult black people. It's a derivative of the word *melanzane,* or eggplant. I knew this because I'd had friends against whom the word was wielded. Assuming that no one knew how wrong the word might be taken, I approached Flint to tell him. I figured, why risk alienating our guests with such an ugly word?

"I don't know if you know, Chef," I told him, broaching the topic as delicately as I could during a quiet moment in prep. "But that grater we use, the *moulie,* that's like the equivalent of the N-word. Maybe we can call it something else in front of guests?"

"What the fuck are you talking about?" Flint snorted.

"I just think it's a little sensitive . . ." I said, realizing this wasn't going well.

"C'mon man," said Flint, "you're just being politically correct."

I started to analogize that we wouldn't refer to a bunch of kindling as a faggot since that word has become so hateful but Flint clapped me on the shoulder and said:

"No black people eat here anyway."

He laughed, and I could tell he expected me to laugh too. This clearly racist aside was either a plank to walk or a bridge to connect us. If I acted as offended as I felt, the label of "difficult" or "politically correct" or really just "problem" would be even more deeply imprinted on me. If I laughed, not only would I be betraying myself, but I'd be giving Flint a pass.

I kept my face still as the night and nodded. It was not a gesture of acceptance. It was not a gesture of resistance. It let Flint know that I recognized his move for what it was: a racist jab masked as a gesture of friendship.

After work, Greg and I would go back to Astoria and talk

about the day. I was working sixty-, seventy-, eighty-hour weeks for $10 an hour and being treated like a piece of garbage, food thrown back at me, perfectly prepared *mis en place* sent back, phantom flaws found. Greg, on the other hand, had moved up the food chain and was now earning considerably more and working considerably less than I was.

Around this time, through a friend I had met at the Hot Bread Kitchen back in the day, I was introduced to Brian Bordainick, a tall guy from New Orleans who reminded me of Kyle Chandler. For the past year Bordainick had been running Dinner Lab, a series of pop-up restaurants in unlikely places across the country. At the end of each dinner, the guests—who had paid a membership fee of from $100 to $175, plus $60 to $80 per meal to attend— would rate each chef and give feedback via comment cards.

When I first met Bordainick, he was impressed with me and with my story. "This is going to be gold," he said. "Everybody loves a rags-to-riches story!" I didn't tell him that I had never been in rags and I certainly wasn't in riches now. I was just happy to hear that someone thought I had a story worth telling.

One of Brian's employees called me up. "Kwame," he said, "I really want you to do a Senegalese dinner." At the time a humanitarian crisis was affecting the region, and he had this idea that the dinner could also serve as a fundraiser.

"That's a good idea," I said, "except that I'm Nigerian, not Senagalese."

"Oh, I know, I know," he responded. "But, you know, it's African."

I was being offered a chance to step out of the shadows and into the spotlight. I was so sick and demoralized by the changes at EMP, I was ready to leave the best kitchen in the world. So what if I had to make a Senagelese fish stew rather than jollof rice from Nigeria? Both came from the Wolof people. But as I thought about it, the idea just didn't sit right with me. It wasn't that I minded making food from Africa—or that I couldn't. But what Dinner Lab promised was a chance to be me, to really showcase who I was as a chef.

I called up Brian directly and said, "You know, I'm grateful for the opportunity, but I just can't do Senegalese food. It's inauthentic."

"Okay," he said. "You want to do Nigerian then?"

"Not really," I told him. "I'm not a master of Nigerian food either."

"Then what do you want to do?"

"I want to cook my own food. I'm Nigerian. I'm American. I grew up on Creole and Jamaican food. I've been working in fine dining now for a long time. I want to cook whatever that is."

Brian, to his credit, took it in stride. Since it was only one dinner—and I'd be judged by the customers at the end of it— the commitment was low on his end. Plus, what I said was undeniably a better idea.

"Okay," he responded, "sounds good. Just make sure you have enough for a hundred and thirty guests."

It was on.

I started to plan the meal in my head right away. There was only one problem: There was no way I could do both Dinner Lab and work eighty hours a week at EMP. It was one or the other. Even though I wasn't moving up the ladder, if I stayed at EMP I had a coveted spot in one of the world's best restaurants. Maybe Flint would be replaced or run off sooner than later and the pathway to promotion promised by Chef Kent would materialize. Maybe if I just kept my head down on the smoke station, eventually someone would notice. On the other hand, if something was going to change, I figured it would have happened already. I was putting up good food and I had been, for months and months. And yet it was always met with indifference at best or hostility at worst. Just as importantly, though I admired Humm's menu it wasn't my food at all. There was no self-expression—at least for me—in any of it, just rote execution. I wanted to cook my own food. I didn't yet have a clear idea of *what* exactly my food would be, but it was too good an opportunity to pass up. I resolved to put in my notice at EMP as soon as I could.

Predictably, the conversation with Flint was not pleasant. It was, however, a little unexpected.

During a quiet moment during prep, I asked if I could speak to him in private. He led me to the dry-storage area in the kitchen.

"What's so important, Kwame?" he demanded irritably.

"Chef," I started, "I'm thinking of leaving. I'm just not happy here."

A flicker of rage crossed his face.

"That's bullshit," he said. "What's really going on? No one leaves EMP just because they're unhappy. It's a fucking professional kitchen, not day care."

Fine, I thought, I'm out anyway. I'll just tell him.

"Look, Chef, I got a crazy opportunity to cook my own food with something called Dinner Lab. It's a great opportunity, and I really want to do it. It would make me really happy."

Something about the word "happy" seemed to enrage the guy. He grew red in the face and looked like he wanted to murder me.

"You're not quitting," he seethed. "That's fucking stupid. Dinner Lab is stupid. You're not a chef. You'll never be a chef. You wanna be great but you can't be. Not yet. You gotta stay here. You need to get yelled at. You need your ass kicked."

"I hear you, Chef, but I don't agree. I want to go off and do my own thing."

"Think of your ancestors!" he exploded. "Think of Carême and Escoffier. Fuck, think of Chang and Keller," he said, reeling off the list of the famous chefs who had shaped the fine-dining world.

There was a great irony in Flint echoing what my grandfather had said about my ancestors when I was living with him in Nigeria: "Your ancestors will never leave you. They are part of who you are." Here was Flint, a guy who I knew thought black chefs had no place atop the kitchen hierarchy, telling me to think of my ancestors, as if my ancestors were his ancestors too. But no, my ancestors aren't Carême or Escoffier or Keller or even Daniel Humm or David Chang. My ancestors are the ones I thanked after Grandad killed Red, back in the dusty courtyard of Ibusa. My ancestors are those who, like Auntie Mi, ground cassava flour for hours, soaked stockfish, and hit kola trees until the nuts fell down. My ancestors are steeped in the curries and jerk of Jamaica and found in the stews and rouxs, gumbos and jambalayas of Louisiana. It wasn't something I'd ever expect Flint to understand, but it was something I couldn't deny any longer.

"I'm sorry, Chef," I said, "but I can't stay."

With my first pop-up dinner only a few weeks away, I buried myself in prep. My idea was simple. I would trace my life's journey through food. The format would be a seven-course tasting menu. It was by far the most ambitious culinary undertaking I had faced. Nothing, none of my catering gigs, nor my cooking jobs, nor my time in culinary school, nor even my experiences at Per Se or EMP, could fully prepare me. I was attempting to execute at a much higher level than I ever had, and at the same time create something much more personal than I'd attempted before. The menu I settled on was truly auto-biographical. I'd start with a gumbo, with Gulf shrimp, crispy okra, and pickled garlic, finished with a little andouille crumble and homemade seafood broth. Then we'd move through to the *egusi* stew of my childhood, travel down to Jamaica with a curried prawn with jasmine rice risotto, and then back up to the Bronx for a take on steak and eggs, using double-cooked beef cheek and quail eggs. Then I'd reimagine the deli breakfast BEC sandwich I ate every day on the way to EMP, this time with toasted brioche mousse, pork jowl, Saint-Marcellin, and a smoked egg yolk before finishing with those goddamn cheesecakes that launched my catering business. It would be, quite literally, my life story told through food.

I spent three solid days prepping. I called my old Coterie crew, now spread out in restaurants throughout the city, and from the kitchens of Le Bernardin and Lamb's Club they reassembled to help me out. On the day of the event I was stressed out and nervous yet at the same time completely focused on the task at hand. The dinner was held at the Green Building, an event space by the Gowanus Canal in Brooklyn. A key part of the dinner involved the chef coming out to talk to the diners. Frequently, the organizers told me, the chefs were too standoffish or busy to make an appearance. I told them that wouldn't be a problem.

Hello," I began. "My name is Kwame Onwuachi. I'm cooking for you tonight."

Some people turned to look, but many of the 130 guests were too busy talking or drinking to notice.

"Hey!" I said, sharper now. "Guys, stand up and come up here!"

To my surprise, people began to drift toward me. I got up on a chair.

"I'm cooking for you tonight," I said, "but before the food starts coming out, let me tell you where the food comes from."

I launched into my life story, which meant not only my story but the stories of my mom and my father and my grandfather too. I invoked the memories of peeling shrimp with my mother in our Bronx apartment and of eating *egusi* stew in Ibusa. I left out the sordid, sad parts, carefully cutting around them like rotten bits of fruit, until what was left was pure addictive sweetness. I could tell the guests were rapt. I held them in my palm for a second, then let them go back to their tables as I disappeared into the kitchen. I had set the stage; now I had to slay.

What can I say? I nailed it. I could never have created this menu if I hadn't bounced around for the past twenty-six years. I could never have handled the flow of the kitchen that night if I hadn't trained myself to keep going no matter what. We had our share of accidents, jus spilled and garnishes missing, but nothing could faze me. I was relentless and drove my team relentlessly too. This went beyond just putting out good food. This was *my* food, an extension of who I am, and so I cared, probably more than I ever had before.

When the time came for the guests to score the meal, I received 4.8 out of 5. Nearly perfect. Brian was impressed. Immediately after the meal he approached me with an idea he had for a ten-city, ten-chef tour. Ten chefs would compete in various cities across America for audiences who would judge them. The chefs with the highest average scores at the end would receive $100,000 in prize money to start their own restaurants. Still exultant from the dinner, I agreed without hesitation, barely considering what spending the next ten weeks on the road might look like.

Even now, I can hardly say. The competition was a whirlwind

of cooking and prepping and travel, of telling my story night after night to a new crowd. Over the next few weeks I learned what resonated and what didn't, how real I should be. I streamlined my narrative, giving my dinners titles like "From Candy Bars to Michelin Stars," until by the end I could neatly present myself, my story, and my food in one tidy and fluid package. And the crowds ate it up. I truly felt like a rock star.

I was clearly the one to beat, and yet no one could. At venue after venue I walked away the winner. But as the competition was coming to an end, Brian called me to deliver some bad news. Dinner Lab had run into financial troubles, burning through $10.5 million without turning a profit. The promised seed funding just wasn't there, even if I did win.

As disappointing as that was, I wasn't sweating it. Everyplace we stopped—Austin, Nashville, New Orleans, New York—investors would show up, cash in hand, eager to join up with the hot young culinary talent. In my mind I already had a restaurant empire, prize money or not. I was untouchable.

At the end, I was declared the winner of the entire competition and I had three offers to open a restaurant, including a particularly intriguing one from a pair of new restaurateurs in Washington, D.C.

Corn Velouté

YIELD: 4–6 servings

---

4 large onions, thinly sliced	2½ cups heavy cream
3 tablespoons canola oil	2½ cups milk
10 large garlic cloves, thinly sliced	10 fresh sage leaves
	10 thyme sprigs
5 large ears corn, kernels removed, cobs reserved	Kosher salt

---

1. In a large saucepan, sweat the onions in oil until translucent. Add the garlic and continue to sweat until the raw flavor is cooked out, about 10 minutes.

2. Add the corn kernels and cobs, cream, milk, and a bouquet garni of the sage and thyme. Simmer on medium-low heat for 30 minutes.

3. Remove the bouquet garni and the corn cobs. Puree in a blender until smooth, then strain.

4. Season with salt to taste. Serve.

Angles

I t was 5:00 a.m. on a hot morning in June, and I was brushing my teeth for the second time. Standing in the marble-and-gold bathroom of a luxurious San Francisco hotel I could never have afforded, I looked at my face in the mirror: watery, sleep-deprived eyes, toothpaste foam bubbling at the edges of my mouth, wrinkled pajamas. Wearily, I began to brush again. Past my own face I eyed the small film crew. The cameraman and the boom operator—a jacked-up dude covered in tattoos—and a no-nonsense lady who had a way with microphones, and a young PA named Sarah, had wedged themselves into this bathroom on the fifth floor of the Fairmont Hotel in San Francisco, where I was staying for the thirteenth season of *Top Chef*. Of the original field of fourteen, I was one of the six contestants remaining.

"That's great, Kwame. You're doing great," Sarah said. "Beautiful!" I brushed for a few more seconds until I heard her say, "Got it, baby, thanks." The camera light switched off and I spat. Welcome to morning reality.

It should come as no surprise that the experience of being a participant on *Top Chef* is a surreal one. In our suite of rooms my fellow contestants and I repeated these mundane tasks over and over again for the benefit of the viewers at home. We gamely pulled back our covers, stumbled and restumbled from our beds, ran and reran brushes through our hair. Capturing all of this were pairs of cameramen and boom operators, overseen by producers who moved before us like shoals of fish, always close by but never making contact. In the evening we repeated this quasi-performance for what was called "night reality." In between, we were wrung through long hours of outlandish high-pressure culinary challenges. Yes, the knives were real and very sharp. Yes, the food had to be delicious. Yes, the pressure was extremely intense. But what chef in the real world has a surf-and-turf challenge sprung on them with no notice? Or must, in fifteen minutes, turn junk food into food porn to please an influencer?

For the last two months, as we traveled throughout California, we had all lived in this twilight world, between reality and performance, populated by an ever dwindling number of contestants—some friendlies, some neutrals, and some enemies. We were accompanied by a large crew, and sometimes we were visited by the judges, who materialized like holy visions to make pronouncements and decide our fates.

Though the audience would never see people like Sarah or the musclebound cameraman—and perhaps *because* the audience would never see them—interacting with the crew was the closest any of us came to being normal while filming. You could have an actual conversation with them, because you could be certain it wouldn't end up on TV. Except, of course, when you forgot that your producer-friend was working you. Then, months later, when the show airs and you see yourself talking trash about a fellow contestant in a confessional, you realize they were just doing their job when they called you "baby."

As long as the cameras were rolling, you couldn't be sure of anyone, neither judges nor fellow contestants. Every interaction was a calculation, on my part and on theirs. Reality television distorts but does not fundamentally alter character. I was still Kwame, the Kwame I was when I woke up that morning, before the cameras came in. But superimposed over this was Kwame the character, the made-for-TV version of myself. He was less likable, perhaps, but acted more comfortable than I felt. He took my own confidence and exaggerated it to the point of arrogance. He was what I assumed the producers wanted. A perfectly three-dimensional person does not make for good television.

Internally, of course, where the cameras couldn't see, I was just as terrified as I'm sure the other contestants were. I was scared to make a mistake, scared to come off as a fool or an amateur, scared to be myself. To cope, as we all did, I had a strategy, one I'd honed for years: pack all that fear, all that self-doubt, all that weakness, tight into a box, close it, padlock it, and then put my head down and work. Don the mask of indifference and get on with it.

As for the other contestants, whether it was Jeremy Ford, who ultimately won the show, or Amar Santana, or anyone else, there was a similar dynamic at work. The characters we played for the cameras were heightened or flattened or distorted versions of our true selves. There was a real and a real plus. Jeremy *was* a laid-back dude, just not quite as laid back as he appeared. Amar *was* exuberant, though perhaps a bit more vivacious before the cameras. Isaac Toups really was a good ol' country boy from Louisiana, but he wasn't nearly as folksy after we wrapped. Each of us had a role to play, and as the show went on, by unspoken agreement with each other and the production team, we became our characters more and more.

And yet, I realized, this wasn't anything new, not to me and not to any other minority. In some ways I had prepared my whole life for reality television. Ever since I was born, I had been made aware that the world saw me in one way, thanks to the color of my skin, regardless of how I saw myself. This was a lesson learned on the streets of the Bronx and in the dining rooms of Baton Rouge and in the kitchens of Per Se and EMP. I would not survive if I didn't know how to play that game, to hustle to get ahead, to write my own story, and to manipulate, to the extent that I could, how I was seen.

But as I was coming to realize, that was only half of the battle. The other, and perhaps the more important part, was how I saw myself. When I closed my eyes, when the cameras were off, when there was no one but myself, who was I then, what Kwame did I want to be? The thing about filming *Top Chef* is that the production company basically quarantines you. Televisions are unplugged, cell phones confiscated, and computers removed. You're in a terrarium, unaware of the world outside.

For relief, I used to sneak out the service elevator of the hotel and wander around the streets. In Los Angeles, where we spent time at the beginning of the season, I walked up and down Hollywood Boulevard. What a bizarre feeling it was, as if I lived in another dimension than the people in their cars or streaming out of the gym or spilling out of bars. Who was real and who wasn't, I couldn't tell. Without cameras around, it felt like everything was a waste of time. Without cameras around, I struggled to know how to just be Kwame. It was unsettling. On those almost-delirious nocturnal wanderings—the only time I was alone for months—it occurred to me that perhaps it was precisely because I didn't know who I was when no one was watching that I sought the spotlight so hard, spending those early mornings in the green room at *Chopped,* fantasizing about becoming a star. When I got back to the hotel, I felt relief not only at not being caught, but also at returning to being seen, stepping back into a character I knew by heart.

When I first got a call from a casting director asking whether I wanted to apply to be on *Top Chef*, I was conflicted. A few years earlier Liz Bacelar, who had been so supportive at Coterie, had set me up with a producer of hers. We were at Liz's weekend house upstate. I made a meal as elegant as the setting: Brussels sprouts petal salad, port-glazed quail with corn velouté, golden cauliflower polenta. The producer, a middle-aged white woman, loved the meal, putting her spoon to the side as she sucked down the velouté. As we sat around surrounded by empty plates, I expectantly awaited her judgment: Was I ready for TV?

"The dinner was amazing, absolutely amazing," she began. "It's clear you know how to cook." I waited as she paused for an uncomfortably long time, searching, it seemed, for what to say next. "The problem is, Kwame, and I hate to say it, but America isn't ready for a black chef who makes this kind of food."

"What kind?" I asked.

"Fine dining: velouté. What the world wants to see is a black chef making black food, you know. Fried chicken and cornbread and collards."

And there it was, finally spoken aloud. I wasn't mad at this woman; she seemed apologetic enough. But as the evening stumbled on, now painfully awkward, I pondered my choice. Fame and maybe fortune dangled before me, but the cost would be my conforming to ignorant stereotypes of what a black chef "should" be. Or I could stay on my own path, applying all the technique I had gleaned to make the best food I knew how. Success, or at least exposure, was less certain. Just before she left, the producer handed me her card and told me to get in touch if I ever changed my mind. I thanked her, never changed my mind, and never called. If the price for being on TV was to become a caricature, I'd rather remain uncast. But because my first restaurant, the Shaw Bijou, was set to open that October in Washington, D.C., I needed all the help I could get. Win or lose, as long as I didn't bomb out in the first episode, *Top Chef* would hugely boost my exposure. As one of my partners put it, "Any press is good press," and so I agreed to appear on *Top Chef.*

A lot of chefs will tell you they grew up loving cooking shows. Julia Child. Jacques Pépin. Ina Garten. I grew up loving cooking shows too, but those gentle chefs weren't for me. No, for as long as I can remember it has been the hard-core competitions, the shows that treated cooking as a blood sport (and along the way somehow made sous-viding pork loin seem heroic) that I loved. *Iron Chef* was my jam. By the time I was eight, the original Japanese version had just begun airing in America. I followed the epic battles of crustaceans and butternut squash like it was March Madness, year round. When my mom was out for her catering gigs at night, as she often was, I stayed home with Tatiana, sitting too close to the television tuned to Food Network. Everything about the show was amazing.

The whole thing was so over-the-top, it was like catnip for a food-obsessed young boy. I followed the chefs as they moved with single-minded purpose under the bright lights of their kitchen stadium, heedless of the cameras shoved in their faces. They were so fearless, unhesitatingly wrenching octopuses from their tanks and twisting lobsters' bodies in two. Then it was a fury of chopping and blending, sautéing and flambéing. These Japanese men (and they were all men) in their shiny clothing and tall hats were my Power Rangers, my personal superheroes.

Sometimes I got so inspired, I headed into the kitchen, pulling down from their high shelves my mothers' pots, bowls, and sheet pans, grabbing from the pantry whatever ingredients I could find and from the refrigerator whatever I could reach. I imitated the techniques I saw on television, albeit with the skill of an eight-year-old. Not infrequently my mother came home late at night to a complete mess of a kitchen with me curled up asleep on the floor. To her credit, she never once yelled at me. She just scooped me up, dusted the flour from my clothes, and put me to bed.

In some circles there's still a stigma attached to reality television, a belief that there are real chefs and TV chefs. The former climb up the ranks, unseen and unheard, in other people's kitchens. They pay their dues slowly and come to fame after years of toil, if at all. The latter, on the other hand, find fame first and figure out the particulars afterward. There are risks to both approaches, but by 2013 reality TV was clearly one of the best ways to build a brand.

With the Shaw Bijou, I was planning to open the most ambitious restaurant D.C. had ever seen. Nonetheless, the highest position I had ever held in a restaurant was only as a line cook at EMP. I didn't have a fancy knife roll, packed with hard carbon steel, to unfurl on set. By this time, I had precisely two knives: a chef's knife and a tourné knife. The rest of my money back then went to rent. Now, if you know one thing about *Top Chef* you know the line delivered by Padma Lakshmi to the unlucky bastard being kicked off: "Pack your knives and go." I had heard it a hundred times as a viewer but hoped I would never hear it as a contestant. If I did, however, I at least needed knives to pack. As a parting gift before I went off to California to start filming that June, Kelly, one of my partners at the Shaw Bijou, handed me a thick roll of bills. "That's for you to get camera ready," he said with a grin. It was like some scene out of *Pretty Woman.* I took the cash and went on a shopping spree at Korin, a high-end Japanese knife shop in Tribeca. A good knife can run more than a grand, so after I bought my set I had only a few hundred dollars left over. Such was the pitiable state of my savings that I used the last of the money to finally replace my glasses, which I had worn crooked for years.

I got eliminated on the thirteenth episode. The elimination challenge was to create a fast casual restaurant concept. The six of us were paired with six of the already eliminated contestants to act as our sous chefs. Marjorie Meek-Bradley, who won the Quickfire challenge, had earned the right to dictate the pairs. Since she saw me as a danger, she paired me with Philip Frankland Lee, who was as close to a villain as the season had. Philip and I didn't get along. In fact, no one got along with him. You can see it on the show; it wasn't clever editing. He was just a guy who refused to take responsibility for anything. But to be fair, it wasn't his fault I went home. It was mine.

My restaurant concept was a bite-sized chicken-and-waffles stand called Waffle Me. The idea was that you could customize your waffle from whole wheat to coriander to sweet potato, customize the level of spiciness on the chicken from mild to fiery, and you could add your own condiments. I'd had thirteen episodes to find my gimmick; now it was time to cash in. We were all in the same boat: Jeremy, a dude, did Taco Dudes. Isaac played up his Creole roots and did a gumbo shop called Gumbo for Y'all; I, the only black contestant, did chicken-and-waffles.

It crossed my mind, of course, that I might be playing into age-old stereotypes of black folks' food. But fast-casual concepts have to be easy to grasp and delicious. There is nothing more comforting when done right than chicken and waffles. I was confident I'd walk away with the win.

Alas, I stumbled, fatally. Frozen waffles were my downfall. I get it now. I had two things to make, the chicken and the waffles. The chicken I nailed, but as all the judges said, the waffles were a problem. I had planned to do my own and had asked the producers to procure a waffle iron for the challenge. This was according to the rules, but they hadn't gotten it until halfway through. By that time I had already made do with the frozen Eggo waffles I had bought as a contingency on our shopping run the day before. I knew it would be an issue, but I was hoping that griddling them with butter and ancho chili powder and adding a maple jus would be enough customization to compensate. I mean, maple jus, for Christ's sake.

I knew I was in trouble at the judges' table when Padma said, "I want to know how you made your waffles." I waffled, naturally. I said I had griddled them in butter, but then, realizing that there was no way out, admitted I hadn't made them; they were frozen. Tom Colicchio fixed me with his blue eyes, and I could feel his dismayed incredulity bearing down on me. Padma gave me one of her sad, disappointed looks. Adam Fleischman, the guest judge and founder of Umami Burger, did a double-take.

After the challenge segment ended, we all headed into the stew room, where contestants waited—fueled by ample booze—to learn our fates. I had a feeling I was going home, and I had plenty of time to rehearse what I wanted to say when Padma asked me to pack my knives. There were two things I wanted to be sure of. First, it was important to me to act with dignity in the last moments. Getting kicked off *Top Chef* is like a public execution. These were my last moments, the last image viewers might ever see of me, so I wanted to comport myself with grace. Second, I wanted to say something to Tom. I had never let on that I had worked at Craft, that I knew him from back in the day. That would be my final reveal.

In the end it was between Jeremy and his undercooked pork belly and me, with my premade waffles. I felt exactly as uncomfortable as I appeared on TV, shifting from foot to foot with no idea what to do with my face or where to look.

When at last Padma spoke the words I had dreaded for so long, I turned to Jeremy for a hug. I had seen enough eliminations to know the rituals expected of us. I approached the judges' tables, said my piece to Tom, and headed out the door. And that was it. The bubble burst immediately and not without relief. After a brief exit interview, the mother of one of the PAs drove me to the elimination house.

Because there's such a long gap between filming and airing, eliminated contestants are kept quarantined together in a house until the season finale is filmed. There was not much we could do but stew in a mixture of boredom and depression. During those blurry days and nights between elimination and the final, a week or so later, I thought a lot about what had happened. The show wouldn't air for months, and I wondered how I would be presented. I wondered how it would change my life. Would I be a hero or a villain? A celebrity or a failure? In the meantime, I had a restaurant to open. Once filming ended, I returned to D.C., to try to figure out who I was as a chef without a camera in my face.

Hot Chicken and Waffles

(What I Wish I'd Made on *Top Chef*)

YIELD: 4 servings

FOR THE FRIED HOT CHICKEN

4 boneless, skinless chicken thighs

2 cups buttermilk

Vegetable oil for frying

2 cups Niter Kibbeh Oil (NKO)

4 tablespoons berbere

4 tablespoons paprika

2 cups cornstarch

Kosher salt

FOR THE CRISPY WAFFLES

1½ cups pastry flour

2½ tablespoons malted milk powder

½ tablespoons dry yeast

2 teaspoons sugar

1 teaspoon Kosher salt

½ teaspoon baking soda

1¼ cups milk, warmed

5½ tablespoons butter, melted

1 egg

1 egg white

FOR THE CHILI HONEY

1 cup honey

1 tablespoon red chili flakes

½ teaspoon Kosher salt

---

1. Marinate the chicken in buttermilk overnight.

2. **For the waffles** Combine all dry ingredients and sift. Mix the warm milk, butter, and whole egg. Combine the wet ingredients with the dry ingredients and allow the yeast to bloom for at least 10 minutes but no longer than 2 hours. Whip the egg white to stiff peaks and fold gently into the batter. Cook the batter in a preheated waffle iron until golden brown. Finished waffles can be held in a 300° F oven for up to 20 minutes.

3. **For the chili honey** Combine honey, red chili flakes, and salt in a small saucepan. Warm on low heat for 15 minutes. Puree and reserve.

4. **For the fried chicken** In a large pot, heat oil to 350° F. Combine the NKO, berbere, and paprika, and set aside. Remove the chicken thighs from the buttermilk, being careful to shake off excess liquid. Dredge the chicken thighs in the cornstarch and fry until the chicken reaches an internal temperature of 165° F. Immediately salt the chicken to taste and dip thighs in the NKO mixture.

5. Serve chicken thighs on top of waffles and top with chili honey.

The Jewel

———

Before *Top Chef,* when I had returned from the Dinner Lab tour, I was full of ideas, bursting with hope and beaming with pride. Greg and I were still living in Astoria, and we used to hang out on the roof of our apartment drinking beers and planning our glorious future. He'd been with me, as a friend and a business partner, since our days at the Culinary Institute. I had relied on him for support at EMP, and he never once let me down. He was nearly the only person I could say that about. Now that I was on the cusp of a new opportunity, I knew that whatever I did, I'd be doing it with Greg.

Dinner Lab had taught me a few things. It gave me confidence in my talent in the kitchen and my ability to connect with guests in the dining room. Some chefs, no knock, are skilled on the line and even leaders in the kitchen. But it's like *Field of Dreams:* When they emerge from the back of house, their personalities all but disappear. They become unbearably shy or surly in public. That wasn't a problem I had at all. After years of adapting to new and difficult situations, I was at ease transitioning from one presentation of myself, as, for example, the no-nonsense chef, to another, a charming storyteller.

The second, more important, lesson I had learned from my

experience with Dinner Lab was that my life story *could* actually be translated into food and that audiences, guests, diners, wanted to consume both. I had found a way to convert, through food, not just the warmth and love of my upbringing but also the struggles I'd faced. Whatever my next step was, I knew I needed to capitalize on this.

Even before the tour wound down, I had received an offer to start a bar with an accompanying menu with a well-established Nashville restaurant group. The idea was that eventually I could expand into a more ambitious food program. It was a good offer, generous financially, and Greg and I both really liked the guys running the project. But just before we signed on and moved south, a Dinner Lab guest got in touch with me.

"Kwame," she wrote, "I was at your dinner in D.C. I loved it. My friend is trying to open a restaurant here. Would you want to talk to him?"

I emailed back that I was already opening a place in Nashville, but I'd be happy to consult.

"Just hear the guy out," she responded.

Not one to say no to an opportunity, I agreed. That's how I met Glenn Paik and Kelly Gorsuch.

The first time we first spoke by phone, Kelly and Glenn told me they wanted to open a fine-dining restaurant serving southern comfort food. Ugh, I thought, of course. The idea of doing upscale riffs on mac and cheese, fried chicken, and collards was not only a played-out concept, it was a step backward for me. More than one step. The belief that African American cuisine couldn't rise above the Mason-Dixon line was exactly the sort of stereotype I wanted to destroy. Though southern cooking had played a huge part in my own upbringing, it wasn't the entire story. To emphasize only that aspect would mean becoming an actor in the long and ugly play of degrading black culture for the benefit of white people. I politely thanked them for thinking of me but said I wasn't interested. I was about to hang up when Kelly said, "Wait, wait, wait. What do *you* want to do?"

In all my conversations with potential partners, this was actually the first time anyone had asked me point-blank what *I* wanted. Now was my chance. I laid out what Greg and I had discussed so often on our rooftop in Queens, an extension of what I had been doing at Dinner Lab. The idea was clear—my autobiography told through food—but by now I had come up with a name. I would call the restaurant Bijou. The word is French for "jewel," and it would be both a homage to my mom and a nod to the painstaking execution and flawless technique I'd bring to the table. "It's a fine-dining, modern American, globally influenced restaurant that tells my life story through food," I explained, allowing the words to roll off my tongue like the smooth pitch it was.

Glenn and Kelly, who were already a little familiar with my narrative, were enthused. I walked them through a few of the courses I had developed during Dinner Lab—steak and eggs made with beef cheek and quail eggs, reimagined fisherman's pie, a lamb sweetbread seasoned like the chicken and rice I had eaten at halal carts growing up—ending with Butterfinger *mignardise,* small hand-made versions of the candy bars I had sold years ago on the subway. When I finished there was a pause on the other end, then both Glenn and Kelly said at once, "We love it!" I couldn't believe how receptive they were to the idea. Two strangers were willing to invest in my life, my story, my vision.

Excited about taking the next step, soon Greg and I were on the train down to D.C. to meet the guys. We met up in a coffee shop in Shaw, the neighborhood in Northwest D.C. where Kelly lived and worked. Glenn was a low-key middle-aged Korean American businessman. What I learned later is that his is a classic immigrant story. His parents had emigrated from Korea and he grew up in Baltimore and made his money in private equity. Now he ran information technoogy for government agencies. Glenn was clearly the business side of things. He exuded a sort of good-natured competence that was comforting, especially after the collapse of Dinner Lab's funding. Here, I thought, was a man who knew his way around pivot tables and PnLs. Glenn was a family guy who lived out in Alexandria. He was quiet and unobtrusive, no flash. Unlike many of the big-watch, hair-gelled bankers I had met on tour, he didn't seem interested in milking the hospitality life for personal glory. That was a good sign.

Sitting next to him was Kelly, an almost comic contrast. Kelly is a big guy with a red beard who owns a slew of businesses in D.C. He's a scion of a local hair salon family and runs a bunch of them in and around the city. Kelly imagines himself a dynamo and has a personality as big as his beard. In some ways he's like me, ambitious and restless, always looking for the next move. As soon as we sat down he told me he saw his salons as a jumping-off point for an entire lifestyle and hospitality brand. He already makes scented candles, furniture, and lighting fixtures. Fine dining, he said, was the next domain to conquer.

Greg and I were pretty straightforward as we reiterated our vision of Bijou to the guys. Greg would be in charge of all things in the dining room. I had to have creative control and absolute discretion on both the concept and the menu in the kitchen. We still had the Nashville option waiting for us, so neither of us was in the mood to compromise. It turned out that we didn't have to play hardball at all. Both Kelly and Glenn seemed totally on board with our conditions. And it got better.

As we were finishing up our coffee, I mentioned money. My idea for Bijou was not cheap. Considering staffing, food cost, and presentation, it would require major investment and it was not without risk.

"What budget do you have in mind?" I asked Kelly, trying to sound casual about it.

"Money's no object," he replied, immediately. "Sky's the limit, bro."

"Yeah," I said, "but you want to *make* money, right?"

Kelly replied, "As long as the quality is up to my standards, I don't care if it ever turns a profit."

Greg stepped in to say, "We're going to need some time to develop the idea."

"That's okay," said Kelly. "Take all the time you want."

In fact, he even offered to put us both on salary as we developed the concept, $70,000 a year. That was way more than I had been making at EMP. I tried to contain the crazy excitement I felt inside.

At Kelly's suggestion the four of us went for a walk before Greg and I hopped on the train back to New York. As Kelly explained while we walked past blocks of quaint rowhouses, the Shaw neighborhood was founded as a free slave encampment in the 1800s. It had been home to D.C.'s black cultural elite for decades. It was a hotbed of jazz and art in the 1920s and 1930s, a sort of Harlem of the South. That burned bright straight through until the 1960s, when D.C. was hit by riots, and by the crack epidemic in the 1990s. Since then, for nearly the past thirty years, the Shaw has been on a slow road to recovery, a road that has sped it toward gentrification. In the past five or six years, Shaw, like so much of D.C., has been rushing toward the new, with fancy condominiums springing up every week. Coffee shops have displaced community centers. Yoga studios have supplanted storefront churches. But the old Shaw still showed through in spots, and certainly in the modest yet beautiful rowhouses that lined the streets.

We walked past rowhouses under construction, and a sign proclaimed that they'd soon be the home of the Carter Woodson Center, devoted to Shaw's own Father of African American History. Kelly hadn't let on where we were going, but he stopped in front of a two-story townhouse on the corner of Q and 9th NW, with dark blue walls covered in ivy.

"We're here," he announced.

"What?" I asked. "Where?"

"This is Bijou."

What? Was he kidding? He already had the place picked out? Sure enough, Kelly produced a set of keys from his pocket and pushed the door open. He had bought the building a few years ago and was living in it until he could figure out what sort of business to use it for. Even as I gazed at Kelly's belongings, I could feel that this sun-flooded room would be Bijou. It felt so right to open up my restaurant in this neighborhood. I would be a continuation of Shaw's proud black culture. In retrospect, I have to admit that Kelly could have pushed open any door pretty much anywhere in the world and I would have seen Bijou. The check he offered was blank, and my dream was so close, I could have imagined Bijou anywhere I looked.

As Greg and I returned to New York, we were stunned at our luck. We had come in hard, but still I don't think either one of us thought these two guys, one a salon entrepreneur and the other a financier, would go all in so fast. Perhaps that should have set off warning bells—it *definitely* should have set off warning bells—but I wasn't in the habit of saying no to wish-fulfilling genies or passing up an opportunity because it looked too damn good.

Greg and I signed papers with Glenn and Kelly shortly thereafter. We would all be partners. Though Glenn and Kelly would be investing the money—exactly how much I didn't know—Greg and I would be in charge, as per the agreement, of everything that took place within the four walls of the restaurant. The four of us sat around a table at Izakaya Seki, one of D.C.'s best Japanese restaurants, drank sake, and toasted our forthcoming success. "Here's to opening the best restaurant in D.C.," I said, hoisting a glass high.

Greg and I wrapped things up in New York. He gave notice at Eleven Madison Park and we gave up our apartment that spring, moving into a place around the corner from the restaurant and exploring our new home's neighborhoods on bright red bikes, laughing and pointing like two dudes in a bromantic comedy.

For the first few months it was like Christmas every single day. True to their word, Kelly and Glenn were incredibly supportive and never stinted on money. As soon as Greg and I got situated, the four of us began an endless dining tour of the best restaurants in D.C., from Rasika, chef Vikram Sunderam's brilliant haute Indian restaurant, to Tom Power's upscale Corduroy, to the granddaddy of all D.C. fine dining, José Andrés's minibar. Sure, the meals were useful in getting to know our competition, but they were also useful in our getting to know each other, and to be honest, a whole lot of fun. Glenn revealed himself to have a sly sense of humor. Kelly was just as gregarious as I had imagined, and wine only brought out more gregariousness and an almost hilarious self-regard. Over these dinners we'd dissect what we liked and what we didn't at each restaurant. We admired the silverware at Kinship and the lighting at Rose's

Luxury, the bathrooms at minibar, the plates at Maketto. They all pointed to the fact that D.C. was ready for an ultra-high-end dining experience.

From the start, my mind had gone to the fine-dining model I had been taught at Per Se and EMP: small, intricate plates— actually small amounts of food on big plates—using high-end ingredients, served in a tasting menu format. Kelly and Glenn were only too happy to push me toward even finer dining. There would be only eight tables at the Shaw Bijou, an insanely low number. These tables would occupy what was now the parlor but would eventually become the dining room. What had been a backroom we would turn into a state-of-the-art kitchen. The basement we'd transform into a prep kitchen that housed the walk-ins, laundry, my "office" (really the crawlspace under- neath the stairs), and storage. The second floor, where Kelly's bedroom was, would be completely demolished. In its place we'd install a bar, and we planned to transform the larger space, closer to the street, into a members-only club. Kelly envisioned a place where the elite of D.C. could come to relax and let loose, with twenty-four-hour access and complete discretion. Mem- bership would start at $2,000 a year. I had my doubts. For one, I didn't want to open a place I couldn't afford and wouldn't feel comfortable in. Second, we could really use the space for more seating. Although I argued for a bar and lounge open to the public, Kelly was firm and I eventually gave in.

Presiding over these changes, I watched the whirl of con- struction crews and the flurry of schematics. Drawing from every element Greg and I had lusted after or experienced or had read about, we were transforming this old 1860s house into an over-the-top den of luxury. We sat with a ceramicist to craft the plates, since each course would have its own flatware. We collaborated with a woodworker, one of Kelly's friends, to create impressive wooden doors with undulating ridges. Repurposing wood from an old Nashville barn, we built the bar upstairs and surrounded it with chairs covered in Icelandic sheepskin. In the kitchen, custom ranges ran along one wall, and underneath the wooden island stacks on stacks of pots and pans grew taller each day. In the prep kitchen in the basement, a battalion of immersion circulators and dehydrators shared space with two walk-ins and a wine room we also used for charcuterie.

We had planned on opening Shaw Bijou in October 2016. But as it turns out, converting a home into a commercial enterprise is a massive logistical and bureaucratic nightmare, one that none of us were ready for. There were zoning issues and infrastructure issues, outdated plumbing plans filed with the government that resulted in torn-up streets that in turn added months and many thousands of dollars onto the build. Even as our opening was delayed, Kelly and Glenn kept Greg and me on salary, and we never lost hope.

When I got the call from the producers of *Top Chef* and took off for two months in the middle of planning, the guys held the line. Both Kelly and Glenn (as well as Greg) had been supersupportive. They guessed correctly, win or lose, that my star would only continue to rise. The exposure would keep the Shaw Bijou on everyone's lips, and that couldn't hurt business.

While I was gone I tried to check in as best I could, but all my phone calls were monitored and could, I knew, be televised. So the team was on its own. Nevertheless, with Greg as my proxy, the restaurant inched closer to completion. When I got back from California, I had to keep the outcome of the show a secret. But people in the industry knew that I had been a contestant, and they also knew what Greg and I were planning. D.C. is a small scene and, even though we hadn't opened our doors yet, we were big fish. So as we began to form a small community among D.C. chefs, our reputation—my reputation—

preceded me. As a new chef in town, especially one who like me who was coming from New York City to a smaller market, you never know exactly what to expect. Reception can sometimes be rocky, especially if anyone senses an attitude of superiority. Luckily for us, though it was smaller than New York's scene—perhaps *because* it was smaller—we found many friendly chefs who made us feel right at home, frequently inviting us out for drinks at their restaurants, drinks that continued long after their doors closed for the night.

Most of the chefs were supportive, but some weren't. I remember going out with a local chef named Haidar Karoum. I didn't know Karoum well. After a few drinks he turned to me and out of the blue said, "Your restaurant's gonna fail, homeboy!" in a tone that was playful, but just barely.

I tried to laugh it off. "Man," I said, "shut the fuck up. You're just jealous."

"No, seriously," Haidar said, his voice turning unfriendlier. "Who do you think you are, homeboy?"

I took a beat. "Don't call me fucking homeboy," I said.

"You're the only homeboy here," he snarled.

Telling me my restaurant was going to fail was already a dick move. Adding a "homeboy" to it just wasn't going to stand. It wasn't as bad as calling me "boy." but it was in the same vein, threading race, if not racism, into a taunt. I wasn't going to let it slide. I got right up in his face, so close I could smell the vodka on his breath and see the broken red veins in the whites of his eyes. I could remember the satisfying feeling of beating the piss out of all those punks who stiffed me at Bridgeport and of the solid telltale smack of fist against jawbone. I thought of Boobie back at Webster, of rolling kids from the block. Who was this asshole who thought I could be trifled with? Then I felt Greg's hand on my shoulder. "Kwame," he said, "forget about it." I snapped out of it. I came to, the room opened up again, and

I remembered who and where I was. I didn't need a headline right now about getting into a chef brawl.

"Fuck you, Haidar," I said. "You just wait and see."

Despite isolated incidents like the fight with Haidar, I walked on sunshine that summer. The press was hyping us and it felt good to be part of D.C., a city getting its groove on. The *Michelin Guide* was coming, and the restaurant scene finally had some serious swagger. Or rather, people were finally waking up to the talent that had been coming up for the past decade. Not only that, but good vibes were in the ether. We were in the victory-lap years of the Obama administration and were all looking forward to greeting the next president, Hillary Clinton. The spirit was hopeful and happy. Most newspapers and bloggers greeted my arrival with excitement.

Then came calamity. Just as Greg and I were sprinting toward the finish line, Glenn made a startling announcement during an operations meeting. He said we had been running behind in our payments to the construction crew and contractors. It wasn't anything to worry about, he assured us, just an issue of money flow and liquidity.

Nevertheless, obviously, I was worried. For the past year we had been operating in accordance with Kelly's assurance that money was no object, and we'd had no feedback from Glenn. I never saw an invoice or a work order, but Glenn assured us we were on track financially. This was the first I had heard that we were in any sort of trouble, and it came as a huge and scary shock.

"We owe them thousands of dollars if they're going to finish the job," said Glenn.

"Why," I asked, trying to make sense of what I was hearing, "are we having this discussion now?"

"We need money now," said Glenn. "We're going to have to use the ticket sales to raise the money." Like many high-end tasting menu restaurants, we had decided to presell tickets in lieu of standard reservations. That way we could guarantee the number of covers we'd have each night *and* protect against no-shows.

"No way," objected Greg. "That's too risky. If we do that we won't have any buffer when we open. That was the whole point of ticket sales in the first place."

"Do you want to open the restaurant or not?" Kelly jumped in. Apparently he had known that we were hard up.

Greg and I looked at each other. We felt trapped. We were in too deep to walk away. Already we had given years of our lives to this project.

We had no choice but to agree. But we still hadn't settled on the price for the menu. In my mind, I had suggested a hundred dollars, with service included, which would make the Shaw Bijou one of the more expensive restaurants in town but not the most expensive. And even that was a bit above what I had initially wanted. I had always had a $60–$70 price point in mind, along the lines of Contra, a restaurant on New York's Lower East Side I very much admired.

Kelly shook his head. "That'll never work. We can't raise enough."

$125?

No.

$150?

No.

After a pause, Kelly, who had clearly had a number in mind all along, said, "It needs to be one eighty-five for the numbers to work. No tip. No tax. No wine."

Greg and I both objected immediately. "That's way too much, man," I said. "We're gonna get killed."

"We need that money to open," said Glenn. "It's one eighty-five or nothing."

Ultimately, Greg and I had to agree. I tried to justify the price to myself. After all, I knew from having dined at three-star restaurants while still living in the projects that if someone really wanted to eat our food, they could save up. So $185 it was.

When *The Washington Post* published an article that mentioned the price for a meal at Bijou, the news was greeted as if I had murdered someone. Immediately it became the only talking point. If you know anything about our restaurant, you probably know that it was extremely expensive. For a dinner for two with drink pairings, you'd probably be looking at close to $1,000. It didn't matter that we had a choose your wine pairing starting at $20 and curated by our sommelier David Blackburn from bottles rarely sold by the glass.

Now, $185 for fifteen courses, without tax, tip, or wine, is admittedly steep. I had never made any secret of the fact that the Shaw Bijou would be a fine-dining destination, and this fact was amply covered—and celebrated—by the press. D.C. had a small but growing cadre of expensive tasting menu restaurants, led by José Andrés minibar. It was in this small but rapidly growing segment of the dining scene that Greg and I wanted our restaurant to exist. But still, $185, with no tax, no tip, no wine.

Soon the tide of D.C. turned against us. "The Shaw Bijou's price tag leaves a sour taste," wrote a journalist at *Washington City Paper*. "Something doesn't feel quite right." Commenters were less discreet: "I have never wanted a restaurant to go down in a spiriling flame than this one," wrote one. (*Sic*, obviously.)

Because of the high price, nearly every food journalist in the D.C. area, not to mention legions of food bloggers, were already pissed at us by the time we opened. I understood it. A chef like José Andrés has earned his right to charge as much as he does. Who were we—who was I—to charge as much?

The pricing left me in an awkward position. Publicly I had to defend it, no matter how much heat we took from the press. After all, I couldn't very well go out and say, "Look, we're actually already broke and we need the money upfront." What's more, I didn't want to undercut the entire premise of Shaw Bijou by appearing apologetic before we even started. But at the same time even I knew it was tone-deaf, so when given the chance to defend ourselves, I tried to blunt the impact by explaining the price in terms of food cost.

What I said then—and it's still true now—is that we were well within standard operating procedure when it came to covering our food and labor costs. In fact, $185 was a bargain, comparatively. In most restaurants, a tasting menu is about 28 to 30 percent food costs. We were operating at 35 to 40 percent food costs. That argument is true on one level, but at the same time no one forced me to use king crab or American Wagyu or uni bottarga. No one dictated that a tasting menu must stretch to more than a dozen courses. No one demanded that we have only eight tables. Or a kitchen staff of ten or a dining room staff of just as many. No one made me order custom-made flatware or aprons or anything. That was on me. Had I known we were broke, I would have made different decisions every step of the way. But I didn't. I wanted to be the best I could be. I wanted the Shaw Bijou to be the best it could be. Given a blank check, why not reach for the stars? Why not upgrade at every turn, select the most expensive, the rarest, the most luxurious ingredients I could? That was, after all, what I had seen at Per Se and at EMP and on my fine-dining travels, and all those restaurants were showered with accolades.

I am certain that the preopening backlash would not have

been as fierce had my skin been lighter and or had my food been drawn from the same style of New American, modernist, or nouvelle cuisine that other top-dollar restaurants favored. None of the other high-priced tasting menu restaurants in town came in for the kind of vicious criticism accorded the Shaw Bijou. Not even a little bit. Maybe it was because I was young. Maybe because it was my first restaurant. Maybe because I was new in town. But the thought still lurks that the hate had something to do with the fact that I was making food that came from my culture, from black culture. I was saying that this culture is worth something, worth a lot, actually. That *I* was worth something. Underneath the reaction to the price tag, this was the white-lash rage that seethed.

D espite all that, opening night that November began auspiciously. A deep plum purple was the official color of the Shaw Bijou, and everything from our aprons to the custom-fabricated range was that hue. The logo, a blackberry, was set against a purple background. I thought it a good omen that on our opening night, the autumn sky was this exact color. The evening was cold but not bitterly cold. A gentle wind blew, and the air crackled with excitement (and the pounding of a jackhammer as the Department of Buildings finished some last-minute repairs on the water main in front of the building). The Shaw Bijou had been two years in the making, and now it was finally open.

A million thoughts ran through my mind on the eve of that first service, everything from how many quarts of chicken jus were in the walk-in, to how many logs of bottarga we had left, to whether the goat faces in the combi oven were crisping up properly. I could envision the entire night's guest list—forty-eight people in two turns, or sittings, who had bought tickets months in advance. There were three birthdays, two pregnancies, a gluten aversion, a dairy aversion, and a dairy-but-soft-cheese-is-okay aversion. I visualized the fifteen-course tasting menu the way a high diver does before he jumps into the pool. I closed my eyes and could see each element of every dish come together. I had been imagining this moment for years.

What I didn't think about, really, was the curious chain of events, years of bootstrapping hustle and sheer luck, that had landed me at age twenty-six in this time, at this place, with these people. I was scared that if I did look back, I'd be like Wile E. Coyote caught in midair, realizing there's no solid ground beneath him.

Without a doubt, this was the most important and significant service of my life. I was finally becoming the restaurateur and chef I knew I could be. I stood at the pass in my own kitchen, as the head of my own staff, as a leader, an enforcer, a coach, the interpreter of centuries of my people's traditions, the guy people said "Oui, Chef" to. "Chef Kwame Onwuachi" was written on my jacket. "Chef Kwame Onwuachi" was written on the menu. No one doubted that I was in charge. It was my ass on the line if things went south, and I'd get the glory if things went well.

In my immediate field of vision I could count at least a score of people who relied on me for their livelihoods. Some, like Greg and Paz, were my closest friends. Others were near strangers. Regardless of where they came from or who they were, they depended on me as much as I depended on them. From porter to commis to sous chef to server, I rode them all hard, but it was me who felt the most weight on my shoulders. My staff, both back and front of house, had picked up their lives and packed up their belongings to come here, to be in this spot right now.

They had come from around the country and arrived at the doors of the Shaw Bijou with ambition and limitless hope. It was my responsibility not to leave them out in the cold.

Why did they come, for this punishing life of little pay and less sleep at a new and unproven restaurant, for a chef they might have seen on television once or twice but about whom they knew almost nothing? Quite simply, they had come because I had publicly proclaimed and damn well meant to open the best restaurant in Washington, D.C. Me, a black kid from the Bronx, new to this town. Yes, that was something I was going to do. It was audacious, ballsy, maybe a little arrogant. But everything I had learned and all that I had experienced had confirmed my belief that I couldn't wait until someone gave me an opportunity. I had to make things happen on my own. I had to force the situation. I've always had to. At Shaw Bijou, all that hustling had paid off. Finally, I had made it. It lasted for all of twenty minutes.

Things began to unravel when I saw D.C.'s most important restaurant critic, Tom Sietsema's, joyless face appear twenty minutes after we had officially opened the doors. Thanks in part to what the man clutching a leather valise and appraising our kitchen with a cold eye would write a few days later in *The Washington Post,* and in part to the cowardly incompetence of my business partners, and in part to my own pride—no getting around that—the restaurant would close its doors after just three months.

When I look back at the three months the Shaw Bijou was open, at the bright months preceding them and the angry ones following, it all gives me a headache, breaks my heart, fills me with intense pride, makes me want to shout and dance and cry with *all* of the emotions. I'm not old now by any stretch, but I was so young when we started working on the Shaw Bijou. I was green, and confident that the arc of my life would be a simple and elegant curve upward. In the story I told myself at the time, I had tunneled through adversity and narrowly avoided bad breaks to emerge triumphant at the apex of fine dining. It was a simple rags-to-riches tale, a narrative as smooth and solid as an on-ramp. I had, in short, come to believe not only in myself, but in the Kwame story I told others. In this telling, the Shaw Bijou would be my home run. Foolish, I now know, and wrong too, to think a story could have a happy ending before it really even began.

By the time Sietsema arrived in the kitchen, he had already been attended to by our burly and bearded bartender Zach on the second floor. He had already enjoyed the first course, a few slices of jerk-marinated duck prosciutto, accompanied by a pastry cigarette full of La Tur cheese and hazelnut oil, served on a small but thick wooden plate custom designed for us by one of Kelly's friends. The duck prosciutto, a nod to my dad's mom, a stern Jamaican woman named Gloria, had been cured, marinated, and then left to hang for two weeks in the walk-in. Sietsema had then been led down the back stairway to continue his meal in the kitchen. Afterward, he'd continue to his dining room seat. This was the progression all diners took when they came to Bijou.

The stairs led to the end of the line. I stood on the far side, expediting at the head of a wooden island. At my back was a wall of spices in neatly labeled Ball jars, from lavender buds to ají amarillo. To my right was a combi oven full of crackling sheep faces and dry-aged quail, and to my left you could see the dining room through a short hallway. In front of me were three chefs working the hotline and two on garde manger. Jong Son

248 Notes from a Young Black Chef

was on the second course, the first served in the kitchen proper. Jong was small, funny, with thick glasses and a furious work ethic. He was supereager and, like the rest of us, nervous as hell.

Jong didn't recognize Sietsema. And at first neither did I. The critic is meant to be anonymous, but as he entered the kitchen a GM from a restaurant around the corner who wanted a job at Bijou snuck in and whispered into my ear who it was. By that point there was nothing I could do but watch Jong and pray he didn't mess it up. I was trying to eye him furiously while at the same time not let on that I knew who he was serving and all the while making sure the kitchen didn't fall behind. Jong, I knew, was a people pleaser, and when he got anxious he tried to please more. I was freaking out, because as I knew firsthand, there's nothing less pleasing than a pleaser trying to please. If he had just been handing the guest a plate, it would have been no big deal. But I had asked each chef to preface the dish with an autobiographical vignette from my life that situated it in my life story. This was the same approach I had used so successfully at Dinner Lab.

"Good evening," Jong began. "Chef Kwame"—here he pointed to me at the end of the kitchen—"often enjoyed chicken or lamb and rice from halal carts while living in the Bronx. This dish is a homage to those days. What we have here are lamb sweetbreads glazed in chicken jus with Kashmiri chili, atop a basmati rice chip, with a smoked sesame seed emulsion."

I shuddered. What had sounded so normal and friendly in preservice run-throughs came across as a little creepy and a little cultish. That I was just a few feet away from him gave the whole spiel a little bit of an "Our Great Leader" feel. This obviously wasn't what I had intended, but there was nothing I could do but watch.

Sietsema listened politely, nodded, and popped the bite in

his mouth. His jaw was the only thing that moved, back and forth, back and forth. I knew the food was good, bursting with flavor, but no smile crossed Sietsema's face. Just chewing back and forth.

He brushed by me, barely making eye contact, and walked into the dining room.

Fortunately, I didn't have the luxury of time to dwell on what had just happened. It was one moment among many, and was soon erased by the next guests, a smiling couple clearly excited to be there. "We bought tickets the first day," said the lady. "Can I take a picture?" asked her date. We all smiled for the camera. Now, this was more like it.

Opening night and the three nights before the review came out were some of the best of my life. After some initial hiccups, which were to be expected, the team was finding its groove. The restaurant was sold out, and we were firing on all cylinders. I thought that despite all the troubles we had run into before opening, we had made it through the hard part. Importantly, we were having fun. Greg and I had talked about taking *every-thing* to the next level, and now we finally had real live guests to try things out on. Greg would research the people coming in, pass me whatever intel he could find, and it was up to me to create something special for them. One night a woman told us her husband had just gotten a tattoo of a beet, so between the courses I snuck in a serving of camembert and beet mole on a flatbread. On another night, a guest mentioned something to her server about being so comfortable she wanted slippers when she walked in. So, during her meal I had my fiancée, Mya, run out to TJ Maxx and return with a pair that we presented on a silver platter.

I could count the hours I slept that first week on two hands, but every morning I woke up excited. My mantra was "Every

Day Is Day One," and as I walked the few blocks from my house to the restaurant, I almost jogged I was so eager to get there.

To his credit, Sietsema didn't keep us in the dark about his feelings for long. We opened November first. His review ran on the fourth. I read it in the alley behind the restaurant with Greg. It was not good. "Shaw Bijou serves a few delights and several duds. Is that worth $500 a head?" ran the headline on WashingtonPost.com. Though he lauded a couple of our dishes—the king crab poached in garlic butter, my haute riff on Steak & Eggs—he slammed the sunchokes, thought the squash velouté was a cliché, the foie was too salty, the service was shoddy, and he hated the desserts. "A waste of tamarind and cranberry powders, not to mention palm oil," he wrote. Most damningly, he took issue with the portion size, which went straight to our price point. "None in my party are linebackers," he wrote, "but all of us end the meal less than sated."

The review came out on a Friday morning after a really good service. We'd had no misfires, no missed aversions, no botched orders, nothing oversalted, nothing panicked, little chaos. We were feeling good. Then, *boom,* a morale bomb. Of the team, probably Gisell, our pastry chef, got hit the hardest. Jon de Paz was gutted because he was on the foie station and I had asked him to watch his salt on the marmalade in prep that night. And though I tried not to let it bleed out, I was hurting too. A lot.

Some elements of his review were undeniably true. The foie, I knew, *was* too salty. The service was rocky also. The only defense I had is that he didn't even give us an hour. He gave us a twenty-minute grace period. I had never gone from feeling so high to feeling so low so quickly. The review was what it was, demolishing, and it was up to us to pick up the pieces.

I called a meeting as soon as the staff had arrived to lay out our situation. As we gathered in the dining room, both the dining room and the kitchen staff, it was on me to motivate the team.

"This fucking sucks, guys," I began. "I know. I feel it too. But this is my dream, this is the shit we've all been working for for months. No one, not even Tom Sietsema, can take that away from us. Use this as a fire under your ass. Use this as motivation. Get angry and use that anger to make the best fucking food in D.C. From here on out, no mistakes. Cook with your heart and fucking crush it. Okay?"

The room echoed with a very loud "Oui, Chef!"

In the days immediately following the review, the vibe inside the kitchen became one more of defiance than defeat. We knew it was unfair to be reviewed based on your first hour of service. We knew there was work to be done. But we all felt that this was a chance to show Sietsema and all the other haters what and who we were. We could get through this.

My optimism was not shared by the other partners. Greg and I were quickly called in to a meeting with Kelly and Glenn. Kelly was furious. He told me he had never liked the desserts anyway and had always thought the menu was too expensive. This was total bull, which he knew as well as I did. He was the one who forced us to price it at $185 to recoup cost overruns. Nevertheless, he gave me a list of things to change. His big idea to save the restaurant was lunch. I told him we couldn't run the restaurant we wanted while serving a whole extra meal. As it was, we were there all day every day prepping for dinner. The sunchokes and the dessert had to go. I told him that he had explicitly given me full rein in the kitchen. He replied, "Everyone has a plan until they're punched in the face."

The review really brought out some ugly, long-simmering tensions between me and Glenn and between me and Kelly. In the run-up to the opening I had been doing a lot of press. On

one television appearance on Fox's local affiliate, I had worn a
T-shirt with the words "We Out," attributed to Harriet Tubman, as I did my cooking segment. The shirt was a lighthearted
but earnest homage to her escape to freedom in 1849. The segment went well, nothing that notable, but when I got to the
restaurant afterward, I saw Glenn waiting for me. This was a
little unusual, since he didn't make too many visits.

He pulled me into my own office, a tiny space in the basement, saying, "We gotta talk."

"You can't be spewing your political viewpoints," he said
point-blank.

"What political viewpoints?" I countered.

He gestured to my shirt. "Those!"

This was during probably the most heated moment of the
presidential campaign cycle, when Donald Trump was broad-
casting his hate speech at an increasingly loud volume. Nevertheless, it was news to me that publicly celebrating Harriet
Tubman had become a political statement. I had thought it was
celebrating a shared history.

"Glenn," I said, "if you think this is political, it's on you."

"It's a subtle jab, Kwame. You don't see me with my MAGA
cap on, and yet I'll be the first in line to vote for Trump."

I was taken aback. Not that Glenn supported Trump; I didn't
agree with him, but that didn't mean we couldn't work together.
What bothered me is that he wanted to control *me,* to stifle my
voice even as I was drawing attention to an American hero.

To make matters even worse, I was experiencing the same
dynamic with Kelly. I can't count the times that he'd come in
during the build-out and make some comment clearly designed
to rile me up. Once, when the subject of Trayvon Martin arose,
Kelly actually told me that he thought Trayvon had ruined
George Zimmerman's life. "That kid was, like, six foot nine and

was running at Zimmerman. Wouldn't you be scared?" Was he saying this just to goad me or because he honestly believed it? Which one is worse? I told him I wasn't having this conversation with him, but it gnawed and gnawed at me. Between that and Glenn's outburst, I was genuinely confused. How, I wondered, could these guys truly support a restaurant like the Shaw Bijou, which was based on the idea that at least one black life mattered, while generally dismissing the idea that all black lives matter? I had the sickening feeling that I had gotten myself into a situation where I wasn't considered a master but a servant. I had been used to this in other kitchens, but that this could happen in my own kitchen was, I don't know how else to put it, soul crushing.

The postreview meeting made this dynamic undeniable. To be fair, some of the changes were for the better, and the sunchokes were on the way out. We were going to add another course that was served in the kitchen, to make the meal more of an "experience." But to have these changes demanded imperiously by Kelly made them all the more difficult to undertake. I felt under assault from within as well as without. I had to ask, or rather tell, Gisell to change the desserts completely. She wasn't happy, but she did it. I increased the portion size. It ate into our margins, but I had to address the criticism, both internally and externally.

Nevertheless, we made the changes—except the lunch part—and soldiered on. When the review first hit, we got some cancellations but not too many. And I don't know if those we did get were in response to the review. The piece went live two days before the presidential election, and all of D.C. had entered a state of shock.

Reservations began to seriously taper off in the beginning of December. And because we were already in the hole, we had no reserves to draw on. In the first few weeks we were doing sixty covers a night, two full turns of the dining room. But by December first, sometimes we'd have just five covers the entire night. It was a ghost town. For a chef, there's nothing more demoralizing than an empty room when you still have to present a happy face. No one wants to eat with a loser. The magical experience we were going for at Bijou relied on the idea that I was a young, supersuccessful phenom. The food, the hospitality, the sense that it was my home, these aspects were so heavily autobiographical that when it became clear that I wasn't this perfect inspirational model, the whole thing, I think, became unappetizing.

I grew deeply depressed. Greg and I were both drinking heavily. We'd split a bottle of whiskey a day, starting at nine in the morning and polishing it off before we shut down. I assume that the rest of the staff had their own ways of getting by—drugs, drink, whatever. I was in no shape to be a leader and wasn't one. But I was *with* the staff, suffering with them. And amazingly, even though I couldn't see straight by the time service rolled around, we weren't missing ticket times, we weren't making errors on dishes. We were running just as smoothly as before. But now there was hardly anyone to notice.

Over the past two years Greg and I had met many times in the alley behind the restaurant for a quick cigarette. Now we'd meet back there to cry. Shivering in winter sun, me in my chef's whites and he in a gray suit, we looked at each other, shell-shocked.

"Shit, I guess black people *shouldn't* have their own fine-dining restaurant," I told him one day.

"Don't say that, man," he responded.

"Feels true, though, doesn't it?"

"Whatever happens," he told me, "I'm here for you."

We finished our cigarettes in silence, ground them into the dirt, and headed back inside.

The visible decline of the Shaw Bijou exacerbated tensions among all of us. Glenn and Kelly were not immune. The two men had known each other for years—Kelly had cut Glenn's hair for a decade—but this was the first time they had been in business together. Money doesn't change you; it just reveals who you truly are. And as it turns out, these two guys didn't like each other much. When things were going really well with the Shaw Bijou, the dynamic was papered over. But when things got tough—and they got extremely tough—the friction ignited a fire.

Glenn was our day-to-day contact during the build-out and in the first month after opening. Kelly was intended to be more of a silent investor. It turns out that he was both loud and silent in the worst way possible. Because we still needed his sign-off for major expenditures it was imperative that we could get in touch with him. He ran a number of other businesses and lived in Richmond, Virginia, an hour away, so I understood that sometimes contact was tough. But starting a few weeks before we opened, Kelly began to disappear more often and for longer and longer stretches. He began to act strangely too. Shortly after the review hit, Kelly told Greg and me we were not to contact him directly; if we needed to get in touch, we should go through Glenn. That was a problem, since we relied on Kelly to cut the checks for everything from payroll to deliveries. When neither Kelly nor Glenn was reachable, Greg and I were forced to pay our staff, bills, purveyors—everything—from our own pockets. The situation was clearly unsustainable.

I drove out to Richmond to meet Kelly and talk face-to-face.

There was no way Bijou would survive if we couldn't resolve this. Sure, our relationship had grown contentious, but it was nothing, I thought, that should endanger the business. We went out to lunch at a diner near his house, and though Kelly never apologized nor explained his long absence, he told me that Glenn was trying to sell the restaurant to another investor. At first I didn't believe him. Why would Glenn do that? I didn't think he would take such a drastic step without talking to me or to Greg first. But then Kelly showed me the emails, and I had no choice but to believe him. I had been so head-down during the opening I hadn't realized it, but the two men were barely on speaking terms. At least that partially explained Kelly's going dark in the past few weeks.

I drove back to D.C. infuriated and quickly called a meeting with Glenn and Greg to force the issue. At first Glenn denied that he was trying to sell, but when I told him I had seen the emails he broke down weeping and admitted that it was true. Then he finally leveled with us. Like a lot of first-time restaurateurs, he had gotten into the Shaw Bijou for fun. He had a high-paying job and close to a million dollars to spend. But as the years wore on and expenses mounted, he told us, his savings had become depleted. He had lost his job and had already dipped into his children's college savings. He and his wife had two young kids and had fallen behind on their mortgage and sold their house. Now they were living in a tiny apartment. In a very concrete way, the Shaw Bijou had ruined him, and he had to get out.

He apologized for lying. I was still mad, but it's hard to stay mad at a guy who is broken. He told us he had agreed to sell his share of the business—close to $700,000—back to Kelly over the next seven years in annual installments. A pit of dread opened up in my stomach. Now Kelly would hold all the cards,

and if the drama of the past few months had taught me anything, it's that this was bad news for me.

As the three of us sat upstairs on the fur-covered chairs in
the Shaw Bijou, we all mourned a dream that was coming apart
before our eyes. Before he left, Glenn asked Greg and me each
for one thing, a souvenir, from the restaurant. I ran downstairs
and grabbed my chef's knife and gave it to him. Greg brought
him a few Zalto glasses. When he walked out the door, it was
the last I would ever see of Glenn.

M iraculously, on those long winter nights we managed to
put out the best food we ever had. The chefs, to their
credit, never flagged or complained, not once. Every morning
they came in, to make their *mise en place* by hand from scratch,
and every night they'd have to throw out the bulk of it and
begin again the next day. Meanwhile I trotted from table to
table during service, thanking our guests for coming in and
trying to project an air of confidence when I felt anything but.

Kelly was freaking out. In one of my last meetings with him,
shortly before the restaurant closed, he demanded that I fire
half the kitchen staff. I told him I couldn't do that so close to
Christmas, but he insisted. Eventually I told the team, each of
whom earned about $26,000 a year, that I had to halve their
salary. Stay if you want, but if you go, I said, I don't blame
you. They all stayed. I also agreed to reduce the menu to just
seven courses for $95—ironically, what I had wanted from the
outset. I wrote a press release at the time that read in part,
"Humility creeps up on you when least expected, and the opening of this restaurant has taught us just that. This being our
first restaurant, and for some a first business venture, we had
a substantial amount of learning and adjusting to do. And we

have, immensely." I hated writing that letter, and I disavow it today. Did we make mistakes? Of course we did. I did. Did I think I needed to publicly humble myself, trot out my apology like a captured runaway slave, promise that I had learned my lesson and that, yes suh, I knew my place? No, I definitely did not. I opened a business that didn't work. I didn't murder anyone. But in Kelly I was working for a guy who once told me Trayvon Martin had what was coming to him, the same Kelly who had initially wanted a high-end fried chicken joint, Kelly who had no interest in my story, who despite what he had said earlier cared only about the money. What makes that statement I issued so infuriating to read now is that it was false and futile. If you want to know the truth, I'm still not humble. I still believe in myself and in my potential. I'm still ambitious, and if the Shaw Bijou taught me anything, it's to pick better partners, never apologize for who you are, and always come out of the corner guns blazing.

If it hadn't been for Kelly, I'm sure the Shaw Bijou would have found its footing. During the last months, despite everything, it was already happening. In the first days of January we saw an uptick in business. Corby Kummer, another critic, gave us a largely positive review in *The Atlantic*. The staff's spirits, which had flagged toward the end of the year, began improving. We were all in this together, me and them. I had found a new way to lead that felt more authentic, that involved listening as much as it did commanding. I let each cook put up a dish of their own that would accompany the tasting menu. Since they weren't getting paid well or getting proper credit—I felt—for their work, I at least needed to make them feel part of the team. And it worked. The kitchen staff was buoyant, and in the dining room the new tasting menu was bringing in huge volume. When I went out to talk to tables, I had that same feeling I did the first few days. I felt good and the room felt good. We had found our groove. We were doing more than $15,000 on the weekends. With those numbers we could sustain a business. I started to allow myself to feel hopeful again.

Not that Kelly was there to see any of this. He had ghosted us. We were used to this, but since payroll was about to hit, whatever was going on had to come to a head soon. With Glenn out of the picture, we were even more reliant on Kelly. The night after what turned out to be the last service, Greg and I went out with the entire kitchen staff for drinks at a local bar. We felt like warriors who had made it through a bruising battle and emerged alive.

I woke up hungover early on Sunday morning to find an email from Kelly to me and Greg. "Meet me at Bijou," it read. I rolled my eyes, not in the mood for another tense conversation with him but we needed to work this out. I texted Greg, but he was still sleeping off the previous night.

I arrived to find Kelly sitting in the dining room alone. I pulled up a chair and sat down across from him.

"Where's Greg?" he asked.

"I dunno," I said. "What's up, Kelly?"

He was looking down at the table, trying to avoid eye contact. I had a feeling about what was coming.

"Kwame," he said, "I'm closing the restaurant."

I'd been waiting for the news for the past month, but still, to hear him say it was painful. And yet at the same time I felt a wave of relief wash over me, that I didn't need to fight anymore, I didn't need to worry, the story had come to an end.

"When?" I asked.

"Yesterday," he said.

I looked at Kelly for a beat, then took one last look around the dining room, at the beautiful lights we had obsessed over for hours, at the curving hand-carved credenzas, beyond the dining room to the wall of spices I had planned to draw from for years to come, and to the spot at the head of the island where I had stood nearly every night for the past three months. I wanted to cry, obviously, but wasn't going to give Kelly the satisfaction of seeing me upset. Nor was I going to give him a handshake and pretend it was all cool. Kelly had absconded with my dream. I turned around and walked out the door. I never looked back and never entered the Shaw Bijou again.

I made my way straight to Greg's apartment, pounding on his door until he woke up.

"Greg," I said, "it's over. Kelly closed Bijou."

Before he could really react we started getting text messages from the staff wondering what was going on. As soon as I had walked out the door, Kelly called an all-staff meeting for later that day to tell them. Greg and I weren't invited. On the spur of the moment, we invited them all to come to my house after the staff meeting for what was essentially a wake.

Greg and I just sat there with so many emotions—rage, sadness, despair, shame—coursing through our bodies that we felt numb. We had failed, and that was that. With the restaurant closed, the game was over.

I headed back to my apartment and soon Jong, Gisell, Paz, Jarren, Russell, and the rest of the staff showed up en masse. All were upset. I didn't know quite how to relate to them. They were once my team and I had been their leader. But now that relationship was over, so I was touched that they still referred to me with respect as "Chef." And I was touched that when I called for silence, there was silence. I told them how deeply grateful I was that they had given their lives over to the Shaw Bijou for the short time it lasted. I told them to never be sorry for doing something different, for trying and failing. That every day is day one.

In the days that followed I fell into the toxic cycle of what-ifs. What if Tom Sietsema had returned for a full review in a few months and lauded our ability to right the ship after a rocky start? What if Greg and I had asked sooner about the financials? What if Kelly wasn't an asshole and Glenn hadn't run out of money? What if Hillary had won? What if I had salted the foie myself? What if? What if? What if? What if all the critics were right? What if my story actually isn't worth being told? What if I am exactly as hubristic as they say I am? And what now?

I wish I had answers, but the truth is, when you go through something as traumatic as a restaurant closing, you're left with a quiver full of clichés to comfort you. Well, I say, I tried my best and that's the best I could do. I told myself that it was short but sweet. I told myself that it was a learning experience. I told myself that I'm stronger for it. None of those things are untrue. None paint the whole picture, either. None of them really captures the heartbreak and the bruises, the excitement, the pride, the despair or the humiliation or the joy or the shades of emotion in between.

After the Shaw Bijou was closed, Greg moved back to Pittsburgh, the team disbanded, and the press moved on. There was nothing for me to do but keep on going too. But how? Everything had been stripped away. All my worst fears had come true. For the first time in my adult life, the Kwame story didn't end happily, and I didn't have any clue what the next chapter would be.

Butter Garlic Crab

YIELD: 6–8 servings

---

4 heads garlic

4 tablespoons olive oil

2 pounds crabs, shelled and cut in half

2 tablespoons canola oil

$3\frac{2}{3}$ cups onions, roughly chopped

1 cup carrots, roughly chopped

1 cup celery, roughly chopped

6 large garlic cloves, roughly chopped

20 thyme sprigs

1 bunch parsley stems

1 tablespoon black peppercorns

12 cups water

2 cups butter, cubed

1 quart king crab meat, picked over to remove any shells and cartilage

Kosher salt

1 lime, cut into wedges

Bottarga

---

1. Preheat oven to 400° F. Cut each garlic head in half horizontally. Drizzle each head of garlic with 1 tablespoon of olive oil and enclose individually in foil. Place in oven and roast for 2 hours. Remove, and allow to cool. Once cooled, remove garlic cloves from roasted head and strain to form a puree. Reserve.

2. Meanwhile, in a stock-pot over medium-high heat, caramelize crab shells in canola oil until fragrant. Add chopped vegetables and sweat for about 10 minutes. Add the aromatics and 12 cups water, and simmer for 2 hours. Strain, discarding the vegetables and aromatics, and return liquid to the pot and reduce for another hour.

3. Place the roasted garlic puree, reduced crab stock, and butter in a blender and puree until smooth. Return to the pot and add king crab meat. Warm through and season to taste with salt.

4. Serve in bowls with a lime wedge and top with grated bottarga to taste.

The Lesson

As soon as the Shaw Bijou closed, I was pretty much paralyzed with depression. I felt humiliated, angry, and sad. It also didn't help that I felt like the entire city—a city I had moved to for the sole purpose of opening this restaurant—seemed overjoyed to see that I had failed so miserably. Just as bad, the sense of personal shame was compounded by a biting frustration, that I had unwittingly played into the narrative of the young black chef who didn't know his place. I was certain that news of the Shaw Bijou's closing was greeted with a self-satisfied roll of the eyes and a snide "Well, I hope he learned his lesson." To be honest, though, I never heard anyone disparage me outright. I didn't have to. There was a part of me that was saying the same thing.

For the first few weeks I just stayed in bed in the condo I shared with Mya, staring into the mirrored glass of the facing apartment complex. I tried to work out in my head what had gone wrong. Clearly it was more than just one thing, more than the price point or the lack of back-office support; more than the precarious financial positions of my partners; more than the fact that the city's food media hadn't been on my side. Maybe it was my cooking, maybe it was me, that didn't measure up. That was the hardest possibility to contemplate, because if I started to doubt myself, everything I had built would crumble. It was my own hustle that had landed me here, with some amount of financial stability (though that was questionable without a job), some amount of fame (or infamy). But it's the end of a hustler if he starts questioning himself. So I didn't. I know I'm a damn good chef.

I could see that one easy way to redemption was to crawl back into the public eye, humbled and chastised. I could play the part of the wayward son who has learned that it's the tortoise, not the hare, who gets ahead, that it is he who pays his dues who ultimately finds success and that respect is not given freely but must be earned over time. But even as I laid low, I couldn't bring myself to do that. It just wasn't true. I hadn't "learned my lesson." The Shaw Bijou failed for a lot of reasons, but if we'd been given more time and been allowed to stay the course, we would have eventually succeeded. I have no doubt that within the year we would have been the best restaurant in D.C. The only lesson I learned in the aftermath of our closing is that there are a bunch of people who seem real concerned about my education, as long as that education is the lesson they want to teach me.

Mya was supportive at first, but, like my mom did back in Baton Rouge, soon enough she pushed me to get off the couch and back out into the world. When I opened my computer and started sifting through unopened emails, I was gratified to find that buried among the sympathetic notes were a few from potential investors. A restaurateur in Oakland was interested in resurrecting the Shaw Bijou with a lower price point. There was an offer to open a fast-casual concept in San Francisco. A deep-pocketed investor in New York dangled carte blanche before me. Then there were the D.C. possibilities: a consulting gig for a local pizza chain, an opportunity at a new hotel being built by the Wharf. Of course, none of these were full-blown or formal offers yet but rather examples of the industry nosing around to see if there was still flesh on my bones or fight in my heart. The answer was that there were both. I wasn't ready to be a has-been at twenty-seven.

Slowly I eased back into the world. I took meetings, listened in on conference calls, responded to emails. I wasn't fully recovered; I still struggled with how to present myself as an up-and-comer when I knew most of the world saw me as a down-and-outer. But I dug deep, remembering the days of selling Butterfingers on a hot subway car in New York City and all the times I stood in front of potential clients during my catering years, when I had absolutely no idea what I was doing yet through sheer bravado convinced people to entrust me with their weddings and meetings and birthdays. I thought back to stories Granddad told me of my ancestors in Ibusa all those years ago: never changing, never shrinking, stoic and steady.

M ya is from Boston and was itching to get closer to home. Boston would be great; New York would be better. The pull of the five boroughs was strong. Returning to the city would be a homecoming, maybe not as triumphant as I would have wanted, but if I made it in New York, restaurant capital of the country, the failure of the Shaw Bijou would be quickly forgotten. San Francisco, where I hadn't been since filming *Top Chef,* didn't sound too bad either. Now *there* was a market that could handle high-priced tasting menus. But of all the offers, the Oakland option seemed the most tantalizing. I could return to fine dining and do so in a city with deep resonance for African American culture. Oakland Bijou had a nice ring to it.

Even as I contemplated relocating, something didn't sit right. It seemed I wasn't done with D.C. yet. To move now would be an admission of defeat, one that I would carry with me for the rest of my life. It wouldn't matter how much success I found elsewhere; the failure to make it in D.C., where I'd given everything I had, would gnaw at me. As tantalizing as those offers were, I turned them all down. I would stay and finish what I'd started.

The next step after figuring out where I'd be was figuring out what I'd be. From a purely financial and workload standpoint, consulting would be the easiest gig. I could come up with a few toppings for pizzas, get paid a couple thousand dollars a month, and have plenty of free time to audition for television shows, or hang out with Mya, or chill with my friends. After hustling nonstop for the past decade, it would be nice to take a little break, sleep more than five hours a night, and not wake up in a panic about who was going to miss their shift.

Nah. That wasn't me either. If the Shaw Bijou had taught me anything, it was that I relished being a leader in the kitchen. What I'm most proud of from that whole debacle wasn't actually the food but the kitchen I—we—had created. Though there was a hierarchy, every voice was heard, and many voices were present. The kitchen of the Shaw Bijou was full of people of color, the kind of kitchen I never saw in fine dining before. That I had had some part in bringing that team together, that I may have given them a model of how to succeed and thrive in a fine-dining environment, means that no matter what, to me the Shaw Bijou was a success. For the past decade I'd been a loner, moving so fast through my career that I hadn't fully experienced what it meant to lead a team, to create a culture. Now that I knew how, I wanted to do it again. A consulting gig would have been fun, but I didn't want to be a solo agent anymore. To be a chef was to be a leader, and to be a leader you needed a team. I realized that whatever my next step was, I wanted the chance to create the kitchen and dining staff I had wanted to see for so long: a diverse and motivated group of people. Who knows, maybe there'll be a future Kwame among them.

That still left a huge blank spot about what kind of food I'd cook. If it had worked out, the Shaw Bijou would have been confirmation that my thesis—transforming my life into fine dining—was viable. In the wreckage, I found myself questioning that premise. Maybe I should have said yes to Kelly and Glenn's original idea: southern comfort food. Maybe that producer was right all those years ago and the world just wasn't ready for a black fine-dining chef.

I toyed with what it would look like for me to go from the Shaw Bijou to shrimp and grits, mac and cheese, and fried chicken. I have absolutely nothing against that good ol' southern food. It's what I ate down in Baton Rouge, what I ate for most of my childhood. But it isn't me; it's simply what the world expects of me. And I would never submit to that.

For as long as I could remember, I had struggled to balance how I saw myself versus how the rest of the world saw me. Whether it was teachers, cops, fathers, chefs, business partners, or restaurant critics, I had been told so many times that I wasn't worth it, that I was too much trouble, too ambitious, too proud. Maybe I was. Maybe I am. But I will never believe that my culture, black culture, African culture, Caribbean culture, the blood of my father and my mother and my granddad, of Auntie Mi, Mother, and Gloria, of Cassie and Bertran, of Boobie and Ruger and Jaquan, doesn't matter. I know that if I cook this food, food that is in me already, the world will come to eat it. All I have to do is stay true to myself, to be the Kwame I am when no one is looking.

Whatever I do, this is what I want to see: I want to see a

kitchen full of white, yellow, brown, and black faces—open faces, not faces closed by fear like mine was for so many years. I want to see a world in which not only the food from the African diaspora but the food from Africa is given the respect it deserves. When I push open the kitchen doors, I want to see a dining room full of diners, but especially brown and black diners, who, looking at their plates, feel seen, celebrated, and recognized. And when I look in the mirror, I want to see a young black chef who made that world a reality.

Grandma Gloria's Oxtails

YIELD: 4 servings

FOR THE JERK PASTE

½ cup soy sauce

2 cups scallions, roughly chopped

4 habanero peppers

Juice of 4 limes

1 cup fresh thyme, roughly chopped, packed

2-inch knob of fresh ginger

½ cup Worcestershire sauce

2 tablespoons brown sugar

1½ tablespoons salt

2 tablespoons allspice

¼ cup parsley, roughly chopped

1 cinnamon stick

2 bay leaves

½ teaspoon cloves

FOR THE OXTAILS

2 pounds oxtails

½ cup jerk paste

1-inch knob of fresh ginger, grated

6 large garlic cloves, whole

1 tablespoon curry powder

1 tablespoon brown sugar

2 cups scallions, roughly chopped

1¼ cups garlic cloves, whole

2-inch knob of fresh ginger, roughly chopped

¼ cup brown sugar

½ cup thyme sprig, roughly chopped

1 tablespoon allspice

2 fresh bay leaves

Chicken stock, as needed

1 Scotch bonnet

Kosher salt

---

1. To make the jerk paste, put all ingredients in a blender and puree.

2. In a 8 x 11–inch baking dish, combine oxtails, ½ cup jerk paste, ginger, garlic, curry powder, and brown sugar, making sure the oxtails are well coated. Marinate the oxtails in the refrigerator overnight.

3. Preheat oven to 525° F. After 24 hours, allow the oxtails to come to room temperature. Sear oxtails in oven for 25 minutes. Remove from oven and reduce oven temperature to 250° F. Add the remaining ingredients, including enough chicken stock to cover the oxtails, and cover dish with two layers of plastic wrap followed by two layers of foil. Braise in oven for 8 hours.

4. After the 8 hours, once the meat is tender, remove meat from pan and reduce cooking liquid with Scotch bonnet pepper until syrup-like, add oxtails back to the pan, and finish reducing the liquid with the oxtails in the sauce.

5. Season to taste with salt and serve with rice.

Acknowledgments

For Jaquan

This book is dedicated to my best friend Jaquan Millien, who was murdered on Tuesday, October 23, 2018, at approximately 4:40 p.m. Jaquan and I shared many things: first tattoos, first girlfriends, first heartbreaks, first parties. The first time I took the train alone, I wasn't alone at all. I was with my friend, Jaquan.

Over the years, we drifted apart. He stayed in the Butler Houses where he grew up and where he eventually died. I moved to D.C. He had a son, Omari, who was also shot but will survive. (Tragically he, like his father, will grow up fatherless.) I opened restaurants. But we never strayed in our hearts. He was my support and I was his. He had absolute faith in me when it felt like no one else did, and I had absolute faith in him.

Now he's gone. And I have only memories of him, of the sound of his laugh, and his wide warm smile. But I have my story and he was—is—a huge part of that story. Jaquan won't be able add any more chapters to his life. So I offer these chapters to him.

From Joshua David Stein

Firstly, I'd like to thank Kwame, for trusting me to help tell his story, and Tom Pold at Knopf for working so closely with us to make it shine. I'd like to thank my family: my wife, Ana Heeren, who in her words, "is a saintly woman of infinite patience who deserves to be bathed in riches and fed chocolate bonbons all day" and my sons, Achilles and Augustus, for loving me even though I am always staring at my shiny boxes.

A NOTE ABOUT THE AUTHORS

KWAME ONWUACHI is the executive chef at Kith and Kin and owner of the Philly Wing Fry franchise in Washington, D.C. He was born on Long Island and raised in New York City, Nigeria, and Louisiana. Onwuachi was first exposed to cooking by his mother, in the family's modest Bronx apartment, and took that spark of passion and turned it into a career. From the bowels of oil clean-up ships to working at some of the best restaurants in the world, he has seen and lived his fair share of diversity.

Onwuachi trained at the Culinary Institute of America and opened five restaurants before turning thirty. A former *Top Chef* contestant, he has been named a 30 Under 30 honoree by both *Zagat* and *Forbes*.

JOSHUA DAVID STEIN is a Brooklyn-based author and journalist. He's the editor-at-large at *Fatherly* and the host of *The Fatherly Podcast*, the coauthor of *Food & Beer*, the U.S. editor of *Where Chefs Eat*, and the author of the children's books *Can I Eat That?*, *What's Cooking?*, and *Brick: Who Found Herself in Architecture*. He was the restaurant critic for the *New York Observer* until he quit in protest in 2016 and a food columnist for *The Village Voice*, before that went mute. joshuadavidstein.com.

A NOTE ON THE TYPE

The text of this book was composed in Apollo, the first typeface ever originated specifically for film composition. Designed by Adrian Frutiger and issued by the Monotype Corporation of London in 1964, Apollo is not only a versatile typeface suitable for many uses but also pleasant to read in all of its sizes.

Typeset by Scribe Inc.,
Philadelphia, Pennsylvania

Printed and bound by Berryville Graphics,
Berryville, Virginia

Designed by Cassandra J. Pappas